# Responsive Communication

## Combining attention to sensory issues with using body language (Intensive Interaction) to interact with autistic adults and children

Phoebe Caldwell, Elspeth Bradley, Janet Gurney, Jennifer Heath, Hope Lightowler, Kate Richardson and Jemma Swales

# Responsive Communication

## Combining attention to sensory issues with using body language (Intensive Interaction) to interact with autistic adults and children



**Published by:**
Pavilion Publishing and Media Ltd
Blue Sky Offices
Cecil Pashley Way
Shoreham by Sea
West Sussex
BN43 5FF

Tel: 01273 434 943
Email: info@pavpub.com

Published 2019



A catalogue record for this book is available from the British Library.

ISBN: 978-1-912755-36-3

*Pavilion Publishing and Media is a leading publisher of books, training materials and digital content in mental health, social care and allied fields. Pavilion and its imprints offer must-have knowledge and innovative learning solutions underpinned by sound research and professional values.*

**Authors:** Phoebe Caldwell, Elspeth Bradley, Janet Gurney, Jennifer Heath, Hope Lightowler, Kate Richardson and Jemma Swales
**Cover design:** Tony Pitt, Pavilion Publishing and Media Ltd.
**Page layout and typesetting:** Emma Dawe, Pavilion Publishing and Media Ltd.
**Printing:** CMP Digital Print Solutions

# Contents

# About the authors

**Professor Sheila the Baroness Hollins** is a crossbench life peer in the House of Lords, Emeritus Professor of Psychiatry of Disability at St George's University of London and President of the Royal College of Occupational Therapists. She has been a clinical specialist, researcher and policy maker in mental health and published both scientific and professional papers and books. In 1989 she founded the long running Books Beyond Words series of picture books for young people and adults with learning disabilities, which includes stories about everyday life as well as physical and mental health, trauma and sexual abuse. Baroness Hollins was President of the Royal College of Psychiatrists (2005–2008) and President of the British Medical Association (2012–2013).

**Phoebe Caldwell DSc**

For over 40 years, Phoebe Caldwell DSc has pioneered the development of communication support for individuals on the autistic spectrum, opening up channels of communication and emotional engagement for thousands of individuals across the UK, whose previous experience had been one of social and emotional isolation. Phoebe's work was recognised nationally when she won The Times/Sternberg Award, which celebrates the achievements of people aged 70 or over who have done most for society in their older age. Internationally, Phoebe collaborates with a range of professionals from countries including Denmark, the Netherlands, Russia, Australia and Canada.

Phoebe's way of working is distinctive in that it is rooted in respect for the identity of the individual as they are. The Caldwell Foundation uses the term Responsive Communication to describe her approach to communication support.

At the heart of Responsive Communication is one-to-one work with individuals on the autistic spectrum who find communication difficult. Phoebe's aim is to reduce the inputs that are causing sensory distress (addressing their particular hyper- and hypo-sensitivities), combining this with stimuli that are easily processed, by using a child or adult's individual body language to engage with them (Intensive Interaction). When Phoebe provides this one-to-one support, she works with family and care-givers so that they can learn the approach and use it themselves with the child or adult, so that they always has a meaningful point of reference.
Phoebe is employed by the NHS, schools, local authorities and families to work with difficult-to-provide-for individuals. As part of this, she trains professionals, therapists, managers, practitioners, parents and carer-givers. Phoebe is the author of twelve books and a number of research papers and has produced several training films.

**Elspeth Bradley**, PhD, FRCPC, FRCPsych
Elspeth Bradley, researcher, psychiatrist and psychotherapist, has supported children and adults with intellectual disabilities and autism over the past 35 years in the UK and in Canada.

She has held tenured clinical academic appointments in intellectual disability psychiatry in both countries: in the UK as Senior Lecturer at St Georges Hospital Medical School, NHS Consultant Normansfield, Richmond and Twickenham and Lead Consultant in Intellectual Disabilities, Cornwall Partnership NHS Trust; and in Canada as Psychiatrist-in-Chief and Post Graduate Education Coordinator in Intellectual Disabilities at Surrey Place Centre/Department of Psychiatry, University of Toronto.

Elspeth's involvement in autism started as a psychiatry trainee at the Maudsley and Bethlem Royal Hospitals and Institute of Psychiatry, London and later consulting to a National Autistic Society School in the UK.

In Canada she received federal funding for the first population-based study of intellectual disabilities, autism and psychiatric disorders in teenagers and young adults. With Canadian colleagues she has studied profiles of adults with autism and intellectual disabilities admitted to psychiatric hospital, as well as diagnostic practices when patients have intellectual disability and autism. Clinical work has permitted a longitudinal appreciation of how mental distress and concerns about behaviour arise in the context of personal, developmental and environmental circumstances, life events and trauma.

Elspeth has been the lead on the mental health and behavioural section of *Primary Care of Adults with Intellectual and Developmental Disabilities: Canadian consensus guidelines*, from initiation in 2006 through two revisions (2011 and 2018) and was the lead author on the *Autism Spectrum Disorder Health Watch Table*, one of several tools to assist family doctors implement these guidelines. She has published over a hundred peer reviewed articles and book chapters.

Currently Elspeth is Associate Professor at the University of Toronto with clinical appointments at the Centre for Addiction and Mental Health and St Michaels Hospital, Toronto. She consults to community agencies supporting adults with intellectual disabilities and autism. She is a Fellow of the Royal College of Psychiatrists, UK and the Royal College of Physicians, Canada.

**Janet Gurney**
Janet Gurney is Director of Training for 'Us in a Bus,' a voluntary organisation that uses social interaction to build relationships with people with profound learning difficulties and complex needs including autism and challenging/distressed behaviour. Janet has been using Intensive Interaction in this work for over 25 years, and has had the privilege of working alongside

Phoebe Caldwell. Janet uses her experience, perception and sensitivity to establish common ground with people who are often isolated, helping them to have more of a positive voice and an impact on their world. She has a post-graduate certificate in training and is skilled at adapting her training approach to meet the needs of participants.

Janet also works as a consultant for organisations wanting to improve the way they connect with their service users, most recently with Caritas, in St Petersburg. In 2013 she was a guest speaker, alongside Dave Hewett and Gina Davies, at an international autism conference in Warsaw. In 2015 she addressed the Chromosome18 Europe conference in Rome. Janet's ability to look at the world from the individual's viewpoint and the challenges they face means she can use her skills to make a real difference to their lives. The therapeutic impact of this can be seen in people's increased confidence and willingness to engage with others.

Her workshops show people how to build and develop support for people who can often seem 'difficult to reach', including people with PMLD and/or autism. Janet explores the principles and theory of Intensive Interaction and Responsive Communication to show how this can be used to build more fulfilling, interactive and equal relationships with people who find communication a huge challenge.

**Jennifer Heath**
Jennifer Heath qualified with an MSc in occupational therapy in 2010. She works as an Occupational Therapist at Underley Garden where she is also a manager for the health and therapy team there. Underley Garden is a school and children's home for children and young people with a range of complex needs, including autism. Underley Garden is based in Kirkby Lonsdale, on the border of Cumbria and Lancashire. Jennifer is also a Sensory Integration Practitioner, currently in training to the advanced level.

**Hope Lightowler**
Hope is 20 years old. When she was 17 she was sectioned, and it was a very difficult and traumatic process to get discharged. A couple of months after discharge she was diagnosed with high functioning autism. Chapter 2 is an account of her journey.

**Kate Richardson**
Kate Richardson is a highly specialist learning disability Speech and Language Therapist. She works part-time in the NHS supporting adults with a learning disability and has co-authored several teaching and learning publications on communication and learning disabilities. Kate is a founding director of Autism Wellbeing CIC (http://autismwellbeing.org.uk/index.html), a not-for-profit social enterprise based in Carmarthenshire which provides a range of services to the autistic community.

**Jemma Swales**

After completing a degree in psychology, Jemma worked at a day centre for autistic adults with learning disabilities in London before moving north to Cumbria. She now works as a self-employed Autism Practitioner and is one of the directors of Autus Cumbria Ltd, a small not-for-profit organisation. Her work includes offering long term support for autistic people and their families, running activity sessions for young people and delivering a range of training. Much of her experience involves supporting people with complex behavioural needs and finding and implementing practical ways forward.

# Foreword

Professor Sheila the Baroness Hollins

Phoebe Caldwell has found some unique paths to achieving deep and meaningful engagement with autistic people and people with profound and multiple learning disabilities. Families and carers are in awe of the deep and intuitive connections she is able to make, adapting her way of being with and responding to each person.

Through her practice of Intensive Interaction over several decades, Phoebe has illuminated the way in which sensory issues can impede communication and emotional engagement of autistic individuals with others. She has shown how both hypo- and hyper-sensitivities can contribute to a scrambled sensory input, and how subsequent anxiety results in either hyperarousal (sometimes seen as 'meltdowns') or hypo-arousal (sometimes seen as 'shutdowns'). These sensory issues are often unrecognised by professionals, families and other observers, as they are not routinely part of the experience of those who do not have autism. When sensory triggers are not anticipated or recognised, distress may manifest as behaviours that challenge.

The authors of this book share their different perspectives, while also all being practitioners of Responsive Communication. One author identifies with autism, and the others bring perspectives from a range of professional backgrounds including biology, service management, speech therapy, occupational therapy and psychiatry. Their own complementary perspectives help to broaden the reader's understanding. Responsive Communication is an approach that combines Intensive Interaction with a necessary attention to the sensory issues described briefly above, both being necessary for effective emotional engagement and reduction of behavioural distress.

From my perspective as a psychodynamic psychotherapist, psychiatrist and parent of an adult autistic man, I see in Phoebe someone who has highly developed listening skills. On World Communication Day in 2016, Pope Francis spoke about listening in a pertinent way, saying: '*Listening means paying attention, wanting to understand, to value, to respect and to ponder...*'. These are the skills a skilled psychotherapist should have and in our own deep listening we should be able to tune in to whatever each person is trying to communicate. My experience living alongside a child with little verbal communication led me to explore the power of pictures as a tool to support my listening and inform my understanding and responding. Later, I began to co-create visual stories with people with intellectual disabilities and autism to explore meaning in relationships and life experiences. In my clinical work I used them as projective tools to help me understand my patients. In training others to share these stories I have noticed that some people are uncomfortable with the silence which often accompanies an encounter that triggers a memory of trauma. Filling the space, finding someone else to chat to while waiting for a response, shows a lack of respect and negates the careful thinking that is under way. But more importantly it shows a lack of awareness of the nature and quality of silence. Being comfortable with empty and full spaces, with close and distant encounters, is an attribute that I suspect Phoebe shares with me and the Beyond Words approach.

# Chapter 1: Attention to sensory issues: hyper- and hypo-sensitivities

Phoebe Caldwell

## Introduction

Responsive Communication is a book about how we can get in touch with children and adults who are struggling to understand and articulate speech. Its authors are Elspeth Bradley (psychotherapist and psychiatrist), Hope Lightowler (expert by experience), Janet Gurney (manager of a service for people with severe and profound learning disabilities) and Kate Richardson (speech and language therapist). Jemma Swales (autism practitioner) is manager of a service for autistic children and adults and the final two authors are Jennifer Heath (occupational therapist) and myself, Phoebe Caldwell (biologist). We have also had valuable assistance on visual sensory problems and Irlen syndrome from Tina Yates, director of Irlen East.

Collectively, we have been using autistic people's personal body language to communicate with them (Intensive Interaction) for well over a hundred years: we know just how helpful this way of working can be to establishing emotional engagement with those who are otherwise cut off from communication.

So if Intensive Interaction is so successful, the obvious question is, why introduce an alternative? What can the approach we are now calling 'Responsive Communication' offer that is not already available?

This book is a cooperative effort. Janet will focus mainly on Intensive Interaction. Hope writes about the problems of being at the receiving end of service provision, when your sensory difficulties go unrecognised. Elspeth considers the neurobiological underpinnings of emotional and mental health issues, including meltdowns and shutdowns. Kate shares insights gained from providing a Responsive Communication service to autistic children and young people and their families. Jemma focuses on her experience of working with people who are able to describe the distressing, traumatic events that arise from the clash between their autistic experience and the demands of society. Jennifer discusses sensory issues and body language at a school and children's home for young people with autism and complex needs. I myself (Phoebe) am writing about engagement with autistic adults and children who have severe sensory process issues. Each of us has a different voice, reflecting the wide variety not only of our personalities, but also of our experience. What we have in common is a sense that before we can address communication, or alongside the process of doing so, we need to attend to the sensory features of autism that are hindering our ability to get in touch with our autistic partners. In so doing, we are trying to marry cutting edge (and sometimes extremely complicated) research with our clinical experience of what can be very moving personal emotional engagement. In writing this book we have and are learning from each other – and, all of us, from the autistic people with whom we engage.

In the 1980s Geraint Ephraim, clinical psychologist, introduced the idea of using body language to interact with people who were struggling to understand speech (Intensive Interaction). Gary, as he was known, was my supervisor for four years while I held a Joseph Rowntree Foundation Fellowship. Drawing on the work of Daniel Stern,[1] he called his approach 'augmented mothering', a title that proved to be unfortunate since it coincided – and got lost in – the then emphasis on normalisation and age appropriateness.[2] Services felt (mistakenly) that the title was inappropriate for interventions with adults and in danger of infantilising them. Relaunched as 'Intensive Interaction' by Nind and Hewett,[3] Intensive Interaction is now widely, and successfully, used to tune into the affective world of our conversation partners, both adults and children. The practical experience of the writers of this book is that immersion in the body language of one's partner is accompanied by a decrease in their level of anxiety and helps to encourage them to use such communication as they have. The general quality of their lives is improved.

Practical experience of working with people with autism led the authors to ask themselves whether there are there additional ways that we can help to reduce stress and improve the conditions that facilitate communication. Can we use these to improve the quality of autistic people's lives?

Spurred on by advances in the neurological understanding of the nature of autism, and the new inclusion of sensory issues in DSM-5,[4] it is increasingly clear that addressing these difficulties opens up further ways of reducing the information processing distress so characteristic of autism, and providing an environment that has meaning for the autistic individual. (While Responsive Communication particularly refers to autistic people, the approach described also has relevance to those with severe and profound learning disabilities, who may equally have sensory issues.)

---

1 Stern DN (1985) *The Interpersonal World of the Infant*. New York: Basic Books Inc.

2 Wolfensberger W (2000) A brief overview of social role valorization. *Mental Retardation* **38** 105–123.

3 Nind and Hewett (2001) *A Practical Guide to Intensive Interaction*. London: British Institute of Learning Disabilities.

4 Described as hyper- or hypo-reactivity to sensory input, or unusual interests in sensory aspects of the environment, in the American Psychiatric Association's Diagnostic and Statistical Manual of Mental Disorders, most recently released as the DSM-5.

So for example, it may be counterproductive to try to engage the attention of an autistic person simply by using their body language, if at the same time we are wearing a jazzy coloured T-shirt that triggers visual processing difficulties. They may try and tear off the offending garment, a response that is misinterpreted as aggressive or even sexual behaviour (instead of self-defence against the real pain engendered by visual sensory overload). We need to look for the underlying triggers to the behaviour: the simple remedy in this case is to wear a plain, dull coloured T-shirt, which does not cause visual sensory processing overload.

While independent of cognitive performance, sensory processing issues show up differently in each autistic adult or child. And importantly, the sensory experience of each will be different from that of the people supporting them who are not on the spectrum. Non-autistic people do not see, hear or feel things in the same way as the autistic people with whom we share the world. This 'difference' is spelled out by the Autistic Self Advocacy Group, ASAN:

'*While all Autistics are as unique as any other human beings, they share some characteristics typical of autism in common, such as, different sensory experiences. For example, heightened sensitivity to light, difficulty interpreting physical internal sensations, hearing loud sounds as soft and soft sounds as loud, or synesthesia.*'[5]

This is how Ben, a clever young man who lacks speech, actually feels. He focuses on phrases he has extracted from a tape and spliced into relevant video, which he plays repetitively with total attention and evident pleasure. One of his favourites is, '*I'm different from all you guys, I'm different from all you guys*'. Ben feels himself to be different, and has found a way of affirming this. Our experience is that it is helpful to engage not only with positive feelings, but even more so with negative affect. As we shall discuss later, validation of feelings helps the individual confirm their feeling of self, the loss of which emerges as a problem for many autistic people.

Unless we in the non-autistic world recognise these differences (and adapt our interventions and the environment to meet the sensory needs of the autistic individual), the sensory overload and consequent meltdown they trigger in the autistic brain can have behavioural consequences. While these may be difficult for their care providers to manage, they can be catastrophic for those who experience them. As the autistic child or adult struggles to keep up with the flood of incoming stimuli, most retreat into their own world of repetitive behaviour in order to isolate themselves from the sources of overload. Or they try and get away from the source of intolerable pain and confusion by aggressive acts. Rather than excluding such children, we need to rethink the design of their environment.

5 ASAN (2019) *About Autism* [online]. Available at: www.autisticadvocacy.org/about-asan/about-autism (accessed March 2019).

In writing this book, the authors have thought carefully about the language we are using. This is partly out of regard for the preferences of the autistic people with whom we are trying to engage and partly because the words we use to describe a condition reflect the nature of personal sensibility, but also because our descriptions can influence how others will interact. What we are looking for is definitions that balance accuracy with respect. So we have rejected 'sensory impairment', 'sensory deficit' and 'sensory deviations' as being seen to have negative overtones, looking instead at 'sensory problems' and 'sensory concerns' before settling for 'sensory issues'. At the same time we recognise that when we ask autistic people about their preferences, those who can tell us are highly articulate, but there are many on the spectrum for whom 'issues' does not truly reflect the gravity of their distress and how this impacts on their quality of life.

We use the term 'people' rather than 'case studies' or 'histories', since they are more than this: if one has been using body language to set up emotional engagement, getting the therapeutic distance between oneself and partner right has become important. As they struggle to make sense of a world that is behaving like a kaleidoscope where the pattern never settles, we have become close to each other; they are people with whom we have opened up a relationship, not examples.

Finally, there is lack of uniformity as to a collective description for those on the autistic spectrum, between those dedicated to 'people first language', who use the term 'people with autism', and those who prefer 'autistic people'. The latter is favoured by articulate self-advocates since they feel that 'people with autism' overlooks the reality which they experience (as if it were somehow separate), and also presents autism as a negative condition. This is a deeply felt emotional quagmire with entrenched arguments on both sides. Lydia Brown, of ASAN offers a fair summary of the different points of view.[6]

In this context it seems important to remind ourselves of the wide variation in presentation of autism. Donna Williams, who was among the first autistic people to write about her life and experiences, emphasises that she cannot be a spokesperson for all people with autism, since everyone is different.[7] Some professionals feel it is disrespectful and dismissive to use 'autistic people' for those who are non-verbal and have severe learning disabilities. While acknowledging that our choice may be regarded as sitting on the fence, the authors of this book have decided to use the terms interchangeably, as appears most respectful to them in any given context.

And as regards personal attitude (while not all professionals would agree and we need to guard against the danger of projecting our own feelings onto

6 Brown L (2011) *The Significance of Semantics: Person-first language: why it matters* [online]. Autistic Hoya. Available at: https://www.autistichoya.com/2011/08/significance-of-semantics-person-first.html (accessed March 2019).

7 Williams D (1995) *Jam-Jar.* Channel 4. Glasgow: Fresh Film and Television.

our partner – and also taking on board their feelings as our own), when we are practicing, we do have to find ways to become as vulnerable as the person we are working with. Otherwise we cannot fully enter the space of intimate mutual attention, where we are open with each other, testing out each other's emotional boundaries and starting to build engagement and trust. This is what we mean when we talk about 'valuing' another person (valuing them not just as we think they should behave to be socially acceptable but as they actually are), so that we take the trouble to learn not only their emotional language, but the nuances of their affective status. Fortunately, this is not as difficult as it sounds, since human body language is a direct route to how we feel. As we shall see, navigating its skill is not new to us, since we have all been through the process of learning to read each other's body language in infancy.

To summarise, 'Responsive Communication' is the name adopted by a combined holistic way of getting in touch with autistic children and adults with whom we struggle to communicate, they with us and we with them. It is an add-on to Intensive Interaction that not only pays attention to and responds to body language but at the same time addresses sensory processing issues. As well as increasing incoming signals that do carry meaning, by using signals the brain recognises easily, it aims to reduce incoming messages that are overloading the processing system. And while seeking to avoid trespassing over professional boundaries, this approach draws together a number of different angles on the most effective ways of tuning in to the lives of those we are trying to engage with. It offers a truly person-centred way of engaging with them, especially with autistic people, one that facilitates the interventions of all parents, therapists and all who support them. We need to pool all our skills.

Some of the people we shall meet will be familiar to readers of my earlier books. I have gathered them together, because collectively they represent the sensory difficulties with which so many autistic people are struggling (even if they personally do not recognise these as out of the ordinary since the sensory overload they experience represents 'normality'). I am revisiting them in order to emphasise the possibility of taking remedial action by paying attention to the individual's sensory issues.

I also need to make a personal apology. My practice spans forty-five years and while my memory of relationships with individuals as people is clear, references to some have been mislaid, although I did have permission to write about them at the time.

I am reintroducing some of the people with whom I have engaged because, rather than dwelling on behavioural outcomes, their stories illustrate the courageous way autistic individuals continue to tackle a world that is not making sense. Most of what I know I have learned from the people with whom it has been my privilege to engage.

# Autism

Autism has always been difficult to diagnose since it presents in so many different ways; it is a cliché drawn from experience that there are as many different varieties of autism as there are autistic people. In each person the autistic condition is impressed upon a unique individual, who may be functioning at almost any level of cognitive ability. The condition of autism is somewhat like a tree, where one can recognise the species by its leaves and general morphology. It has many different roots (causes) and multiple branches (consequences). Its final shape, contours and size will be unique, depending on all sorts of inner disconnections and environmental factors. We are trying to put into one category what is truly a wide spectrum with many underlying causes. In addressing some of the sensory issues, Responsive Communication does not expect to cure the autism, but rather to moderate particular effects and reduce the anxiety that goes with it.

Ever since Leo Kanner published his study of eleven children[8] in which he described the autistic child as having '*a powerful desire for aloneness*' and '*an obsessive insistence on persistent sameness*' and made the distinction between autism and schizophrenia, the one diagnostic feature that is consistent is the wide differences in presentation.

Diagnosis of the autistic condition has tended to focus on behaviours. In the 1970s, Lorna Wing and Judith Gould defined the 'triad of impairments' (difficulties in social interaction, social imagination and social communication), which came to be recognised as the gold standard for diagnosis. However, until recently, focus on behaviour led it to be thought that more boys were autistic than girls; it is only lately that it has it been understood that girls have been missed out, since they tend to be more socially interactive than boys, or better at masking their symptoms. For this reason, quite a number of autistic women are receiving a late diagnosis: one that normally comes as a relief to an individual who has recognised their difference (and even been told they are 'mad' or 'bad') but not been helped to understand why they have specific difficulties.[9]

The number of children diagnosed with autism is roughly one in one hundred in the UK but in America, the figure is thought to be higher, one in sixty eight – the discrepancy being attributed to different criteria used in diagnosis.[10] Exactly what underlies these figures is a matter of dispute – how much is environmental and how much genetic? One study in Scandinavia suggests that it is about half and half. Other studies point towards diesel and fire retardants and organic

8 Kanner L (1943) Autistic disturbances of affective contact. *The Nervous Child* **2** 217–250.

9 '*It all made sense when we found out that we were autistic*' http://bbc.in/2GRcBRa

10 Earl RK, Peterson JL, Wallace AS, Fox E, Ma R, Pepper M and Haidar G (2017) *Autism Spectrum Disorder: A reference guide* [online]. Bernier Lab, University of Washington. Available at: http://depts.washington.edu/rablab/wordpress/wp-content/uploads/2017/07/Bernier-Lab-UW-Autism-Spectrum-Disorder-Reference-Guide-2017.pdf (accessed March 2019).

chemicals in the environment as responsible. In favour of genetic aetiology, 'an exhaustive review of genetics has so far identified over a hundred different mutations and imbalances associated with autism spectrum disorders'. Autism is not a single clinical identity but '... a behavioural manifestation of tens and perhaps hundreds of genetic and genomic disorders'.[11]

While the exact cause of autism is unclear, dramatic strides in scanning techniques and accompanying neurosciences have made it possible to see what is actually happening inside the brain, even to the extent of highlighting individual fibres in the brain. This research is ongoing and in some cases contested. For this reason, some of the ideas and associations put forward in this book may be speculative. But anatomical studies make it clear that the structure of the brain is affected, both at a gross level and in terms of cellular structure. For example, cells in some autistic brains in the evolutionary, earlier part of the brain (the limbic system) may be smaller and very tightly compacted.

*'Autism Spectrum Disorder (ASD) is arguably one of the most puzzling, yet intriguing neurodevelopmental disorders. The first description of this disease 60 years ago suggested a significant malfunction in cognition and behaviour in affected children. For a period of time it was believed that parenting and environmental factors were responsible for the absence of social interactions, repetitive behaviour, impaired language and an obsessive need for "sameness"... More detailed and careful analysis of post-mortem and imaging studies instead implicated fundamental defects in brain pathology, in regions including the limbic system, hippocampus, amygdala, cerebellum, corpus callosum, basal ganglia and brainstem.'*[12]

As one parent from that era put it to me, 'it was bad enough having a child who one loved but was out of reach, without being told it was my fault'.

And while autism is associated with such well-known genetic conditions as Fragile X and Tuberous Sclerosis,[13] Temple Grandin points out, and I agree, that there do seem to be two major different groups of what we are calling autism. The first is evident when the mother (or mother figure) knows that there is something 'wrong' from the first time that she picks up her baby; the baby is not cuddling in and relating in a way that might be expected. The other group of babies appear to develop normally and then suddenly 'become autistic', sometimes almost overnight. Onset may be later but typically is around age of two and a half to three. Occasionally late onset can be confused with schizophrenia.

11 Betancur C (2011) Etiological heterogeneity in autism spectrum disorders: more than 100 genetic and genomic disorders and still counting. *Brain Research* **1380** 41–77.

12 Sudarov A (2013) Defining the role of cerebellar Purkinje cells in autism spectrum disorders. *The Cerebellum* **12** (6) 950.

13 Grandin T and Panek R (2013) *The Autistic Brain: Thinking across the spectrum*. Boston, MA: Houghton Mifflin Harcourt.

Whatever the underlying cause or causes of autism, the nervous system is being affected. In the case of babies that appear to have it from birth, it is probable that the damage begins during the first four weeks after conception (not birth), when the neural tube is being formed, with knock-on effects to later development. This infantile autism may be inherited, but could also be the result of environmental insult damaging the genes prior to conception. If this is the case, there is a possibility that an environmental trigger could be getting built into genetic sequences and therefore becoming hereditable.

Onset in toddlers appears to have a different aetiology. Autistic or not, in an effort to make sense of what is going on around us, all of us grow billions of connections (synapses) in our brains during the first few years. Brain cells (neurons) are grabbing hold of each other in an effort to establish neural circuits that will help us to make sense of the world in which we find ourselves placed. Quite a lot of these tentative connections are never used and, in a process known as 'synaptic pruning', are tidied away by a different type of brain cell (the brain's domestic cleaners), known as glial cells. Under-pruning leaves too many connections, so that the brain is indiscriminately overactive when it fires. Temple Grandin says *'It's like having a lion in the head'*. Another description is of a Catherine wheel. Alternatively disconnection may be the outcome of over-enthusiastic pruning, when useful links between different parts of the brain are cut away.

As we learn more about the neuroanatomy of autism, attention has shifted from the 'what' questions (what is this child or adult doing, what is their behaviour – and usually, 'how can we change it?'), to 'why are they doing this?'. Why does Jimmy endlessly focus on lining up cars, or have what appear to be outbursts of inexplicable distress? And is Mike correct to say, *'My brain is not wired up properly'*?

These days we are used to thinking of our brains as resembling vast computers. In order to function smoothly, the different compartments need to be able to talk to each other.[14] But we do now know that autism arises during periods of neuroplasticity, when nerve cells in the foetal and infant brain are growing connections both with each other and between different parts of the brain. Underpinned by both genetic and environmental triggers, while some areas become over-connected or under-connected, others are misrouted entirely. These variations will be different in different individuals, according to how the brain wires up or has failed to do so; this in itself could account for the astonishing diversity in presentation of autism in the spectrum. However the overall problem appears to relate to a failure in connectivity.[15]

---

14 In others the two parts concerned with speech (reception and production) are not linked, and in yet others a disconnect separates sensations gathered in the body from emotions perceived in the brain.

15 Kana RL, Libero LE, Moore MS (2011) Disrupted cortical connectivity theory as an explanatory model for autism spectrum disorders. *Physics of Life Reviews* **8** (4) 410–437.

Connectivity failures are at the root of a number of problems. If we take off the top of our heads and look inside, we see the familiar walnut shaped brain, separated into two halves joined by the corpus callosum, a thick band consisting of two hundred million fibres, a figure that gives us some idea of the scope of the possibilities for variation. It appears that in many autistic people, the corpus callosum link is damaged so the two halves of the brain may have difficulty communicating with each other. The corpus callosum could be smaller or have parts missing, or could even be totally absent. While not everyone who has corpus callosum agenesis (complete or partial absence of the corpus callosum) is on the spectrum, where this is so, it is accompanied by difficulties in social behaviour similar to those present in autism.[16]

But it is worth pausing to look at the effects of damage to the corpus callosum, or what is known as having a 'split brain'. In itself, this condition is not as drastic as one might think. Studies by the cognitive neuroscientist Michael Gazziniga into people who had the connection between the two halves of the brain deliberately separated in order to treat severe epilepsy (in the past – this treatment is no longer carried out) indicate that they can live reasonably normal lives and hold down a job. Michael and his team spent forty years investigating the neural functioning of patients with severe epilepsy who have undergone surgical treatment to sever the corpus callosum, effectively cutting off the two sides of the brain from each other.

For all of us, there is a crossover between the eyes and the visual processing area of the brain so that what our right eye sees is processed by the left brain, and what we see on our left side is processed by the right brain. When Joe (who is not autistic but who has had the corpus callosum severed to treat his epilepsy) is presented with a picture of a phone – arranged so that he can only see it on his left side – he recognises and processes this in his right brain, but can only say the word 'phone' after he has drawn it. (Knowing what a phone is and being able to name it are lodged in opposite sides of the brain.) So Joe needs to give himself an external clue before he can say what is already known to him in the right half of his brain.

External clues may be important for a number of autistic people. In this context it seems quite possible that Donna Williams also had a problem with her corpus callosum. Compare Joe's inability to articulate what he already knows with Donna's account of how she wrote her first book.

*'What happened was I just got a typewriter and then, once it was on the table I put a page in and it all just came out. And I am sitting there, my fingers going and I'm reading it as its coming out at me and telling me what is in me.*

---

16 Lau YC, Hinkley LB, Bukshpun P, Strominger ZA, Wakahiro ML, Baron-Cohen S, Allison C, Auyeung B, Jeremy RJ, Nagarajan SS, Sherr EH, Marco EJ (2013) Autism traits in individuals with agenesis of the corpus callosum. *Journal of Autism and Developmental Disorders* **43** (5) 1106–1118.

*So it wasn't really that I talked to the pages of my book but it was that the pages of my book came from up here* [touches forehead] *back through my eyes and talked to me. And I listened very big and I thought I'm going to take care of myself now that I own it.'*[17]

So once it was on paper, what she had recognised as feelings lodged in her right brain, could inform her left brain and allowed her to articulate what she felt. Although she knew her own story, she needed to see it before she could articulate it. (Perhaps this is where social stories may be helpful; the left brain may recognise and be able to formulate what the right brain knows, when it sees the correct prompt.)

In later chapters we shall come across other disconnections between different areas of the brain, which have a direct impact on the way that the brain as a whole is able to function, such as that between the part of the brain concerned with speech reception (Wernicke's area) and speech production (Broca's area). These two need to work together, in order to receive, configure and articulate responses. Yet another disconnection has been identified in autistic people in the interoceptive system, which gathers information about temperature, feelings and pain and feeds them to the brain, which then builds an overall picture of the state of the body.

But while some connectivity variations have the potential for adding to confusion, others may actually be helpful. About 10% of autistic people are what is known as 'savants', who have remarkable abilities in particular fields. Temple Gradin,[18] Professor of Animal Science at Colorado State University, has severe autism. She is famous for being able to visualise complex engineering blueprints in her brain, down to the last screw, without resorting to pen and paper. That is, her visual processing capacity is phenomenal. High definition fibre tracking scans of her brain show that unsurprisingly, her visual processing tract is huge, while her speech production processing area is disorganised. When she speaks, it is clear that she has had to work hard on this; it does not flow easily.

However, as well as exceptional brilliance, autism in around half of people on the spectrum is accompanied by intellectual difficulties, sometimes severe or profound. Perhaps it is more useful to think of this the other way round; that some children and adults with severe and profound intellectual issues also show autistic behaviours. Again, it depends which part of the brain is affected.

As well as disconnects and issues with the strength of signals, once in the brain messages can also be sent in the inappropriate directions so that

---

17 Williams D (1995) *Jam-Jar*. Channel 4. Glasgow: Fresh Film and Television. For a more detailed account of the right brain–left brain story, see Caldwell P (2017) *Hall of Mirrors – Shards of Clarity: Autism, neuroscience and finding a sense of self*. Brighton: Pavilion Publishing & Media Ltd.

18 Grandin T (2013) *The Autistic Brain*. Boston: Houghton Mifflin Harcourt.

they arrive at the wrong processing area. For example, incoming auditory signals may end up at the visual processing area, so that sound may be 'seen' as coloured light streamers, described as a kind of aurora. Cytowic[19] reports a crossover between taste and shape: soup that was too salty and is described as containing too many triangles. The experience of synaesthesia is not confined to the autistic spectrum and may seem bizarre to the non-synesthete, because we all, autistic or not, take our own sensory experience to be objective reality.

The outcome of failures in connectivity and misrouting is that the brain cannot keep up with sorting incoming stimuli and experiences sensory overload in the processing systems. In a clip in her film, *Jam-Jar*,[20] Donna Williams shows her walking past the crisp packet aisle in a supermarket, each brand with a different colour packet. She shows us how she can process the first colour and up to a point the second, but then as the camera slips past, the colours become a blur and '*her brain keeps running, running, running, trying to keep up*', resulting in sensory overload and confusion.

There are many descriptions by autistic people as to what it is like to experience sensory overload. These are complicated by the term being used loosely to describe different phases of an experience, whereby the sympathetic nervous system (the parts of our nervous system not under voluntary control such as heart rate, breathing rate, stomach churning and sweating) becomes overactive and the person may be subjected to sometimes severe pain. Some will use 'sensory overload' to describe the omnipresent background experience of unfiltered incoming information, and the intrusive anxiety that accompanies their inability to keep up with sensory processing, while others use the term sensory overload to describe the onset and build-up of sympathetic activity in what is variously known as a 'meltdown', 'fragmentation', 'crisis', 'tantrum' or 'autonomic storm'. In simple terms the latter is like a magnified panic attack where the autonomic nervous system blows its fuses. A small boy says, '*My head's running away, my head's running away*'. Sam says, '*It's like having my head in a car crusher*'. Peter says, '*I would do anything to stop it, run in front of a car*'.[21] For some, their bodily response to stimulus seems to be all over the place; Wes says '*It's a struggle to respond proportionally to stimulus*'. He likens it to '*an allergic reaction, the emotional equivalent to anaphylactic shock*'.[22] And Donna Williams adds it feels like death coming to get her. She continues, 'it's amazing how many times a day I could be dying and still be alive'.[23]

19 Cytowic R (1998) *The Man who Tasted Shapes*. Cambridge, MA: The MIT Press.

20 Williams D (1995) *Jam-Jar.* Channel 4. Glasgow: Fresh Film and Television.

21 Speaker in 'A Bridge of Voices'. Radio Documentary. BBC Radio4.

22 Personal communication.

23 Williams D (1998) *Nobody Nowhere: The remarkable autobiography of an autistic girl.* London: Jessica Kingsley Publishers.

In order to avoid the anxiety that accompanies even the anticipation of sensory overload and consequent confusion, distress and pain, the autistic person may retreat into their own world, with all their attention focused on special interests, or a self-regulating repetitive behaviour. Such a focus on repetitive behaviour provides a stimulus that can be described as 'hard-wired in': a desperate search for an activity that the brain recognises, without adding to processing confusion.

Known as 'stimming', these repetitive behaviours are often physical activities such as scratching their fingers, flapping hands, even something as simple as clicking the tongue or listening to their own breathing rhythm. When an autistic person stims, they know what they are doing. Those who are more self-aware may resort to these activities quite deliberately, using the activity as a precautionary defence against overload.

In a conference situation there are a number of people milling around and potentially a situation that will trigger sensory processing overload. I meet Jo, who takes out some French knitting. She looks at me and laughs, '*socially acceptable stimming!*'.

In most autistic people, the threshold for triggering the body's self-defence system appears to be set at an unusually low level, so they feel threatened by levels of incoming stimuli that non-autistic people might find benign. If stimming or repetitive activities do not protect them sufficiently, their self-defence system may be triggered.

*'There is growing evidence that autism spectrum disorder is associated with dysregulation of the autonomic nervous system, where the sympathetic branch of the autonomic nervous system is activated in response to events that are experienced as stressful.'*[24]

Stress is not only triggered by immediate sensory assault, but also by anticipatory anxiety that it may happen at any time; that the autistic person will be placed in a situation that will tip them into a painful autonomic storm, involving sensations such as heart racing, accelerated breathing rhythm, stomach churning, etc. These are associated with pain, confusion and, quite often, heat. Ramachandran describes this over-activity of the sympathetic system activity, which is prompted by an over aroused amygdala, as triggering an 'autonomic blitzkrieg', which sweeps away all control.[25] Anticipation walks along a crumbling cliff edge: Judith Bluestone says, '*For those of us on the autistic spectrum, every event also causes discomfort and distress. Just the thought of these events can elicit anxiety.*'[26]

---

24 Panju S, Brian J, Dupuis A, Anagnostou E, Kushki A (2015) Atypical sympathetic arousal in children with autism spectrum disorder and its association with anxiety symptomatology. *Molecular Autism* **11** (6) 64.

25 Ramachandran VS (2012) *The Tell-tale Brain: Unlocking the mystery of human nature.* London: Windmill Books.

26 Bluestone J (2005) *The Fabric of Autism: Weaving threads into a cogent theory.* New York: The Handle Institute.

Under these circumstances, the autistic person may feel themselves to be in mortal danger and respond with 'exit strategies', trying to remove themselves from what they perceive as the source of their overload by hiding or running away. Ros Blackburn found it very effective to throw the handbag of a particularly stress inducing key worker out of the window. She says it was a strategy that worked every time.

Or people may self-injure to distract themselves from the confusion and pain. Donna Williams spells out the sensory build-up to self-injury in graphic terms:

*'There was a rip through the centre of my soul. Self-abuse was the outward sign of an earthquake nobody saw. I was like an appliance during a power surge. As I blew fuses, my hands pulled out my hair and slapped my face. My teeth bit my flesh like an animal bites the bars of its cage, not realising the cage was my own body. My legs ran round in manic circles, as though they could outrun the body they were attached to. My head hit whatever was next to it, like someone trying to crack a nut that had grown too large for its shell. There was an overwhelming feeling of inner deafness – deafness to self that would consume all that was left in a fever pitch of silent screaming.'*[27]

Alternatively, people may become aggressive, in the hope of persuading the (rightly or wrongly) perceived source of their sensory overload to go away. Although this may apparently 'come out of the blue', it is more usual that we have missed the signs of sensory build-up, which may be increased agitation reflected in the rate of stimming, or a change in skin colour or even just a twitch of the head. Each person has their own signs and we need to look out for them and remember that it is we (or environmental factors) that are triggering their anxiety and pain. The autistic person is now in a situation where they are overwhelmed by sensory distress.

More rarely, the brain goes into 'immobilisation' or 'shutdown'. Mary cannot move from her classroom to the hall – at the threshold she stops with one leg in the air. No amount of verbal encouragement can get her to walk through the doorway. In this case, she is helped by giving her a heavy chair to carry which she will use to sit on when she is in the hall: a physical clue overrides the confusion triggered by transition overload.

The classic study on shutdowns is by Ingrid Loos Miller and Hendricus Loos,[28] who made extensive observations of a child in school. When pressured by an adult to complete a difficult task:

---

27 Williams D (1995) *Somebody Somewhere: Breaking free from the world of autism.* New York: Broadway Books.

28 Loos Miller IM and Loos HG (2019) *Shutdowns and Stress in Autism* [online]. Autism Awareness Centre Inc. Available at: https://autismawarenesscentre.com/shutdowns-stress-autism (accessed March 2019).

*'We observed a predictable sequence of behaviour. She looked away from the work area and became distracted with objects around her; became unresponsive, sleepy, immobile, and limp to the touch for several minutes, and then fell asleep in a chair for as briefly as 10 min. and up to 2 hours.*

*She also did this after being corrected for a mistake, such as making a letter incorrectly. When directed back to the task, she had difficulty looking at the page; she kept looking away. She rubbed her eyes and kept them closed. We identified eye rubbing as the threshold stress reaction. Once she rubbed her eyes, if the adult continued to press her, shutdown was inevitable. Offered a reward to finish the task, she appeared to want it, tried to finish but was still too disorientated to continue.'*

They suggest that her shutdowns were caused by an abnormal, unstable response to stress, which they call 'stress instability':

*'The stress instability causes the magnitude of the body's stress response to far exceed that which is normal. If severe enough, the child will go into shutdown so that her body can recover. The levels of stress hormone are higher than normal and they remain elevated for a prolonged period, both of which causes damage to the child's brain.'*

Tim Tuff, who is autistic, gives us an inside view of what shutdown feels like. He senses when this is going to happen to him and says that *'I go unusually quiet and may flap my hands or fiddle with my hair. Sometimes my face goes a little red'* (this latter suggests a build up of activity in the sympathetic nervous system, which alters the size of the capillaries and hence facial colouring). When this happens to him he 'zones out', switching to a form of absence that helps him cope with the overload. He becomes unconscious of the world around him, cannot see and is disorientated, cannot hear what is going on round him and physically cannot run away from the overload although he would like to.[29]

Asked why he got stuck turning the pages of a book, another young man said that 'he needed time to think', that is, time to organise his muscles so that he could proceed.

Apart from aggression, there seem to be two responses that our autonomic nervous systems have evolved to get out of danger: in her chapter, Elspeth will point to a distinction between 'freezing' and immobilisation (shutdown). Freezing is associated with the sympathetic nervous system – when the brain no longer issues motor instructions so that (no matter what it is trying to do) the body comes to a halt. Immobilisation is associated with the parasympathetic nervous system, when the body 'plays dead' (in the hope that the perceived danger will lose interest and go away).

29 Tuff T (2018) Shutdowns: the invisible enemy. *Aukids* **39** 9.

Feelings and responses vary. Gunilla Gerland describes a fluctuation in sensory overload intensity from a 'normal' state of spinal distress to the spread of pain into her arms.

*'All the time I was growing up I experienced a constant shudder down my spine. Periodically the shuddering grew worse, while at other times it kept relatively quiet so I could live with it. It was like the feeling you get before you sneeze, only as if it had got stuck and was suspended in my spine in order to turn into something permanent ... I became slightly used to it but it was a constant torture, most noticeably when it changed in intensity. It was like cold steel down my spine. It was hard and fluid at the same time, with metallic fingers drumming and tickling the outside. Like sharp clips in my spins and lemonade inside. Icy heat and digging fiery cold. It was like the sound of screeching chalk on a blackboard turned into a silent concentration of feeling, then placed in the back of my neck. From there, so metallic, the feeling radiated out into my arms, clipped itself into my elbows but never came to an end, never came to an end.'*[30]

In 'The Anger Box', William also describes the spread of painful sensation where, once the box which he says 'lives in his chest' opens, the pain spreads from his core to all his limbs. As he describes this, his hand runs down to the tips of his fingers as he shudders. He says that once it has started he has absolutely no control over what he is doing.

How can we non-autistics understand, or rather internalise, what these sensory sensations feel like and the stress which they engender? It is extremely difficult for us to take on board in ourselves the state of being autistic (our own theory of mind lets us down badly when it comes to perception of a completely different experience). We can inform ourselves through journals, through written accounts by autistic people and by listening to what autistic people have to say, but this does not allow us to share feeling. In this respect I have found it helpful to enter the affective experience of autism through immersion in their creative art and poetry, where 'conscious intention breaks up and ceases to be the driving force'.[31]

Grace Igoe is primarily an artist and a very fine one indeed, who happens to be on the spectrum. Her autism is incidental to who she feels herself to be. She works freelance and also teaches at the Manchester School of Art. The nature of her autism is only one of the themes she explores in her ceramics. In an interview she says:

*'I am not autistic when I am making. I am me: creative, imaginative. My ceramic work aims to communicate and show awareness of the autistic condition. I use the form of human heads in my work because facial features are a vehicle for*

30 Gerland G (2003) A *Real Person: Life on the outside*. London: Souvenir Press.

31 Andrew Marr in a review of Martin Gayford's book, *Modernists and Mavericks*.

*expression; the face tells us most about an individual's mood, personality and state of mind ... My work aims to explore and express issue based narratives, questioning and challenging the concepts of everyday life and things that you can't see but are there. Clay as a medium has given me a voice. As a ceramicist, my practice aims to communicate and show awareness about the autistic condition through exploring common traits and behaviours, such as difficulty expressing emotion, struggling managing changes and a strong sense of not fitting in.*'[32]

It is not only to those interested in the autistic world that Grace speaks: by any standards her ceramic heads are stunning – and also shocking; I strongly recommend visiting her website, particularly to view the three almost life size crania which bring home the struggle to maintain 'normality'.

Body language allows us to share affect in a way that words do not; it is only when conscious explanations are put aside and unconscious drives are revealed in body language that we can begin to empathise and share what the author/poet/painter is experiencing.

Some people would argue that in order to maintain professional detachment those who are not on the spectrum should protect ourselves and not even try to go there emotionally. I disagree, and believe that we need to explore the interior struggle since it is so shockingly removed from our own. I need to understand this out of respect for my autistic partner, who may otherwise be judged from an emotional distance by their distressed and 'odd' responses to an unpredictable and frightening battle with sensory distortions. As we shall see, we need to look not only at the physical sensory difficulties that are underpinning their experience, but also at the psychological difficulties caused, both by trauma and the responses and rejection feedback that the autistic person is receiving from society as they go through life.

Autistic or not, we are all people, and all of us spend our lives trying to make sense of what is going on in the world around us and inside ourselves. In the interests of survival, we are trying to define the boundary between what is 'me' and 'not me' and what is going on 'out there'. But how would it be if our sensory intake was so garbled that our brain greets every event with suspicion, so that it is not allowing us to make accurate life preserving decisions?

Again, what all of us are experiencing of the world outside ourselves, is an approximation (some would even call it a hallucination) of the reality of our environment. We see with our eyes and hear with our ears; at least we think we do. But surprisingly, our eyes and ears are only receptive organs, picking up electromagnetic or pressure signals, converting them into electrical signals

32 Igoe G (2018) 'I am not autistic when I am making. I am me: creative, imaginative.' [online] Learning Disability Today. Available at: https://www.learningdisabilitytoday.co.uk/i-am-not-autistic-when-i-am-making-i-am-me-creative-imaginative.

and forwarding them onto the visual or auditory processing centres in the brain, where they are turned into pictures or soundscapes, telling us what is going on in our world. In his book *The Brain*, David Eagleman presents us with a reality that is both fascinating and, since it is so unexpected, almost unbelievable. Our world, with all its sensory delights, is grey and silent and has no smell. '*The dull truth is that, the real world is not full of rich sensory events: instead our brains light up the world with their own sensuality.*'[33]

If the real seeing and hearing goes on in our brains rather than in our sense organs, any deviation from the norm during the processes of reception, transmission and processing in autistic people will confuse the brain in various ways. If there are issues with connectivity, if the wiring is faulty in any way, there is going to be a problem with assembling a coherent picture of the surrounding environment and all its pressures.

Their perceptual experience translates differently in different individuals. At a conference, Richard McGuire tried to give his audience an idea of what his autistic visual experience is like. He took a photograph of the room and distorted it so that the audience could compare what they were seeing with his visual experience of the same point of view. What the audience was looking at was a typical lecture hall with staggered rows of seats rising to the back. But the picture Richard showed of his visual experience is that of looking down a tube with a blurry periphery slipping inwards towards a couple of central chairs. The rest is indistinct and vaguely menacing.

This is in itself stressful because, in order to function, we rely on a world picture of an environment that is sensorily predictable. It is unsurprising that anxiety is such a feature of autism.

'*... an important role for the amygdala is in the detection of threats and mobilizing an appropriate behavioural response, part of which is fear. If the amygdala is pathological in subjects with autism, it may contribute to their abnormal fears and increased anxiety rather than their abnormal social behaviour.*'[34]

Identification of the particular sensory issue is a first step but we also need to think about ways in which we can avoid triggering them.

While it would be simple to say 'avoid all triggers', and while there are circumstances where avoiding environmental stress is an option, this is often not practical when autistic people are living in the community. This is especially a problem in inclusive schools, where the non-autistic population requires the very stimulation that is disturbing for people on the spectrum.

33 Eagleman D (2015) *The Brain: The story of you.* London: Canongate Books.

34 Amaral DG and Corbett BA (2003) The amygdala, autism and anxiety. *Novartis Foundation Symposium* **251** 177–187.

In the northwest England, 4,485 autistic children were excluded from school in 2015–2016 for unmanageable behaviour. A classic example is of an autistic child who hits a teaching assistant and is excluded from school and sent to a pupil referral unit.[35] Many teachers are untrained in the sensory difficulties experienced by children with autism and have no idea how to support them. And the current design of schools, with their high echoing ceilings, their strip lighting, the constant overlapping speech, the clutter on the walls, even down to boards with corrugated edges, is a sensory catastrophe for most children with autism. The new build schools are in many cases as bad or worse than some of the older buildings. We shall see that remedial strategies fall into a number of categories.

We need to look at how we can reduce triggers, either by ensuring a tranquil environment (for example by using acoustic panelling), or by addressing the particular deficit with assistive devices (tinted lenses, noise reduction headphones and pressure clothing), which cut down a particular cause of distress.

In a known sequence leading to meltdown, if we spot an initial sign of distress such as increased tension, changing colour of cheeks, we can sometimes step in and anticipate the climax, deflecting attention from the build-up; relocating attention from the perseverant internal neural messaging onto external and meaningful relationship.

Some people can be distracted by offering alternatives that do have meaning, such as trampolining, which can address the problem of weak messages to the brain, telling it what it is doing. (The distraction must be something that is part of the autistic person's repertoire, something the brain recognises.)

In the next sections we shall be looking at some of the sensory issues that autistic people struggle with and listening to what they tell us about their experience. Where possible we shall try to tie their experience into theory. Most importantly, we must ask ourselves what we can do in the way of alleviation. How can we help reduce the impact of these sensory difficulties?

## Sensory issue 1: visual processing difficulties (Irlen syndrome/scotopic sensitivity)

Most of what is known about the special visual processing problems relating to autism originates from the study of dyslexia and the visual perceptual difficulties which are known as Irlen syndrome; in common parlance there is some confusion over which is which and how they overlap. And there are still many professionals (whose attitude to dyslexia was originally sceptical) who are dismissive of the reality of Irlen syndrome. So, while admitting that there

35 Hazell W (2018) *Exclusions of autistic pupils up 60 percent* [online]. Tes. Available at: https://www.tes.com/news/exclusions-autistic-pupils-60-cent (accessed March 2019).

is still a great need for research and empirical evidence, we need to have a look at what clinical evidence exists for Irlen syndrome.

Tina Yates, who currently runs the Irlen Centre in the UK, says:

*'The distinction between dyslexia and Irlen syndrome is often blurred. They may co-exist but either may be present on its own. Words moving or floating are caused by Irlen syndrome; so spectral filtration should help those with this processing difference whether they are dyslexic or not. Many erroneously believe that colour can aid reading in dyslexia, whilst others dispute that colour helps at all. Much of this confusion arises from the frequent co-morbidity of the two conditions.'*[36]

As an example of this confusion, teams from Bristol and Newcastle universities carried out eye tests on more than 5,800 children and did not find any differences in the vision of those with dyslexia.[37] They concluded that this finding *'raised doubts about the value of using coloured overlays or lenses to help dyslexic children with reading, since eyesight was very unlikely to be the cause of such reading problems'*. A large majority of dyslexic children were defined as having 'perfect vision'. The inference is that these children are just slow readers and were best helped by phonic remediation, rather than expensive colour filters and lenses.

However this is a conclusion which overlooks the part played by the eye in collecting and forwarding signals, which are not transformed into visual experience until they reach the appropriate brain processing area. The eyes may be in good order: the problem lies somewhere in the transport of the signals to the brain, or in their visual processing destination (as we shall see, a shortage of Purkinje cells may be a suspect).

The arguments continue. Bruce Evans, director of research at the Institute of Optometry, says:

*'It is a great shame that in interpreting their results the authors seem to only consider two options: that visual issues either cause reading disability or are irrelevant to reading disability. Such extreme views were popular in the 1970s, but nowadays most practitioners recognise that children who struggle at school need to have sensory factors ruled out as possible contributory factors (for example tests of eyesight and hearing).'*[38]

John Rack, director of education and policy at Dyslexia Action says:

*'The confusion comes in part from the fact that a minority of people who are dyslexic do find that text is significantly clearer when viewed through*

36 Tina Yates, personal communication.

37 Coughlan S (2015) Dyslexia not linked to eyesight, says study [online]. *BBC News* **27 May.** Available at: https://www.bbc.co.uk/news/education-32836733 (accessed March 2019).

38 *Ibid* Coughlan.

*a coloured filter or lens. And some who are not dyslexic experience the same kind of benefit.'*[39]

Personally, I did witness a dramatic change in reading skill when a child came to the house of a teacher for remedial coaching where I was staying. Aged 12, he was unable to read. It happened that I had recently been given some used theatre gels. We tried these without success until we came to an orange filter. It then appeared he could read perfectly well. But then it is probable that he had Irlen syndrome and not dyslexia, that is, the letters in front of him were on the move. Or possibly he had both.

Interesting evidence comes from scans that highlight the difference in brain activity between an individual (see Figure 1) whose Irlen syndrome is uncorrected by tinted lenses (left hand scan) doing a task, with the same child doing the same task when she is wearing her corrective tinted lenses (right hand scan). Using SPECT scans (single proton emission computed tomography) to compare brain activity in 42 people diagnosed with Irlen syndrome with 100 control individuals, Dr Amen found that, while attending to a visual task, the brain in the Irlen group was having to work much harder in the brain's emotional and visual processing centres. When using the correct colour filter, the brain returns to 'normal' levels of activity.[40]

What emerges is that, yes, the visual distortions attributed to Irlen syndrome are not related to eye structure, but rather to brain processing of the information it receives from the eyes. And for some reason, coloured filtration in the form of tinted filters or lenses, or even of ambient light, is cutting out the frequencies that underlie the confusion.

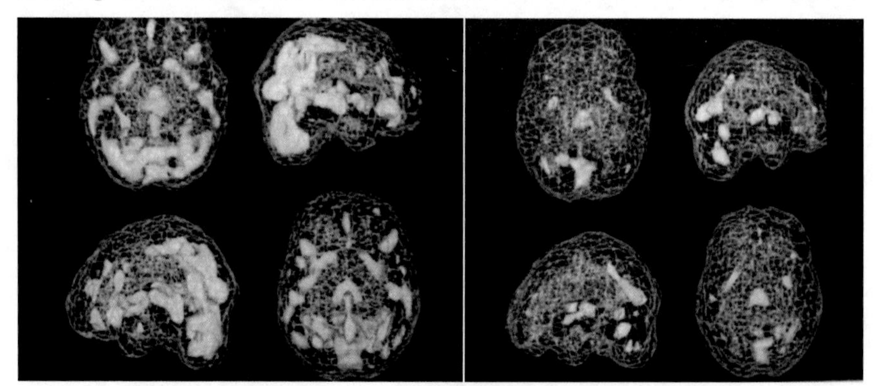

**Figure 1: SPECT Scans from the Amen Clinic, California, USA**. Two individuals with Irlen syndrome reading from a computer screen whilst undergoing SPECT scans. Left hand side: uncorrected, right hand side: wearing corrective Irlen Spectral Filters. Reprinted with kind permission from the Irlen Institute.

39 Coughlan S (2015) Dyslexia not linked to eyesight, says study [online]. BBC News 27 May. Available at: https://www.bbc.co.uk/news/education-32836733 (accessed March 2019).

40 Irlen H (2010) *The Irlen Revolution: A guide to changing your perception and your life.* New York: Square One Publishers.

So how does this affect autistic people in terms of their visual experience? Several years ago I was asked by her mother to visit Alice, who has Down's syndrome and autism. She looked at me sideways and pointed to my nose and said, *'Piggy nose, Piggy nose'*. I did not realise how specific this was, until recently shown pairs of pictures (drawn to order by the mother of a different child, one who had never met Alice).[41] The first shows what the child saw when she looked at her class at school when they were assembled in rows for a photograph (see Figure 2). First of all, she could not see white, so she failed to see fair hair. Secondly, all the children had what quite clearly resembled piggy noses. Finally, she saw a central black disc, a constant feature of her visual field. Tinted lenses corrected these unusual distortions (Figure 3).[42] No wonder Alice had looked at me sideways (so she could see me) and called me piggy nose'. She was telling me what she saw.

Figure 2

Figure 3

41 Story courtesy of Tina Yates Irlen Centre.

42 Presentation at an international Irlen conference in Australia in 2000.

Another connection between Irlen syndrome and autism was made by Donna Williams. Realising that she had extreme visual fragmentation (hundreds of pixilating odd bits floating round her visual field all the time rather than just individual letters moving), Donna describes what happened when she first tried on her (pink) coloured lenses. '*It was as if the whole world went shunt*' and she looked up and around and said, '*Oh my God, that's what the rest of the world is seeing*'. This was an on the move effect directly related to wearing or not wearing the tinted lenses, since when she took them off, '*everything started to slither away again*'.

The changes in perception (and behaviour) can be very dramatic. Miles is six years old. He is severely autistic. He has no eye contact, does not relate to his parents and spends most of his time tearing up cardboard. It is difficult to get him to eat and he is extremely distressed when required to leave the house. I tried using Miles' sounds to connect with him (Intensive Interaction), without getting a response (see **Chapter 3** on Intensive Interaction by Janet Gurney). So I tried different coloured ambient lights.[43] At first he took no notice but when I switched to blue he looked up, dropped his cardboard, came over and took my hand, gave me full eye contact, played with my hands, gave his parents eye contact and engaged with an iPad on the table. Interestingly, he then also responded when I answered his sounds. It is reasonable to suppose that in blue light his sensory processing overload is reduced and he can now distinguish what is going on in his environment. Since blue is a colour that appears to have meaning for him, we tried offering his meal on a blue plate – and he appeared to be comfortable eating his meals. By extension, we tried a blue jacket and he was then happy to go outside, since he now had a colour to which he could refer when his brain is becoming overwhelmed. And from then on, he manipulated the (quite complicated) remote control to choose blue light if it is on the 'wrong' colour when he comes into the room. In blue light he can make visual sense of his surroundings. It does not trigger the difficulty he has with visual processing.

There is more than a single cause of what we know as Irlen syndrome, since it appears to be triggered by intense light and certain colours and patterns. Some people have not just one but multiple triggers. I suspect that it all depends on which part of the visual processing system is affected. Research is urgently needed into just what proportion of autistic people have this type of visual processing overload.

'J' was thirteen when I first saw him. He was in the slow lane of his special school and was easily upset. He could barely read or write. Noticing he flinched when he looked out of the window into bright light, I sent him for an Irlen test. He came back with tinted lenses. A few months later, he emailed me (written by himself and perfectly spelled), saying that I would not believe what a difference these lenses had made to his life, since he had been moved out of the slow lane

43 Using optimum colour changing light bulbs (available at B&M stores).

and into the talented stream. Subsequently he was sent to a school for especially talented children because his teachers could not keep with him. With his permission, I include an email from J, after he had been for a later testing:

*'I just wanted to let you know how I got on at the Irlen centre yesterday. Having tested a lot of lenses, I have found a particular pair which started to cause improvement in certain symptoms and behaviours. Firstly, I was able to read in a straight line without any deficits such as shimmering or losing my pace. I then revisited these afterwards and then started to notice more significant differences, such as a sharp increase in my eye contact, my attention to detail and subtleties in the environment (without just glancing at it until it became distorted) as well as my balance, anxiety and my overall speech. I felt that as I looked around the environment, I could physically detect the blood flow in the back of my head shift, as the architecture of my brain began to shift to accommodate for this new way of functioning. I acutely remember the experience and I can't wait to get the lenses (there is a delay of a couple of months while the prescription is sent to America to be made up), as I couldn't ascertain the full amount of benefits in the time I had. The colour I am compatible with is grey.'*

(J's first lenses were blue. Now he is older it has altered to grey: the most effective tint changes as the eye matures. Regular retesting is necessary).

Interestingly, when J broke his glasses recently, he was plunged back into all the distortions. Now he has the replacement lenses, he tells me that he realises that he was completely misinterpreting the environment, especially outside (where the light is bright): *'It was like a camera lens that can never pick the right focus'*. J was sensitive to bright light and this was corrected using a particular tinted lens. The colour is very specific to the individual: the remedial colour can be any one of the colour spectrum. For example, Hope always draws the curtains when she goes into a room and sits in what the rest of us would see as a dark room. The colour she needs to correct this condition turns out to be a dark plum colour.

Testing is not easy, especially if the autistic child or adult is non-verbal or like one child who cheerfully responded positively to each tinted trial lens that each one made his seeing 'much better!'. However, careful observation of his behaviour made it clear that there was one coloured lens where he stopped fiddling with his sock and relaxed. When the tester returned to this tint, she was able to confirm the change in body language and relaxation.[44]

44 It is recommended that rather than using a Colorometric test, which employs a Colorometric machine, testers of children and adults with severe autism should be Irlen trained to make a hands-on assessment since they may need to be able to spot behavioural changes to support which tint is helping a non-verbal child. Tina Yates at info@irleneast.com has a list of regional assessors who are capable of assessing children with severe autism.

Research at Cornell University suggests that the visual distortions that come under the umbrella of Irlen syndrome alter brain activity in ways that extend well beyond colour perception to influence brain regions supporting perception, thought, language and motion.[45] For example, a man who finds it difficult to balance is sent to Tai Chi classes in the hope that it will help him regain control. These make his condition worse and he hates it. However, after his visual processing difficulties are corrected using tinted lenses, there is a dramatic improvement. He is now able to stand on one leg and hold an arabesque.

## What should we look out for to spot visual overload?

An autistic person with Irlen syndrome may squint when they look out of the window or be distressed in bright light, especially strip lighting – some children are so overwhelmed by this, or by flickering light at school, that they become 'school refusers'. Some will wear caps with the peak pulled down or only sit in darkened rooms. Others will choose to sit in rooms painted a certain colour, or they try to avoid rooms painted in other colours.

Visual clutter may be a problem, such as 'stuff' on the walls; this is a particular problem in schools where children's work is displayed on the walls. Especially difficult to process are the brightly coloured display boards with corrugated edges to be found in almost every school in the country. The rippled border is particularly difficult to process. (Some children may fixate on them in an effort to try and make sense of the visual disturbance.) Autistic children are getting into trouble for tearing them down.

Bright white walls and ceilings can cause visual processing distress and we need to avoid bright colours and patterns and sparkly jewellery and wear plain block colours. Above all, we have to provide visual simplicity.

A resource centre with some autistic attendees called in an artist to decorate the walls of the hall in their centre, to cheer the place up. Her design was an unfortunate choice: orange and purple diagonal stripes. The staff admitted that most of the behavioural incidents took place in that area. Those of us who support autistic people need to remember that sensory overload *hurts*, so that it is almost a form of abuse to knowingly provide environments that trigger pain. We have a duty to inform ourselves.

# Sensory issue 2: Auditory processing difficulties

Like visual processing difficulties, auditory processing overload, 'hyperacusis', can be triggered by a variety of sounds, noises and certain frequencies, sudden loud noises, certain tones and overlapping speech: this overload can be extremely painful. The problem is partly pain due to oversensitivity to certain

45 https://hdtoday.human.cornell.edu/.../update-on-irlen-research-at-cornell-university/

frequencies, but also that some sudden sounds, such as a barking dog, can trigger a 'danger signal' associated with past trauma.

While non-autistic people focus on what the brain needs to hear, filtering out the confusion and pain caused by unwanted hums and unexpected and overwhelming noises, autistic people may lack this capacity. Unfortunately schools have large echoing halls and noisy classrooms and are notoriously difficult places for autistic children. Although expensive, acoustic panelling can cut down the auditory overload significantly and the children's behaviour is calmer. In an effort to cut down the sensory hubbub, one student, Mike, comes into school with a large open book over his head.

Avoidance is one strategy for dealing with overwhelming noise. David, a large man in his thirties, is clearly in distress. He has breakfast in his residential home with ten other autistic men. Afterwards, he retreats to his room and starts to bellow and beat his head against the wall. It is difficult to find anyone willing to support him since he head butts those who try to intervene. This behaviour continues for up to ten hours.

I stood outside David's room: every time he bellowed, I responded with empathy. After a few minutes he opened the door and put his head out. By way of introducing myself, I nodded and placed my hands on my chest (in terms of body language, I am introducing myself – 'I am here'). He returned to his room and continued his sounds. This pattern (he bellowed, I responded, he opened the door and looked at me) continued for about ten minutes and then someone walked down the corridor and slammed the door. To him it must have sounded as if I had left. He shot right out immediately – and again, using mime, I reassured him, I am here. This time he left his room and walked down the passage and downstairs, something the home's manager said he had never done in the morning before.

David went and sat in a room he had never used up until that time. I stood outside and continued to respond to his sounds. These quietened over a period of twenty minutes. He appeared to be calm. At this point, under pressure to teach in ten minutes' time, I made a mistake and, against my better judgement, entered the room and stood close to him. He head butted me. However the manager said this was not a particularly severe attack and that he was so impressed by the difference in David's response that he will use the technique in the future. I suggested to him that the real problem starts at breakfast in a small noisy room where the noises are getting into David's head and perseverating,[46] so that he goes on hearing them long after the actual sounds have ceased. David beats his head in despair, trying to stop the endless pain. David needs a quiet breakfast.

---

46 Perseveration is when a stimulus (sound or rhythm), continues to be heard or issued in the brain, after the source has discontinued. We say a tune is 'catchy' when we continue to go on hearing it after it is played. It sticks in our head: this is perseveration.

The manager agrees and says he will take David to breakfast at McDonald's next door and bring him back when the other residents have gone to work. While this may seem a slightly odd solution, McDonald's is actually very quiet at breakfast. There are few people, no-one is screaming and everything is quiet and predictable. Avoiding the stimulus means that the trigger to David's pain is removed and his behaviour calms down.

We do not realise how penetrating our voices can be, especially if we produce a high hard voice from the front of our mouths: it is wise to always speak quietly to a child with autism (but not whisper, since the sibilance can be painful).

I was asked to see Neil (aged 8), but was told he will not let strangers into the house. I stood on the doorstep where he could see me from the sitting room, but do not speak. After a while I pointed to myself and to the hall, and speaking very softly asked him if I may come in. I said that I would speak quietly. He nodded and allowed me to come in.

Ian is nine. His distress is acute. Every day when he arrives at school in the morning, he is distraught. He goes straight to the quiet room, which is totally dark blue with a dark blue mattress and with an arch rather than a doorway so his teacher, while sufficiently separated, can remain in touch. There he has a total meltdown which lasts for about an hour, at the end of which he calms down. He manages quite well for the rest of the day. When he goes home, his mother greets him affectionately but the quality of her voice is overwhelming, loud and sharp: '*Hello Ian, how are you?*'. Ian says, '*No talking*' and pushes her away into the kitchen, the farthest room from his bedroom. He then retreats to his own room. Here he climbs on the table and has to be prevented by four support staff from crash-diving off onto the top of his head. They are afraid that he will fracture his skull.

It seems likely that his mother's voice carries a certain quality which sets off acute pain in Ian's head. The sound keeps ringing in his ears. It really hurts, and even continues until the following day when he goes to school and has a 'meltdown', after which he calms down. When I suggest to his mother that she speaks to him quietly, she protests that she wants him to know that she loves him – which she clearly does. But sometimes we love people so much that we have to alter our behaviour towards them, even in ways that are counterintuitive. Once she began to speak to him quietly, his drastic self-injurious behaviour stopped. Instead of pushing her away, he began to invite her to read him stories. His behaviour showed less distress at school.

Curiously enough, the fact that Ian was actually telling people that the problem was with the quality of her speech when he said 'no talking' was somehow being overlooked. It is extremely important to pay careful attention to any hints that throw light on our interactions.

A number of people with auditory overload gravitate towards using headphones, of which there are two basic types: ear protectors that cut out all sound indiscriminately, and acoustic noise reduction headphones. The latter cut down background noise and were originally designed for helicopter pilots, so that they could talk to each other over the engine noise. The model we have used, for reasons of comfort and durability, is the BOSE series, 15 and 25, which cut out 80% of the background noise, but there are now a number of different brands. Since they are expensive, it is worth shopping around. Personally I have found the BOSE refurbished ones reliable. Normal ear protectors are not recommended, since it is suggested that in cutting out all sound, there is a danger the child will stop listening. (This may be so but a child who is hypersensitive to sound is so acutely aware of the sound that he may well still be hearing them through the muffs.)

If the child cannot cope with the headphones, an alternative route is that of 'auditory training', where the child is progressively exposed to a sound so that the brain learns to tolerate it. Unfortunately, this approach takes time, time during which the child may be falling behind at school. It is a question of which approach is more easily tolerated by the child. But in particular, which route raises the least anxiety, since stress undermines all our efforts to communicate with the autistic child.

At school, children may be underperforming due to sound being scrambled as it comes in. In some cases, the headphones can make a major difference to their work. It is a question of trying the headphones out to see if the child can tolerate them. The advantage of the headphones is that if they are going to help, they work immediately, with an instant and sometimes dramatic improvement both in intellectual performance and in behaviour. However, not all children can bear the pressure on the head and it may take time for them to get used to wearing them.

The first time I used them was with an eight-year-old boy, Timmy, who I had seen previously and was convinced that his distressed behaviour related to auditory overload. I took a pair of headphones into his class and asked his teacher if I might try them on him. There were four children lined up watching a noisy video. Three had their fingers in their ears. Timmy was wandering round in a daze. His teacher responded that she did not think he had a problem with noise although the others might. So we tried them on the other three first and they all wanted them: I had a fight to get the headphones back. Eventually I tried them on Timmy. He sat down, put them on, looked thoughtful and then took them off again. He then replaced them on his head and, holding the right earpiece, moved it on and off his ear. His teacher remarked that he was playing with them: actually he was testing them carefully with great concentration. He now wears them most of the time and his behaviour is much calmer.

Pam is ten years old. In order to do homework, she has to build herself a cave under the table and surround it with chairs to keep out as much stimuli as possible. I lend her some headphones.

She writes me a letter:

*'Normally in class I can hear everything, others whispering, noise outside, people tapping pencils and dropping things. It's hard to hear the teacher's voice unless she's shouting which isn't often. With earphones on, I couldn't hear anything that disrupted me, I wrote more than usual and I could concentrate on learning and could listen. I took them off and was astonished at how different it was.'*

It appears that cutting out the background noise allows Pam to discriminate and concentrate on the sounds that are important to her. Her teachers were distressed: no one had told them about the possibilities of using headphones and so they had not realised the potential level of her ability. They say within half an hour of starting to wear them, the standard of her work 'shot through the roof'.

Some children become selective as to when they use headphones. Robbie and Peter are both five. In a noisy environment, Robbie was lent a pair of headphones. At first he tore them off but as the noise increased he kept them on and now chooses when to wear them. Peter cried a lot in class. Given a pair of headphones to wear, his distress decreases. He starts to make friends. His problem is that, not only is the noise distressing, but he is anticipating the possibility of painful noise. Now he is calm even if he just has them available on his desk, so that he can put them on if it becomes noisy.

Aged five, David is initially responsive to the headphones but then throws them off. David's mother and father decide that the best way to get him used to wearing the headphones is direct exposure to noise. While his mother models wearing the headphones, she takes him into the city centre and walks his pram up and down in front of a bagpiper. When it is obvious that David is stressed by this, she hands him the headphones.

*'As soon as they are on he stops rocking, still disturbed but much calmer and we walk on. After about 5 minutes (lots of amplified music) he takes them off and throws them away again on the ground. Then we hear a generator nearby, so we walk to that, very, very loud and David starts to get distressed again. I face him and tell him again the headphones will help, and put them on. Almost immediately he looks around and calms down, so we walk on and on – he wears them much longer and then takes them off and hands them to me! Next we are nearing the central railway station and it is clear that David is exhausted, not now with the sound but the sheer volume of human beings, colours, structures, lines and distortions in his vision. As we approach, he calls out, looking at me – I said, "You want the headphones*

*David?". I put them on him, he immediately leans forward, changes his demeanour to more interest than stress and hugs his pillow and starts to laugh and looks up at my husband and me. As we walked through the station he continues, it is as if he has "got it".'*

While not everyone might feel strong-minded enough to be able to take such a direct approach, David's mother knows her son and a recent email from her tells me that she now has a happy child.

Using the already widely used headphone noise reduction technology, researchers are currently working on noise reduction windows, which can reduce sound such as busy roads and railways by 50%.[47] (The noise cancelling waves that are sent out are sufficiently wide-cast for it not to matter if the windows are open.) This will make it possible not only to have quieter rooms but also to reduce the need for air conditioning, which, apart from decreasing costs would cut out its hum, a sound which can be painful for some autistic people who are hypersensitive to sound.

An interesting point is that a number of autistic people say that when they are wearing their coloured lenses, they can hear better. If one looks at the scans in Figure 1 it is obvious that the random firing must be setting off interference, not just in the visual processing area. Maybe this is one explanation. The other is rather more complex.

Research has shown that on the way from the sense organs to the brain, visual and auditory signals pass along a pathway that involves traversing from cells know as 'climbing cells' to Purkinje cells. In an undamaged pathway, one sound message, or one visual signal, passes from one climbing cell to one Purkinje cell. But some autistic people have a shortage of Purkinje cells, so it is no longer a one-to-one situation:[48] several climbing cells carrying different messages may be scrambling to pass their signals on to a single Purkinje cell. There is therefore the potential for audio and visual signals to become scrambled before they reach their respective processing areas.

*'In the limbic system, the hippocampus, amygdala and entorhinal cortex have shown small cell size and increased cell packing density at all ages, suggesting a pattern consistent with development curtailment. Findings in the cerebellum have included significantly reduced numbers of Purkinje cells, primarily in the posterior inferior regions of the hemispheres.'*[49]

With more donor climbing cells than receptor Purkinje cells, it seems that the sound and visual messages may get mixed up before they even reach their respective processing areas.

47 Gibbons K (2018) Noise-cancelling windows could be the next boom industry. *The Times* **1 May.**

48 Palmen SJMC, Engeland HV, Hof PR and Schmitz C (2004) Neuropathological findings in autism. *Brain* **127** (12) 2572–2583.

49 *Ibid.*

And it is not always the obvious sounds that are problematic. Emma is hypersensitive to a particular frequency, which is so muted that no-one else can hear it.

Finally, there is sixteen-year-old Gareth, who I sat next to on a bench while he waited for his mother to finish work and take him home. The hall was extremely noisy, full of excited and competing voices. Gareth was sitting head down with his hood over his head; he looked utterly miserable. And then the bell went off. His face creased up in pain, hands came up over his ears immediately and he curled up into a ball. It so happened that I had a pair of headphones on my lap and I passed them to him. He put them on at once, straightened up and stood, walked down the passage, turned round and came back with a broad grin on his face. '*Now I can go to college*'; I couldn't go before because of all the noise and the people.'

Gareth now has access to higher education and is doing well, except for one weekend when he left the headphones behind and fell into panic that someone will have taken them. (It is worth noting that Gareth's distress is not just triggered by noise but includes the melee of students, so there is too much to process all round. Reducing the auditory overload allows him to manage the crowd.) If we return to Figure 1, we see that overload from one sensory input appears to affect the whole brain: everything 'blows' like a Catherine wheel in the head.

While these stories and others are anecdotal and not empirical evidence, they bear witness not only to calmer behaviour and improved cognitive performance but also to changed lives, both for children and their families. What is clear is that, as Gail Gillingham said many years ago in her book *Autism – Handle with Care*, 'autistic people need visual and auditory tranquillity'. It is also clear that we should not be making cognitive assessments until we have addressed sensory issues: we cannot tell how able a child is if they are struggling to process their sensory intake.

## Sensory issues 3: 'feelings'

In this section I have borrowed extensively from accounts of autistic people's physical and affective experiences, both from books and also from personal conversations. These open a door on the perceptual experiences of autistic people and supplement research accounts in journals. They enrich our understanding.

It is not only sounds and visual stimuli which bring on sensory overload. Autistic people can be over sensitive to feelings, which set off painful sensations, or under-sensitive, so they just do not feel them. Or they can be aware that they have a sensation but cannot identify it.[50]

50 Johansson Iris (2012) *A Different Childhood*. Scottsdale, AZ: Inkwell Productions.

Feelings are difficult to write about for two reasons. Firstly, it is not always clear what we mean when we talk about feelings. Are we referring to feelings as 'physical sensations' ('I feel pain if I sit on a pin'), or feelings as 'felt emotions' ('I feel annoyed that you left a pin on the chair after you had been sewing')? This confusion is not only reflected when we talk to each other but also in articles in journals where the authors do not always make clear which they are writing about. The second reason is that the biology of how we perceive sensation, whether physical or emotional, is immensely complicated: in an exciting field of ongoing research there is no way of simplifying it. But at least we need to try and understand some of the background to difficulties with which autistic people have to struggle.

Feelings are subjective. The level at which we perceive sensation and emotion is personal. While one person may sense a stimulus as mildly irritating, the same stimulus makes another person angry. The depth to which we personally experience our feelings – and exactly how we respond – is dependent not only on our perceptive threshold but also on the feedback from our mapped previous experiences; the gut feelings from our viscera. For example, if we have been traumatised, post-traumatic stress is likely to colour our responses to any event we perceive as even mildly threatening.

While this simple account cannot cover all the ways we feel, it will try to will pick out some of the ways that impact on how we feel and discuss their relevance to autism.

It so happened that at the time I was working my way through the fascinating new research which is illuminating how we feel, I came across two autistic adults who told me that when they were getting upset (or to try and prevent themselves reaching that stage), they would scrunch up their toes inside their trainers. In this way, they could give themselves feedback that was meaningful without drawing public attention to their rising anxiety. Both accounts drew my attention to their need for a point of meaningful focus: I began to speculate as to whether I could enhance that stimulus so they could more easily stay in contact. I wanted to break into the cycle of anxiety and loss of connection with their environment. As soon as I tried scrunching up my own toes inside my shoes, I realised that providing a textured insole might 'turn up the volume' of the stimulus to the point at which they felt more connected to their surroundings and therefore less anxious.[51]

Grace is a professional artist friend with autism. She says she has 'twitchy toes'. She tells me that when she feels herself starting to overload, she deliberately wrinkles her toes inside her shoes. The sensation gives her something to focus on

51 As a general rule, if one needs to understand the effects of a hyposensitivity – and therefore look for some way of helping to address the issue – it is essential to try the stimulus on oneself. This is also true of any repetitive behaviour: if one tries it oneself one quickly learns what feedback the person is giving themselves, and therefore what it is that has meaning for their brain.

without being noticeable in public. It is clear that she is giving herself a stimulus on which she can focus when her brain processing is becoming confused. We look for something that will give her more of that sensation, so she always has meaningful feedback available. By chance, I come across some heavy duty ridged rubber matting, like hard corduroy with very fine ridges. We cut out insoles for her shoes. A few weeks later, she emails me to say *'The textured rubber material for insoles in my shoes has made a massive difference to my twitchy toes and nerves. I was very surprised for something so simple to work'*.

And a month later:

*'The best way I can explain the way the insoles work; it's like the texture of tough stretchy rubber massages my feet (whilst walking), after a while it then seems to tire out all my nerves and overloaded sensory energy, which then allows my tense muscles and some emotions to relax and become more calmer. Even my feet no longer seem to twitch when I'm having a daydream or watching the TV. There are times now I have to take the insoles out, as I'm used to working under pressure (like putting up exhibitions or providing talks) I kinda need the adrenaline to push me through tiredness and lack of motivation. I only just realised this is one of my strategies. I wouldn't advise running with them in, as they can cause my feet to get sore. It took me a while to get use to them and see the difference they made, but I can now safely say I wouldn't go back to wearing shoes without them.'*

Hope, the author of the next chapter in this book, also tries the insoles. When she first puts them on, she says:

*'Before, I knew I was walking but could not feel it, but now I can feel I am walking. The ridged insoles are incredibly helpful. They help to ground me. I can actually feel my feet for once in my shoes. The only time I used to be able to feel my feet was when I was in pain with them. Or if I was wearing new (or uncomfortable), shoes which sometimes meant I would purposely wear these uncomfortable shoes just to get that pressure on my feet. Just so I could feel my feet. I now don't feel like a floating head like I normally do. Or sometimes my feet felt like jelly. Which not only leads to clumsiness, but feeling weird. I liked my feet to feel things, especially the ground, which is why I didn't like wearing shoes. I like to not wear shoes, but don't like not wearing socks, as I don't like my feet getting mucky. Because with socks on only, you can feel the ground. But with the insoles I can get the feeling I crave. The insoles also help when going into overload. As before when I was getting overloaded I would scrunch up my toes which I now understand was my body trying to grasp onto something and get the much-needed feeling I required. Without this, I would continue to spiral further into overload and panic. But now it almost brings me back to where I am and stops me from getting me overloaded – and helps me to calm down. It also stops overload from occurring in the first place.'*

I want to highlight this transition that Hope is talking about – the change from the experience of feeling she is a disembodied 'floating head', to feeling connected with the ground she is standing on. The insoles help her to feel grounded and know what she is doing; she feels embodied. The implications are that without extra input, the messages from her feet to her brain telling her what she was doing are not getting through. Either they were too weak, or they were being drowned out by other signals, like being in a noisy crowd when you cannot hear what the person you are trying to talk to is saying.

Richard says that he did not expect them to have the effect they did. His gait is much smoother, there is less tiredness in his gait and he has a better sense when he is cycling that his feet are resting on the pedals.

Paul says he has a better stride, a better sense of body connectivity, his posture has improved, he is not slamming his feet down when he walks and his right hemiplegia has benefited.

Not everybody who has tried the insoles has found them helpful, but Bridget writes that after a week her brother's motivation and health improved and this has been sustained to a remarkable level.[52]

While current indications are that for a person who is hyposensitive to proprioception and is self-stimulating their feet in order to increase the sensory feedback they are giving themselves (so that they can keep track of what they are doing), the actual site of the self-stimulus may vary.

Tessa rubs her hands together when we are talking about a subject that she finds uncomfortable. When she tries on a pair of 'gripping gloves', with the knobbles turned inside out to face the palm of her hand, and presses them on the arm of the chair, she says her brain stops 'pinging'. When I ask what this means, she says that normally she has a number of different conversations going on in her brain at the same time and that this stops when she has a physical stimulus to her hands to focus on.

Currently, feedback from individuals who are using the insoles has been sufficiently favourable to suggest they are worth trying if the individual is hyposensitive to proprioception and particularly those who rub their feet (and possibly hands) in some way to obtain the stimulus they require.

Autistic or not, the basic distinction is between signals that come from outside us, 'exteroception', and those originating from inside our bodies, 'interoception'. So touch is definitely exteroceptive and many autistic people are hyper (over)

---

52 The textured insoles do not cure autism but they do seem to moderate some of the more unpleasant sensory issues for some people. The ones we are currently using are Revs insoles: https://revsstore.com/. These do require careful introduction for some people, who need to wear them an hour a day at first and work up the time gradually. Others find instant benefit.

sensitive to light touch. They flinch if brushed lightly and may push people away or even lash out. All the sensors in the skin seem to fire at once. A child says, 'it feels like a whole load of spiders trying to crawl out of my skin'.

Hypersensitivity to touch underlies some of what is perceived by the non-autistic world as the most 'odd' sensory responses. Emma simply cannot bear the sensation of cling film. She has to get her mother to unwrap a pack of sandwiches. She says some bath soaps leave her fingers feeling funny so she has to lick them to make them feel normal. And Mike, who cannot bear edges, has to have his fingernails trimmed every evening before he goes to bed or he has a complete meltdown. Others cannot bear the feeling of a shower: '*It feels like red hot needles being fired at my skin*'. On the other hand, some people are calmed by 'brushing' the skin. The particular way that a hypersensitivity or hyposensitivity manifests is personal: everyone is different.

While touch is exteroceptive, it is more difficult to see why proprioception (the physical sensations from our muscles and joints to our brains that tell us what we are doing), also falls in this category. This apparent anomaly is because, although originating within the body, proprioceptive messages signal the state of the body in relation to the world outside, and they  are using same neural pathways to the brain as the more obviously exteroceptive stimuli.[53]

Interoception is a relatively new concept and there is much interest and research into its implications, particularly in the field of mental health. Interoceptive signalling is a component process of reflexes, urges, feelings, drives, adaptive responses, and cognitive and emotional experiences. Summing up at a major conference held in 2016, Garfinkle says, '*Interoception refers to the process by which the nervous system senses, interprets, and integrates signals originating from within the body, providing a moment-by-moment mapping of the body's internal landscape across conscious and unconscious levels*'.[54]

By way of warning, the scientific research relating to interoception is extremely complicated, partly because of the complexity of our neural systems, partly because research is still ongoing, and partly because of the use of alternative definitions used at different times by different neuroscientists. Rather than focusing on where the stimulus originates, Bud Craig, neurobiologist, directs our attention to the anatomical structure of the routes used to deliver incoming signals to the brain.[55] Fibres conducting exteroceptive and interoceptive signals are wired up to take different routes to different parts of the brain.[56]

53 Craig AD (Bud) (2015) *How Do You Feel? An interoceptive moment with your neurobiological self*. New Jersey: Princeton University Press.

54 Garfinkel  SN, Tiley C, O'Keeffe S, Harrison NA, Seth AK, Critchley HD (2016) Discrepancies between dimensions of interoception in autism: Implications for emotion and anxiety. *Biology Psychology* **114** 117–126.

55 Craig AD (Bud) (2015) *How Do You Feel? An interoceptive moment with your neurobiological self*. New Jersey: Princeton University Press.

56 Carreiro JE (2009) *An Osteopathic Approach for Children* (2nd edition). Amsterdam: Elsevier.

Exteroceptive messages, capable of mobilising the whole body quickly in response to events in the outside world, are fast-tracked to the brain through myelinated fibres. Interoceptive messages conduct messages more slowly along unmyelinated small diameter fibres. This difference in speed of conduction relates to a difference in structure of the nerve cells (neurons), in the two different pathways.

Broadly speaking, our brain is a receiving office, taking in messages from the world outside the body and those originating inside the body. It has to integrate these, decide what action is needed and put in place a muscular response. For this to work, the systems have to be connected up properly, but they also need to be in balance.

Starting with proprioception, what does it feel like and what does it tell us?

To get the feeling of proprioception, stand on your toes and focus on what you can sense in the way of tension and pressure: in the toes, calves, knees, and thighs. All these separate messages add up to the feeling of standing on your toes. Now sit down. What proprioceptive messages can you feel now? Be aware of the pressure on your backside, back and, if your feet reach the floor, on the soles of your feet, and possibly your back pressing against the chair back. Even if they are not consciously spelling it out, all these sensations are combining to tell you that you are sitting down. And again, even if you are standing perfectly still, the muscles in your feet are making minute adjustments all the time, just to keep you upright.[57]

But for some autistic people like Grace and Hope, who feels as if she is a floating head, these proprioceptive signals are not getting through to the brain. And these people tell us they feel disconnected, so that they don't know what they are doing.

There are many ways that people with autism try and 'get through' to themselves by self-stimulation to the areas of their body they cannot feel, which implies that they do have some awareness of the deficiency. They will try and compensate for this disconnectedness, especially if they feel themselves becoming sensorily overloaded. Damian Milton tells us he walks on his toes when his brain is getting overloaded. Richard McGuire tells us that he gets his best feedback from bicycling, with five points of physical contact, feet, hands and groin, anchoring him in his body. When he is speaking at a crowded conference, a situation guaranteed to overload the processing system, it may be sufficient just even to have the bicycle present, so he can keep his hands on the handlebars.

On the other hand, and without wishing to complicate matters further, this rather highlights the situation that those of us not on the spectrum normally

57 'Fear of falling', clip from the 2014 BBC film *Dissected –The Incredible Human Foot.* https://www.bbc.co.uk/programmes/p01pmcfw

walk about without being consciously aware of our 'earthed' connectedness. It is not that we feel disconnected but that we take our earthed feeling for granted. It would seem that we are 'unconsciously aware' of what we are doing. And there is evidence for what Guy Claxton calls 'the undermind', the place where we are aware, but not consciously aware; where we store up ideas and sensations.[58]

Autistic children or adults who are hyposensitive (undersensitive) to physical sensation (so that their sensory perception of their environment is completely distorted and on the move) may initiate at least one activity that has meaning for them, deliberately giving themselves strong, sometimes violent physical stimuli, a sensation which is predictable and tells them what they are doing. So we see them bounce on a trampoline, swing, jump or rock, even bang their heads. Judith Bluestone says she used a pogo stick to give herself a meaningful jerk. At least when autistic people do these activities they are giving themselves one sensation that has meaning.[59] Mike runs everywhere and it is difficult to keep up with him. He does this because the sensory feedback he gets from his pounding feet tells him what he is doing. Filling a rucksack with full drink cans on the way to a picnic gives him weight that gives him an alternative feedback.

When the brain is losing its ability to process (or when, as a small boy cried out, '*My head's running away, my head's running away*'), these deliberate strategies enable the individual to be in touch with – and focus on – at least one sensation that has meaning for them.

In the same way, when they are getting sensorily overloaded, or in a situation that they interpret as being likely to bring on sensory overload, we can sometimes help autistic people who are hyposensitive to proprioception by giving them heavy objects to carry. Like the ridged insoles, these act as an anchor that helps them to embody their feeling of themselves and what they are doing. This reduces anxiety.

Debbie lashes out at other children in the playground. She is bewildered and frightened by all the noise and random movement. Her occupational therapist suggests she wears a rucksack filled with books, a weight she can focus on when she is becoming confused. She no longer hits the other children. Marc finds it impossible to cross the back-to-back lane that separates his house from his granny's. I suggest to his mother that when they next return from shopping, she hands him two shopping bags loaded with heavy goods and points to his grandmother's house, asking him to take them over. Instead of perceiving the lane he has to cross as a threatening endless space, off he goes, his mind focused on delivering the weight he is carrying.

58 Claxton G (1998) *Hare Brain, Tortoise Mind: Why intelligence increases when you think less.* New York: Harper Collins Publishers.

59 Bluestone J (2005) *The Fabric of Autism: Weaving threads into a cogent theory.* New York: The Handle Institute.

Meet Carlo, who is eight years old. He is in a busy classroom. It is extremely noisy, next door to a building site, heaving with rumbling earthmovers and diggers. He comes into his class in the morning, picks up and cuddles a cushion, chooses a corner to sit in, where he scratches his cushion and rocks and cries for the rest of the day. He will not join in circle time or any other classroom activity.

Normally I see children in situ, since this is the situation where they are faced with trying to cope and it is easier to see what the sensory issues are. But in Carlo's classroom, there is so much noise going on both inside and outside that I cannot distinguish his sounds from all the rest of the noises, so decide to take him to a quiet(ish) room next door. Carlo struggles at first, thinking we (myself and the psychologist) are trying to incorporate him back into class activities; he needs the security of his corner. When the psychologist takes his hand, he wrestles free and bolts for another corner. However, when he sees me pick up his chair and move it to the door, out of the room, Carlo understands and comes quietly. Once in the adjacent room and relative calm, he settles into a swinging office chair. I start to use his sounds and hand movements scratching his cushion, to communicate with him (see Janet Gurney's chapter on Intensive Interaction). He calms down and responds for a short while, then moves off. At this point I try talking to him from his right hand side and it appears that he is hypersensitive to sound in one ear – he flinches when I talk to him from this side. He runs over to the curtains and starts to swing on them; backwards and forwards, backwards and forwards, giving himself a jolt.

In answer to my query, Carlo's teacher says he loves to go on the swings. It has become clear that Carlo is deliberately setting up activities that help him to focus when his brain is overloading. I ask the teacher to outline what happens when he comes to school. She tells me that he has to be escorted off the bus (he does not want to come in). He is taken to the hall (which is echoing and noisy) and from there to his class, where he settles himself in his corner (the only space that he can manage and where he can press himself against the wall) and starts to cry.

So far we have identified two sources of Carlo's distress. The first is his acute sensitivity to sound which causes him physical distress, and the second is that he is under sensitive to the proprioceptive signals that would help him to make sense of what is going on round him. He is both in pain and confused.

I suggest that when he comes off the bus, he is taken into school via a quiet side entrance, avoiding the noisy hall, and put on the trampoline for ten minutes, where he can activate the necessary physical jerks that he uses to calm himself. The outcome of this intervention is that he is now content to sit with the rest of his class.

One might wonder why this approach continues to be effective after Carlo gets off the trampoline and is no longer receiving the physical stimulus he needs to focus. A possible answer is that while he is on the trampoline he gets his jolts, but when he gets off the same jolt sensation perseverates,[60] continuing to be sent after the trigger is inactivated. Research indicates that after a while, the signal fades and needs to be 'topped up', rather like using a Smart Card. So, he needs to be put back on the trampoline a number of times a day. This is not recreational activity, it is an essential way of helping Carlo deal with his hyposensitivity to proprioception.

Some autistic people find relief and can feel what they are doing if they wear tight clothing. J tells me that wearing a Squease Vest (which has air pockets that can be pumped up to the required pressure) 'stops his body feeling as if it is actively blowing itself apart'.

To confuse the situation further, we frequently measure our sensations by our reactions to them. To return to Carlo, not only does he feel the consequences of his hypersensitivity to sound (a pain that can be acute and is described as like knives going through your head)[61] but also confusion and fear (that he is in danger). He also anticipates and is afraid of circumstances that will trigger these. When he gets to school he does not get off willingly. He has to be picked up and removed from the bus, indicating his reluctance to leave the safety of a sensorily well-defined boundary of his seat, for the noisy open spaces of the school). So, not only is Carlo perceiving his immediate interoceptive sensations, but these trigger the emotions of anxiety and fear. To quote Damasio, feelings are what arise as the brain interprets emotions, which are themselves purely physical signs of the body reacting to stimuli.[62]

These people are all hyposensitive to proprioception; they are not getting an adequate picture of what their body is doing. The sensory picture they are receiving of their condition is scrambled. The probability is that the integration going on between the systems of interoceptive and exteroceptive messages is unbalanced so that one drowns out the other. It may be that the proprioceptive signals themselves are weak, or there is a break somewhere in the pathway that conducts the signals to the brain – but there also seems to be a link between anxiety and the ability to process proprioceptive signals.

This is demonstrated by George McGavin (not on the spectrum), in a simple experiment which shows the link between anxiety and the capability to process proprioceptive messages. Wired up in a laboratory, he walks along a plank resting on the floor with no difficulty. When the plank is hoisted to six feet, he tries again, but even harnessed, fear of falling rapidly brings him to a halt. He says that while he knows that what he is trying to do is just as easy as when he is on the ground, he finds he cannot move his legs. His muscles are tensing up and drowning out the proprioceptive messages to the brain, and this

60 Perseveration is when the brain continues to fire a signal, after the signal itself has stopped.

61 Josephine Marriage, personal correspondence.

62 Lenzen M (2005) Feeling our emotions. *Scientific American Mind* **16** (1) 14–15.

affects his balance. His anxiety is over-riding the messages that tell his muscles what to do, so he cannot proceed.[63]

So if a person with autism is self-stimulating to give themselves meaningful physical feedback, are they doing this because the proprioceptive messages in autism are too weak to reach the brain, or like George McGavin's, they are normal strength but are drowned out by the anxiety messages which are such a feature of autism, or perhaps both? Either way, to counteract this 'lack of bodily awareness', many people with autism resort to giving themselves an activity which involves strong physical stimuli, especially when they feel themselves starting to become sensorily overloaded, particularly those that involve jolts. One of the ways we can help is to 'turn up the volume' of the proprioceptive input, putting in extra input to the point where the person feels anchored, rather than a 'floating head', as Hope describes it.[64]

Assuming for the time being that incoming interoceptive stimuli do reach the brain, this brings us to what is known as the 'hard problem'. How do we get a conscious minute-by-minute picture of what is happening in terms of pain, temperature, itch, sensual touch, muscular and visceral sensations, acidity, vasomotor activity, hunger and thirst?[65] How do we turn our two-dimensional sensory sensations into the all-embracing three-dimensional experience of feeling? And why is it so vitally important that we do feel an embodied sense of self?

Looking at the 'hard problem' first, I find it helpful to visualise a large-scale local ordinance map, with the multitude of detail it represents, the ridges and valleys, the rivers and roads, villages and towns, including such minutiae as the location of post offices and churches, with their towers or spires defined by a cross with a square or circles. Take a lump of clay and, using the map contours, model the shape of the hills with their elevations and depressions, until you have built a three dimensional representation of the countryside you can see out of the window. From two dimensions on the map to a three dimensional landscape: but also you now have this landscape impressed into your fingertips. You can feel it.[66]

63 'Fear of falling', clip from the 2014 BBC film *Dissected –The Incredible Human Foot.* https://www.bbc.co.uk/programmes/p01pmcfw

64 If we are trying to identify the sensory feedback that a person is giving themselves, we need to try the physical activity they are doing ourselves. The sensation is not always what we expect – they may be stimulating an area which is not immediately obvious. For example, Gabriel flicks his left hand with string or gloves or something – but it is not only in his left hand that he feels it; he also has a sensation in his right upper arm. It is these sensations that we can enhance so they can form the basis of a mutual conversation.

65 Craig AD (2003) Interoception: the sense of the physiological condition of the body. *Current Opinion in Neurobiology* **13** 500–505.

66 Drawn from a personal memory of an inspired geography lesson given by Miss Guillam to my class when I was eight years old.

In effect, state of the art scanners are beginning to unravel a picture of a body full of cells acting as spy cameras, gathering sensations and delivering a rolling 'now', 'state of the body at this instant'[67] and reporting to the insula[68]. The insula consists of a small part of the cerebral cortex, or rather two, one on each side of the head, buried in a deep cleft (sulcus). According to Damasio, the insula plays an important part in processing bodily sensations, so they can be used to influence decision making.

The insula is the map room of the brain, responsible for monitoring the balance (or imbalance) of the physiology of the body, a picture which is felt as valence[69], what is 'good for me' or 'bad for me'. In the insula, the sensation of balance or imbalance is translated, embodied and felt as an affective state: the experience of emotion and the feeling of 'me'. Afferent information is translated into feelings. Now I have a contour map, I know what my body is doing and have a general feeling of what myself is doing. I am conscious of myself.

The insula, which is constantly updating itself, works hand in glove with the anterior cingulate cortex, which decides how to respond in order to maintain the best possible outcome in terms of energy expenditure: sensations come in they get transcribed, a to-do list is prepared and action is taken. The brain works as an algorithm that makes sure it operates in terms of maximum efficiency (homeostasis).

However, in practice, there is a bargain to be struck between the messages the brain now has and the older map that it holds of similar received situations it experienced in the past.

*'Although we may intuit that our perceptions follow sensation, our actual interoceptive experience may be modified by afferent signals from the limbic system about the state of the body'*,[70] Seth goes so far as to say that the brain 'hallucinates' our conscious reality (in the sense of perceiving something that is not really there).[71]

*'Each emotion feels differently in the body. For example, before speaking in public, your body may feel a certain way: the heart may race, the muscles may feel tense and shaky, the breathing may become shallow, and the stomach may feel fluttery. These sensations let us know that we are feeling a bit nervous.*

67 'Now' is probably an illusion, since by the time the brain recognises it, the present is passed and past. But thinking about this highlights the importance of recognition in the process of interoception.

68 Von Boehmer H (1990) Self recognition by the immune system. *European.Journal of Biochemistry* **194** 693–698.

69 Damasio A (2003) The person within. *Nature* **423** 227.

70 Barratt LF and Simmons WK (2015) Interoceptive predictions in the brain. *Nature Reviews Neuroscience* **16** (7) 419–429.

71 Seth AK (2017) Ted Talk: *Your brain hallucinates your conscious reality.*

*Without clearly feeling these sensations, it is difficult to identify emotions with a high degree of clarity.*'[72]

So, autistic or not, in all of us interoception is a two-way process, the outcome of which is for the brain to make a 'best guess' interpretation of meaning; one that can then effect subsequent interpretations of sensation. Interoception locks us intimately into a chicken and egg system, where sensations give rise to emotions – which effect how we perceive and react to sensations. The question is, how good is our brain at approximating to our experience?

We have already referred to the classic example of George McGavin coming to a halt when trying to walk a plank hoisted six feet up off the ground. His proprioceptive sensory perception of himself in relation to his situation as being in danger paralysed him to the extent he couldn't move. Fear triggered his self-defence mode and anxiety causes him to misread the degree of danger that he is in and ignore the reality that he is harnessed and perfectly safe. Anxiety overrides mobility.

This ties in with the sensory hyper- and hyposensitivities that make it so difficult for autistic people to perceive an accurate 'state of self and surroundings' picture, since, as Mahler says, '*When the interoceptive system is operating properly, the sensations alert us that our internal balance is off and motivates us to take action to correct the situation*'.[73] But the opposite can also apply – if there is a flaw in the interoceptive system we shall not recognise our sensations and so be able to take remedial action, frustrating the body's struggle to maintain homeostasis.

And here lies at least one of the difficulties for some autistic people: somewhere in the afferent/efferent balance, there appears to be a disconnect between perception and interpretation: they may receive a stimulus through the sense organs, even feel it as a sensation but not connect with what it signifies.

In Iris Johansson's fascinating account of her autistic childhood, she talks about this absence of connection between sensation and interpretation. She says she felt hungry, '*but did not understand that this sensation meant she should eat*'. '*I was unable to get food if I was hungry and anyway, hunger did not signal to me that food was what I needed.*'[74]

And, '*The peeing business worked only now and then. When the feeling of pee-urge arose, I could feel it in my body but I didn't understand it. It wasn't*

---

72 Mahler K (2016) *Interoception: The eighth sensory system* [online]. Available at: https://autismawarenesscentre.com/what-is-interoception-and-how-does-it-impact-autism/ (accessed March 2019).

73 *Ibid* Mahler.

74 Johansson Iris (2012) *A Different Childhood*. Scottsdale, AZ: Inkwell Productions.

*connected to peeing. Little by little I was able to get the thought in my head that when I had this feeling in my body it was time to pee. It took until I was eleven before I understood that the feeling in my body was pee-urge.'*[75]

In addition to failure to interpret physical sensations, Iris was unable to connect with the sensations of emotions:

*'Nobody grasped that I had no contact with the emotion field, none that would give me information that other people seemed to have access to. It was not like this field was missing but a bridge was missing, some kind of transfer, some kind of feeling for others. The peculiar thing about my condition is that there is so often emptiness, a standing still, no impulse whatever, and even though I can see everything and understand everything around me, it doesn't give me any impulses for action. It's like being in an invisible glass box'.*[76]

(In this case one can speculate that there may have been a disconnect between the insula and the anterior cingulate cortex. She had the feeling but could not recognise and take appropriate action on it.)

Tom says he wishes he could feel happy or excited. *'I can sympathise but not empathise, so I can understand that someone might feel sad, while at the same time not feeling sad with him ... I get told off by my partner because she wants me to be excited or happy when I just look like a cardboard cut-out'.*[77]

Comparisons of autistic people and non-autistic people demonstrate a significantly lower awareness of their interoceptive signals.[78] Research suggests that teaching autistic people to focus on their heartbeat is relaxing and that the processing difficulties encountered by autistic people are at least in part due to anxiety messages overwhelming those of sensation.[79] What is on offer is teaching people to recognise their embodied feelings.

Just to complicate matters even further, another study suggests that, rather than a direct relationship between autism and impaired interoception, the link is between an inability to recognise emotions from internal bodily sensations and coexistent alexithymia.[80]

---

75 Johansson Iris (2012) *A Different Childhood*. Scottsdale, AZ: Inkwell Productions

76 *Ibid* Johansson.

77 'Listening to your heartbeat can help with your feelings' BBC News: https://www.bbc.co.uk/news/av/stories-43869170/listening-to-your-heartbeat-can-help-with-your-feelings.

78 Garfinkel SN, Tiley C, O'Keeffe S, Harrison NA, Seth AK, Critchley HD (2016) Discrepancies between dimensions of interoception in autism: implications for emotion and anxiety. *Biological Psychology* **114** 117–26.

79 Mahler K (2016) *Interoception: The eighth sensory system* [online]. Available at: https://autismawarenesscentre.com/what-is-interoception-and-how-does-it-impact-autism/ (accessed March 2019).

80 Shah P, Hall R, Catmur C and Bird G (2016) Alexithymia, not autism, is associated with impaired interoception. *Cortex* **81** 215–220.

In a sensory processing blogpost, 'Aspie' clarifies how being unable to recognise your own feelings feels:

*'What if you are alexithymic? What if forget to eat when you are hungry, or stare in wonder at your bleeding toes, or don't realize you might be in pain until you pass out? Many of us have dampened or muted interoception. We just don't seem to notice what's going on in our bodies until it reaches a level that other people would find intolerable. And often when we do notice it, it goes from, "oh that's happening" to "intolerable" really darn fast.'*[81]

She continues:

*'Recently I had a urinary tract infection coming on for days before I picked up on the symptoms. One of the main symptoms is pain and other than a vague cramp feeling, I wasn't experiencing any. Easy to ignore, so I did. My body had gone from zero to "MAKE IT STOP" in less than an hour. And thanks to my body's poor interoceptive workings, I was rewarded with a kidney infection because unlike most women who dash off to the doctor at those first signs of a UTI, I wasn't getting enough data to trigger my internal alarms. By the time I started getting the right antibiotics in my body, a common minor ailment has progressed to a potentially serious illness that I'm just starting to recover from two weeks later. Our nonstandard brain wiring can mean that we miss common warning signs or have difficulty knowing when to act on distress signals.'*

Izaak, a man with Asperger's syndrome, throws light on his struggles to recognise his feelings using finely targeted metaphor:[82]

*'If I am feeling sensorily overloaded at College and can't face going to a class, I can only feel it is 'bad'; I cannot argue myself out of it by telling myself, 'I was really upset at the time and it would have been worse if I had gone in regardless. For me, I can only think of things in terms of absolutes … I can do binary, 1 or 0, good or bad, nothing in between.'*

Izaak adds a final explanation as to how it feels. *'Emotions are like algebra, except you aren't given any of the values.'*[83]

Before leaving the subject of feelings, a word about practice.

Look for the feedback a person is giving to themselves; see if it is possible to find a way of enhancing this by trying it out on yourself. Ask yourself what sensation this person are giving to themselves? When Grace talked about how her toes

81 Musings of an Aspie (2013) *Acceptance as a Well-being Practice* [online]. Available at: https://musingsofanaspie.com/author/musingsofanaspie/ (accessed March 2019).

82 It is always dangerous to generalise as to what autistic people can or cannot do: one of the things they are supposed to be unable to do is to use metaphors.

83 Personal communication.

itched when she was becoming sensorily overloaded, I physically scrunched up my toes and could feel that it would be more interesting if they were doing this on a textured surface. I wanted to shift attention from pure self-stimulation to a texture outside the body that would be a more affective stimulus.

Also it is extremely important when engaged in body language conversations to take notice of any 'flinches', since these are a clear indication of sensory hypersensitivity.

## Sensory issue 4: emotional overload

If the interoceptive emotional world is a jungle for some people with autism, the diversity of ways that autism presents appears infinitely complicated to us. We call it a spectrum; the divergences referring to exactly where the wiring connections are flawed, which are different in any particular individual.

Having focused on emotional hyposensitivity, under-sensitivity, we come to the contradiction of emotional overload, which is often overlooked.

While some autistic people are under sensitive to feelings – there are others who are overwhelmed by them. (These autistic individuals do not seem to feature in published research.) They may learn to repress their feelings and, to the outsider, present an unfeeling persona to the world, appearing to lack a normal emotional response. But Therese Jolliffe says, 'we do love people and we do feel lonely but cannot handle the emotional feedback we are getting from our bodies which swamps us, so we retreat into our own world'.

Names can have emotional tags, setting off sensory overload and even meltdowns in some autistic people. J had a real problem with names because they were so powerful, particularly his own, which is why we ended up using each other's initial. Maria told me that as a child she had dreaded being called out in class to join in an educational game that involved using the other children's names and she had never understood before why this was so.

Many will find Christmas and birthdays difficult, not only because of the changes in routines and the hustle and bustle, but because of the emotional demands that accompany them. Hope is upset when well-wishers sing 'Happy Birthday'. It is too personal and she shrinks away.

Jo recognises that her hypersensitive responses can be disproportionate when she tells me that when she sees a broken deckchair she is swamped by sadness and bursts into tears. Yet other autistic people may have labile emotions; sometimes they feel as if they are being drowned in a tsunami of feeling, but at other times they are unmoved. If this unreliability of their response system to emotions is related to a flaw in the afferent system taking information to the brain, perhaps one can think of it as behaving like a plug that sparks intermittently.

Emotional engagements are two-way and those who support autistic people are sometimes surprised when their own expressions of emotional warmth and praise are rejected, sometimes even aggressively. Their friendly overtures have triggered an avalanche of sympathetic overload: the autistic person can feel as if they are being attacked and respond as if this is the case, by retreating, shut-down, self-harm or aggression.

An autistic child is kicking her teacher when she is praised. The advice she receives is to ignore the child's negative behaviour and reward her when she is positive. In the case of emotional overload, this is precisely the wrong advice, since 'being ignored' (left alone) is rewarding, whereas praise is threatening and triggers the pain and confusion of a negative sympathetic nervous system over-reaction.

This can be a major problem for teachers who naturally praise students in order to encourage them. The question is how can teachers encourage autistic children who experience emotional overload? Richard McGuire, himself on the spectrum, says, '*If a child has done work well (and normally in this situation the teacher would praise them), use an indirect approach. Walk away and as you leave say casually, 'that seems to have gone well', and leave the child to work it out*'.[84]

When trying to engage with people who are emotionally hypersensitive, indirect speech can be helpful: rather than addressing the autistic person directly, use third person speech.

Winnie, an autistic woman in her twenties, is easily upset and attacks people, particularly strangers. She is sitting on her bed running her hands through her hair and avoiding my gaze. I stand by the door of her room. Remembering that Donna Williams had said about how intrusive direct speech could be, I run my hands through my hair and, using indirect speech, say, '*If I had been doing this for some time, I should want to brush my hair – and if I wanted to brush my hair, I should put my hairbrush on the bed*'. This is a complex sentence for someone with severe autism, but Winnie reaches out immediately, picks up her hairbrush and puts it on the bed. I walk over to her bed, pick up the brush and brush her hair. She leans forwards, puts her arms round me and rocks me gently back and forth. Winnie has been attacking people because the use of direct speech sets off painful sensory overload: she is trying to stop them in the only way she can. When I address her indirectly, she can understand that here is someone who has picked up her difficulty with direct speech and with whom she can communicate, without triggering sensory overload. Once her support staff understand this they adopt an indirect approach. Winnie is able to work in a café doing the washing up after everyone has gone home and it is quiet. Her problem is that first person direct speech sets off sensory

84 Personal communication.

overload. Attacking people was her only way of avoiding what her body interpreted as painful.

## Sensory issue 5: smell and taste

For this section I am relying heavily on Professor Barry Smith[85], Director of the Institute of Philosophy, London University, since as he points out, we give little attention to our olfactory sense; smell is the one we feel is least necessary to our well-being. It is – as he quotes Kant – '*fleeting and transient*' and many would rather lose their olfactory sense than their iPhone. This view is mistaken, since odour is intimately connected with how we feel.

It is not just when we sniff that we smell, we are taking in chemical molecules floating in the air and processing their odour all the time. We are surprisingly good at it: if we get down on our hands and knees we can trace a smell of chocolate powder as well as a dog – although not so fast, since we are no longer designed to move around on all fours.

But we don't really notice smell until we lose it through age or sickness. Its loss changes how we feel and there is a danger that we become depressed, since we lose the hidden familiarity of places that we unconsciously assess by smell.

Barry Smith explains that the olfactory cortex is unique among the senses in that it is linked directly to the centre of emotional memory, the amygdala and the entorhinal cortex. He says, '*Smell is emotionally loaded, some of our most powerful memories return when we get a brief whiff again*'. On a personal note, one of my most powerful memories is the curious mixture of the delicate smell of sea lavender together with the powerful smell of mud saturated with iodine. Immediately I am back, a child running barefoot, leaving a trail of footprints across sun-baked muddy pools on the marsh.

And there are social signals: we smell each other's body odour and will be attracted to those whose immune system is signalling that it is different from our own (all in the interests of good genetic selection). But we also use subliminal smell to detect fear in others. An experiment asked people to sniff the T-shirts worn by two groups of people. The first had been worn by people who were training to skydive, the second by a group who had been doing vigorous physical exercise. Participants from neither group were conscious of the odour difference, but using a skin conductance test (which measures sympathetic nervous response), their bodies responded to the fear smell in the sky diver's shirts.

85 Smith B (2018) Ted Talk: *The Role of Smell in Consciousness:* https://www.youtube.com/watch?v=V34N9YJAMsY.

This result is in contrast to those of a similar study carried out with volunteers who had high functioning autism.[86] The autistic group were compared with non-autistic controls to make sure that their sense of smell (including their ability to detect the smell of sweat) was the same. Next they were asked to smell the T-shirts; again, as before, one set had been collected from sky divers and the other from people who were just exercising. Both groups were monitored for skin conductance.

*'This is where differences emerged: although neither group reported physically detecting dissimilarities between the two smells, their bodies reacted to each in a different way. In the control group, smelling the fear-induced sweat produced measurable increases in the fear response in skin conductivity, while the everyday sweat did not. In the autistic men, fear-induced sweat lowered their fear responses, while the odour of 'calm sweat' did the opposite: it raised their measurable anxiety levels. In other words, the autistic volunteers did not display an inability to smell – but were misreading subliminal but vital olfactory social clues.'*[87]

As Barry Smith says, odour occupies the space between us, and is as vital as facial and postural non-verbal language in emotional cueing: if these olfactory cues are misconstrued, the autistic individual is at a disadvantage in reading their social situation. In the case of fear, they may feel afraid when there is no threat, or miss out when they should be fearful and take steps to avoid danger. Another overlooked feature of smell is the integral role it plays with taste. As Barry points out, while taste has sensors for salt, sweet, sour, bitter and savoury, it is smell that allows us, for example, to make the more subtle distinction between a peach and a grape. And the single experience that we call 'flavour' is a combination of smell, touch, taste and temperature.

Through a taste/smell combination we return to the idea that our brains makes a best guess at interpreting sensory information in the light of previous associations. If we smell a vanilla pod our brain 'best guesses' and tells us that it smells sweet. But if we chew the same pod, it tastes bitter. In the first case, our brain has opted for associated vanilla foods such as ice-cream and custard which do contain sugar ('whenever I get that whiff of smell it is usually accompanied by sugar'), and tells us it smells sweet. Smell can even be integrated with touch. It is the smell of certain shampoos that make the hair feel softer to touch.[88]

86 Weizmann Institute of Science (2017) *Autism and the Smell of Fear* [online] EurekAlert! Available at: https://www.eurekalert.org/pub_releases/2017-11/wios-aat112717.php (accessed March 2019).

87 Endevelt-Shapira Y, Perl O, Ravia A, Amir D, Eisen A, Bezalel V, Rozenkrantz L, Mishor E, Pinchover L, Soroka T, Honigstein D and Sobel N (2017). Altered responses to social chemosignals in autism spectrum disorder. *Nature Neuroscience* **21** 111–119.

88 Smith B (2018) Ted Talk: *The Role Of Smell in Consciousness:* https://www.youtube.com/watch?v=V34N9YJAMsY

Research is ongoing but Sobel suggests that it is possible that the sensing of subtle chemical olfactory signals may go awry at crucial stages in the brain's development in autism.[89]

When it comes to autism, taste is normally bracketed with eating disorders. Moving beyond the idea that food refusal is triggered by behavioural issues, it is now recognised that it relates mainly to sensory issues. The difficulty lies in trying to isolate exactly what the problem is. And the list of issues involved is complicated.

I am standing in the dinner queue for lunch and overhear the cook say to a server, 'Don't give Sam a red plate, he'll throw it on the floor, give him a grey one'. Immediately this raises the suspicion that Sam has Irlen syndrome, one confirmed when he swaps his red chair for a grey one. Later on, his teacher tells me that he has frequent meltdowns when put in the sandpit, an area lined with brilliant orange tiles. These tiles need to be overpainted.

This story recalls the story of Miles (related in the section on Irlen syndrome), whose preferred colour was blue and who had completely withdrawn into his own world, including being unable to eat almost anything, until we offered it on a blue plate.

So Miles' and Sam's eating difficulties refer to visual hypersensitivity. However, Meg, who throws her food on the floor shouting, 'Can't eat that, it's too black', is probably experiencing synaesthesia, since there is nothing that is black on her plate: or it was some kind of visual confusion.

Judith Bluestone, a neurologist who had autism, writes about the difficulties she had chewing food:[90]

*'Most people with autism have irregular tactile sensations in their mouths so they do not like the feel of food. They may have weak muscle tone in general and especially in the muscles in the mouth used for sucking and chewing. They are not ready for the coordinated series of movements involved in chewing and swallowing'* ... and she continues to relate this to pain in the trigeminal nerve, which innervates the teeth, gums, tongue, nose, cheeks, eyebrows, forehead and corneas.

She says: '*The movement of food in the mouth when it is being chewed hurts the trigeminal nerve and you cannot focus on anything else*'. And she introduces yet another food-related problem for people who are hypersensitive to sound, '*it is the noise made when food is chewed that causes the problems*'.

89 Weizmann Institute of Science (2017) *Autism and the Smell of Fear* [online] EurekAlert! Available at: https://www.eurekalert.org/pub_releases/2017-11/wios-aat112717.php (accessed March 2019).

90 Bluestone J (2005) *The Fabric of Autism: Weaving threads into a cogent theory*. New York: The Handle Institute.

On the other hand, a child who is under sensitive to sound may prefer crunchy foods that make a noise, seeking a stimulus that tells them what they are doing (chewing). Or they may have a problem with the idea of change, such as changes in body shape during puberty, which leads them into anorexia in an effort to stop themselves growing up.

The list of triggers to eating difficulties continues to grow…

We have already met Iris Johansson who knew she had a feeling but could not interpret it as hunger and needing to eat. She had a problem with her interoceptive system.

In addition, some children have never got past weaning and are afraid to try something new. Sean Barron says: '*I had a big problem with food. I liked to eat things that were bland and uncomplicated. I didn't want to try anything new. I was supersensitive to texture and I had to touch everything with my fingers and see how it felt before I could put it in my mouth.*'[91]

People may need different foods such as meat and vegetables placed separately on the plate. Perhaps the most extreme case of restricted eating is of a child who would quite literally only eat the crumbs from fish fingers, and then only if they had been bought at Tesco's.

Listing the variety of possible causes of food restriction makes clear the difficulties in finding remedial strategies. One strategy does not fit all, and it is necessary to try and work out what the problem is first.

Most experts recommend building on what the child will eat, but this is not easy. They usually spot it when one tries to hide a 'new' taste in their favourite food.

We need to be ingenious and work from what the child can do. I met a child who sat on the floor and would not eat but kept pawing at her mouth with her fingers. A colleague suggested her parents sit on the floor with her playing with jelly, getting it on their fingers and eventually putting them (and it) in their mouths.

On the question of gluten free diets, a clinical psychologist told me that he had decided to try all his autistic 'patients' on a gluten free diet to see if it helped them. Around 13% showed a distinct improvement – but the quality of life of the others was unchanged. His advice was that if there was no improvement in two or three months, the diet should be withdrawn, since it was extremely restrictive.

All the sensory issues we have looked at so far arise directly from difficulties in processing sensory information. The sympathetic nervous system over (or under)

91 Barron J and Barron S (1992) *There's a Boy in Here: Emerging from the bonds of autism.* Arlington, TX: Future Horizons.

reacts to what it perceives (rightly or wrongly) as life-threatening, triggering anxiety and the body's self defence system. We still need to look at what other features in an autistic person's life are particularly stressful, such as choices and change, trauma, speech and a consequential loss of 'sense of self'.

## Processing issues triggered by choices, time and change

Autistic people are struggling to make sense of a sensorily un-meaningful world. If the picture they have managed to assemble (one that just about makes sense) is altered, or extra demands are laid on it, they are tipped back into chaos and the threat of autonomic storm. It is particularly important to try to structure their environment, so that the individual is not faced with sudden changes of plan. This not always possible in daily living but I do always try and let people know what I would like to do, and get their agreement before I do it, so I know they are aware of what of what is going to happen, giving the brain time to process.

For example, and particularly if a person has a reputation for being easily upset, when I come to their house or room, I stand outside the door and, using gesture, ask if I may come in. I then wait until I get a nod or affirmatory gesture. This may be only the slightest nod, but it is vital that they know that I am not going to invade what they feel to be their personal territory and therefore do not represent a threat. This may take time. While I stood outside in the rain, Sandra said 'No' for twenty minutes before admitting me. The wait was worthwhile because, when she finally let me in, she did not feel afraid and attack me, as she was liable to do to strangers.

When I do get in, I use a person's body language and mime, rather than speech, to introduce myself. Many times, parents have said they cannot understand how it is that their child has accepted my presence and engaged with me, when they normally become sensorily overloaded and often aggressive in the presence of strangers.

Our days are ruled by time and while they may understand sequence, that is, B comes after A, a number of autistic people have absolutely no idea of the interval lapse between A and B.

Sandra knows that the taxi to go home comes after lunch, in that order, so as soon as her meal is finished she goes and stands by the door, regardless of the two-hour wait. As time passes, she becomes increasingly anxious and hits anyone who comes near her. Similarly, Andrew knows that a bus comes to his centre before lunchtime. So he leaves his day room and stands in the dining area as soon as he hears it come. He bellows with increasing distress during the twenty minute wait for the meal. Neither Sandra nor Andrew are able to read the time. Fortunately, Andrew loves to go for walks, so it is simple to arrange that he goes out before the bus come, and comes back after his meal is on the table, avoiding the clues that trigger his distress.

Digital timepieces may make reading the time easy, but they give even less idea of the intervals involved than clocks, since there is no spatial element to which to refer. And telling the time on a clock face is complicated by having a minute and an hour hand.

It is not difficult to make a simple clock by removing the minute hand on a large kitchen clock and just using the hour hand. For example, even the numbers on the face can be obscured using white card, in favour of a picture of the bus, or other visual clue to which the hour hand will align when it is time to go home.[92]

Timetables can help but they do need to be designed so that they are visually clear to a child who may have difficulty processing visual input. They may not know automatically that they should read from left to right, or be able to discriminate an object from the background in a picture.[93] Squeezing a whole load of information about the week on a piece of A4 may be meaningless, whereas separating the activities or days onto card or ply, so that they can be held in different hands, can make all the difference. We have to be careful not to design timetables based on our own sensory experience of reality but to take into account what our partner can make sense of.

One of the important features of independent living is the ability to be able to make choices, and a great deal of work goes into trying to assist autistic people to be able to indicate their preferences. Difficulties arise when the process of making a choice simply overloads the brain, so that there is no way the autistic person can indicate a preference. This is not necessarily a question of intellectual capability – asking a person if they would prefer orange or apple juice to drink can throw even the most able person into confusion. In such cases, we need to simplify the options from 'would you like A or B?' to 'would you like A?' If this is refused we ask, 'would you like B?'

Some people with Asperger's can teach themselves to use alternative strategies – if A does not happen, then try Plan B. For others, they are terrified because they cannot work out what is happening; all they know is that their world is falling apart.

As already mentioned, many autistic people dislike alterations in routine since their need for predictability in a sensorily chaotic world is so urgent. This includes body changes characteristic of puberty. For example, an autistic girl may rebel internally against menstruation, the acquisition of breasts and pubic

92 Caldwell P (2008) *Using Intensive Interaction and Sensory Integration*. London: Jessica Kingsley.

93 *Ibid.*

hair. In order to stop this happening, the brain will initiate steps to prevent growing up, such as becoming anorexic.[94] It is essential that those who support her work towards the promotion of a strong sense of embodiment to guide her through puberty. They need her to feel comfortable with her body. She may be helped by (enjoyable) exercise, such as dance or sport, to reinstate connection with her newly emerging body. Those people who support the individual need to understand and be sensitive to what is happening. Each person is an individual. Social stories can help but support needs to be tailored to preferences.

## Phobia and trauma

One of the commonest autistic phobias is a phobia of dogs, sometimes following an incident when a barking dog jumped up on a child. Unfortunately, while the less well-disposed bark and growl, even friendly dogs want to run up and bounce and play, both of which can be frightening and unpredictable for the child, so that it can be extremely difficult to take them out for walks. Following such an incident, one terrified young man retreated to bed and would only come out of his room for meals. His phobia had also traumatised him.

Recently an autism magazine, *Aukids*, ran an advice column asking the experts for help with this particular problem.[95] All the proposed strategies assumed that the child understood speech and was open to rational strategies, which makes it difficult to help those who are non-verbal and just as scared. But they generally recommended gradual introduction to a user friendly pet and trying to make the child aware of dog body language. For those that live by the sea, Luke Beardon suggested visiting beaches where dogs were not allowed, and two people mentioned visiting carefully selected dog sanctuaries where the dog can be viewed while caged. Noise reduction headphones can help if noise is the problem. Unfortunately, like all hypersensitivities, dog phobia is triggered not just by the noise and general bounciness and the fear that these engender, but at times by something quite different – Donna Williams says that hers was set off by the 'feeling of dog's hair'.

A promising new approach to treating phobias has been developed by Newcastle University using 'virtual reality therapy'. In controlled randomised trials involving 32 children, 40 percent showed improvement in two weeks. An eleven-year-old boy who became hysterical and ran away screaming if he saw a dog had four sessions in the 'blue room' where he learned through progressive control. He now has his own dog and will stroke other dogs.[96]

Trauma is triggered when the stress generated by an event exceeds the ability to cope with the emotions associated with the experience. These 'on-the-loose

94 Ustaszewski A. *Autism and Puberty*. Conference talk.

95 Aukids (2018) Issue 39. www.aukids.co.uk

96 Newcastle University Press Office (2019) Blue room for overcoming phobias in autism. Available at: https://www.ncl.ac.uk/press/articles/archive/2017/02/blueroomautismnhstreatment/ (accessed March 2019).

emotions' perseverate and provide a background of continuing distress which effects behaviour.

There are numerous triggers to trauma which relate to autism itself. At school, autistic children may be particularly vulnerable to trauma since autistic behaviour can cause the individual to stand out as 'different' and therefore lay them open to bullying, with long-term traumatic effects.

Even more deep seated are the traumas experienced in the past by many old autistic people who may have spent long periods of their lives literally abandoned in 'mental handicap institutions', where three quarters of 'patients' were physically or sexually abused. Their persistent distress may be revealed through delayed echolalia and (when the person is upset), the repetition of perseverant phrases such as 'I will be good, I will be good' or, 'Don't lock me in the coal shed'.

At home, Alice is totally traumatised when her beloved grandmother dies suddenly in the night. It appears that she feels it is her fault and somehow she should have prevented this. Refusing to go to bed, she starts an elaborate ritual in the evenings which goes on through the night until she drops from exhaustion around four o'clock. This behaviour ceases immediately when her family move house. It may seem drastic, but for Alice, changing the context removes the trigger to her extreme distress.

In addition, one can regard autism in itself as traumatic, in that neurological connectivity difficulties and consequent misreading of incoming signals may make it difficult or impossible to develop a trusting dyadic relationship. The autistic baby may physically not be able to pick up the parent's loving overtures and responses, with consequent attachment issues.[97]

## Pain and self-injury

When I am teaching, people often ask me what I mean by pain experienced by autistic people, since they do not necessarily show signs of it. The first thing the observer knows is that the person is in trouble, maybe self-injuring or acting aggressively towards other people.

How can we measure the depth of other people's pain? Donna Williams says hers starts in the back of the neck, a tingling feeling, like having eaten lemons, that spreads to every fibre of her body. Other people talk about it starting as a 'fizzy' feeling. Elsewhere Donna describes it as agony. On the other hand, William, who at the time was around eight years old, told me about the anger box that lived in his chest. Once it had opened, pain spread down his arms to

97 Yi C and Zhou T (2017) Autism as infantile post trauma stress disorder: a hypothesis. *Journal of Mental Disorders and Treatment* **3** 142.

the tips of his fingers. He made a gesture of stretching out his arm stiffly and trying to wipe it away. There seems little doubt that, while it may start as a fizzy feeling, what it progresses to is raw nerve pain. Gunilla Gerland talks about 'a silent concentration of feeling placed in the back of my neck. From there, so metallic, the feeling radiated out into my arms, clipped itself into my elbows but never came to an end, never ever came to an end'.

Chris has Asperger's syndrome. We met and talked sporadically for over a year before it transpired that she experienced extremely severe pain in her face and jaw to the extent that when she went to bed, she had to force her head against the bed head and tense her jaw hard in order to sleep. Later she was diagnosed as having trigeminal neuralgia (TN).[98] When I asked her why she had not talked about the pain before, she found it difficult to explain. It seemed that while she was experiencing it, she had not really recognised her pain as such or that the sensation was related to anything specific. Like Iris, she had sensations but did not recognise their meaning. She also said, in a kind of puzzled way, that she thought everyone had it.

Trigeminal neuralgia is a problem with the fifth cranial nerve (the trigeminal nerve). It can cause extreme pain in the jaw, nose and front of the head. It is usually but not always inherited, sometimes skipping a generation or two. Autistic people who have it may chew almost anything and have bouts of unexplained screaming, and many put pressure with their fingers just under the lobes of their ears, which is where the nerve emerges from the skull. They will often bang their heads.

TN occurs in non-autistic people as well: in the past the headaches were sometimes mis-diagnosed as migraine, epilepsy related or cluster headaches. In autistic people TN it is still often dismissed on the grounds that the behaviours such as chewing and head banging are just something that autistic people do (this misdiagnosis is called diagnostic overshadowing). It may be difficult to get a diagnosis since traditionally it was thought that TN only occurred in people over fifty years old, although in the US it is now being

diagnosed in children, even in infants. If you suspect TN, it is important to see a neurologist. TN occurs because the 'padding' between a vein and the TN nerve is worn away, or absent. One treatment is a keyhole operation which replaces the absent tissue with a small piece of foam, so that when the vein throbs it no longer impacts on the nerve. It is very important to try as far as possible to live a stress-free life, since stress affects the sympathetic nervous system and makes the symptoms worse.

Research into self-injury in people with autism at the Cerebra unit,

98 A more detailed account of our conversations with Chris about pain and trigeminal neuralgia appears in Caldwell P (2014) *The Anger Box: Sensory turmoil and pain in autism*. Brighton Pavilion Publishing & Media Ltd.

Birmingham University, links self-injury with pain. Using skin conductance to monitor a rise in activity in the sympathetic nervous system,[99] they found there was a ten second lag between its onset and the self-injurious behaviour. Sometimes, this internal onset of overactivity is accompanied by an external sign such as a flinch or a sound. In this case, it may be possible to intervene with distraction during the ten second lag period.

Mike has very severe autism. Periodically he will crash his head on the table, to the extent that he has damaged his sight. Before he starts to bang his head there is a short interval during which he goes to a table and lays his head on it and looks at you. The next time he does this, acting on the predication of what he is going to do, I bang the table in the rhythm of his anticipated self-injurious behaviour. Instead of going on to hurt himself, Mike stands up, looks at me, laughs and walks away. My intervention, which anticipates the climax of his sympathetic arousal in an autonomic storm, is sufficiently like his to divert his attention away from the perseverant arousal in his brain, and onto a rhythm he recognises in the world outside himself.

Since self-aggression is just one of the ways in which the body arms itself by setting off its self-defence system, I strongly suspect that this alteration of sympathetic activity and its concurrent confusion and pain will be found to precede some autonomic storms which involve aggressive behaviour towards others, as well as aggressive behaviour which is self-directed.

Jeanie pinches people hard, to the extent that one member of her support staff has required hospital treatment. When Jeanie does this, she is not only hurting them (and in this case indicating that her flatmate's radio is on so loud it is hurting her), but as she pinches, she is also giving herself pressure. Her 'attacks' are preceded by a quick flick of her head to the right. I suggest that next time staff observe this, they walk over to her and grasp her arm firmly, pressing it without hurting her, release it and walk away. When staff tried this, like Mike, Jeanie stopped in her tracks and laughed. For both Mike and Jeanie, we had exploited the time lag and interrupted the escalating sympathetic arousal, offering a diversion that was 'like enough' to the climax of their behavioural response to divert their attention away from their storm, and back on to something sourced outside themselves that had meaning for them.

The other problem with autistic pain is that, like Chris, some may have the pain feeling but do not recognise it, which makes it difficult to know whether or not they are ill. Again, this is an interoceptive problem. At least we can recognise it.

99 Specially designed mittens record sweat levels on the palms of the hands which measures the sympathetic nervous system activity.

## Communication, speech, boundaries and a sense of self

Most people with autism are getting mixed messages from the world outside. They do want to communicate, but trying to process scrambled speech is sensorily overloading and may threaten to bring on an autonomic storm. One of the first things those who support people with autism are taught is to use simple speech.

Communication is a two-way process. We communicate (or fail to communicate) with each other in two different ways. The first is 'functional communication', which relates to giving each other information such as 'do you want a cup of tea?' While functional communication addresses needs, the other way we communicate with each other is through emotional engagement; tuning into our partner's body language. Emotional engagement reflects how we feel.

Teaching functional communication normally uses flash cards and sign, with the focus on communication of needs, but the greater part of what we actually learn from each other is through observation of our partner's body language, which tells us how the other is feeling. (We do not want to listen to people unless we feel we can trust them.)

Nevertheless, we do tend to continue to think of communication in terms of speech, so it is extremely important that we become aware of the importance of focus on their affective state and the body language of our partners. For most of us this requires a deliberate shift. We have to learn to listen with all our senses, with total attention to all the inflexions and subtleties of our partner's prosody and posture. It is not so much what they are saying and the sounds and rhythms and movements they are making, but how they are using these. Becoming familiar with their emotional body language is the doorway to how they feel. All our engagements are subjective and what each partnership builds together will be subtly different from another: while using the same 'tools', each will have a quality of its own.

Speech is the end product of all sorts of different processes coming together and working in the correct order. We have ideas in our head and we want to tell other people about them, so we talk to each other. We receive and make sense of the words we hear in Wernicke's area (located in the parietal and temporal lobes of the brain). But in order to reply, we use a different area, Broca's area (in the frontal lobe of the brain), to organise our muscles in the correct order so that we can express what we want to say. These two areas of comprehension and speech production, which may seem to work together seamlessly, need to be able to talk to each other in the brain. In autism, it is not just that Wernicke's or Broca's area may be damaged, but that the links between them may be damaged.[100]

100 Broca's and Wernicke's areas are cortical areas specialised for production and comprehension, respectively, of human language. Broca's area is found in the left inferior frontal gyrus and Wernicke's area is located in the left posterior superior temporal gyrus.

The ability to understand and to produce speech varies widely in autistic people and is intimately linked with sensory discrimination as well. It is not only dependent on the level of the autistic person's sensory issues (how well they are able to assimilate and process sound for example), but also on the level of sensory threat presented by their non-autistic partner (for example, what clothes they are wearing), because stress of any sort will make sound more difficult to process.

First of all, in order to communicate, autistic people need to be able to disentangle the incoming voice from the background sounds. Overlapping voices (as at shift change-over time in residential houses), or sounds from the TV or radio, make it difficult to sort out what is being said. Secondly, if the autistic person is anxious, because of some other sensory difficulties (for example the effects of visual hypersensitivity), they are going to find it difficult to focus on sound. Or, they may have a shortage of Purkinje cells, so the visual and auditory signals get confused on the way to the processing system, as previously discussed. In addition, if they are synaesthetic, sound may be being directed away from the sound processing system to some other part of the brain.

When it comes to replying to speech, there are many stages involved before an idea can be spoken: having decided what they want to say, Broca's area has to organise the muscles to move the tongue and jaw, shape the mouth and synchronise the breathing in order to speak. Often our partners will recognise the rhythm of what has been said to them, and also know what they want to say, without being able to articulate the words. Sometimes they can piggyback the words on the rhythm of songs.

Pranve is 23. He has autism, is extremely nervous and attacks people frequently. His parents and his speech therapist say that the only words that he can say are, 'Where's Charlene?' (Charlene is Pranve's sister who no longer lives with the family).[101] Over a period of about three hours, responding to his sounds, hand movements and general body language, Pranve visibly relaxes, smiling, laughing and looking at me, indicating what he wants and showing me that he enjoys rhythm by clapping his hands in rhythmic patterns. Eventually he starts to hum the song and words of 'Baa Baa Black Sheep', which both his parents and his speech therapist say he has never done before. Struggling to get the words out, he utters sounds in the rhythm of the song first; next he hums the notes. He moves his head round in a way that prompts one to visualise the phrase 'getting your head round a problem'. Then his chin wobbles. Finally he sings the first line, followed by the second. One can follow the whole process, from wanting to show us what he can do, to the final achievement. His parents and therapist are amazed.[102]

101 There are 26 short films on the Caldwell Autism Foundation website that can be viewed for free, including a film of the interactions with Pranve: http://thecaldwellautismfoundation.org.uk/index.php/responsive-communication-the-films/.

102 http://thecaldwellautismfoundation.org.uk/index.php/pranve/.

While Janet Gurney is going to be writing about using non-verbal language to set up emotional engagement in her chapter on Intensive Interaction, I want to highlight the importance of our communication partner being able to recognise our intent to communicate, and the potential of using their own signals to get a response from us. Our partner must be able to recognise our overtures to them as meaningful.

Teddy is five years old. He gives no eye contact and spends his time running round the house and banging himself on the wall. He does not respond when I try using his sounds to get in touch with him. I ask myself what it is that has meaning for him – what feedback is he giving to himself? Put this way it is obvious that impact and pressure are meaningful. I ask his mother to hold him between her knees. Every time he makes a sound, she responds in kind, but she also tugs on his belt, so as well as an auditory response he is getting a pressure response to his sounds. He recognises this at once, turns towards her, looks at her, smiles and places his finger on his lips and then on hers. He becomes completely calm. It turns out that he has had glue ear and possibly has never learned that his sounds can be used for communication.

While some autistic people may have little or no speech, others may be able to understand but not respond. Even people who are very able may struggle to keep up with speech, particularly overlapping speech. The more anxious a person is, the more difficult it is for them to process what is being said and organise a reply.

Speech is especially difficult if the brain is struggling with anxiety: time and again clinical experience demonstrates that processing becomes easier when anxiety is reduced and our partner relaxes. One can see the anxiety falling away.

Eight-year-old April is extremely distressed. She has had some speech in the past but no longer uses it. She has broken her nose and fingers when hitting herself. She scratches the quilt under which she is hiding. She does not respond when I answer her sounds but gradually pushes back the quilt when I use my fingers to scratch the quilt, interleaving her scratch episodes with my own. We start to play with each other's fingers.

While April is scratching, she is putting pressure on her fingers; so I decide to use vibration to interact with her. Since I have no vibration units to hand, I use two electric vibrating toothbrushes, one for each of us. This is a proprioceptive sensation that has meaning for April. She throws off her quilt and comes to life almost at once, laughing and engaging with full eye contact. At lunch, when her Granny phones, April (who is virtually non-verbal), surprises her mother by seizing the phone and announcing she wants cream cheese for her lunch. The following day she tells her mother that she loves her.

To sum up, to speak to each other we have to know what we want to say, and piece together the many different processes in the right order to produce meaningful communication. While we may not be able to recognise words, even if we have severe autism, we almost always recognise rhythm. (Pressure is the first sense to come 'online' in the womb, when we align our heartbeat with the pressure of our mother's transmitted through the amniotic fluid, some time before our ears start to hear).

Echolalia seems to happen for two different reasons. The first is when the autistic child endlessly repeats a single word or phrase that relates to what we have said. Temple Grandin tells us she constantly repeated the phrase, 'the street lights are coming on'. It reassured and confirmed for her that the particular event was happening. The second happens when an autistic person wants to say something, but all they can articulate is a perseverant repetitive phrase a neuronal circuit has become stuck in the brain. As with some people who have had a stroke, a particular phrase seems to be the single porthole through which all communication has to be channelled. As we saw with Pranve, his ability to recognise rhythm meant that we could engage through song.

We can also use this strategy to engage with autistic people who have delayed echolalia, where they endlessly repeat certain phrases (quite often learned from TV or linked to past – sometimes traumatic – episodes). Repeating back the rhythm, cadence and lilt but not the words offers something the brain recognises as their own but comes from elsewhere, and can shift attention out of the internal perseverant circuit in which the brain is stuck. People recognise 'their' rhythm coming from outside themselves and direct their attention towards it. At the same time, they often appear relieved to have escaped from their inner trap and shifted out of their inner world.

Mary gets stuck in a perseverant loop and will go on for hours saying, 'it's all right to hold the childer, it's all right to hold the childer'. I respond with the rhythm: 'Da-da-Da-da, da-da-da-da' and she stops at once, looks at me and puts her arms round me.

This is not so easy when the autistic person is repeating a single word like 'Goodbye' or the last word of your sentence, but it can help to capture attention if one alters the pitch or rhythm slightly when responding to the single word. The brain recognises 'enough' of the utterance but it is also sufficiently different to shift attention outwards.

How we speak to each other reveals our affective state, so we need to listen, not just to the words our partner uses but (if they have speech) to the quality of their voice, since there is often more than one voice – a 'good voice' and a 'bad voice'. The first is cheerful and reflects the socially acceptable way the person has been taught to interact. The second is quite often negative and may be verbally aggressive, reflecting how they feel. (This split may also apply to the sounds non-verbal children or adults make, indicating how they feel, sometimes happy and sometimes, distressed.) Many parents and teachers will recognise this split, which seems to arise from the way we reject their negative thoughts and feelings.

Some autistic people will actually project these positive and negative emotions out from their inner world onto objects, which 'speak for them'. Josh uses one of his hands as a 'good hand' (Mr Pal) and the other speaks for 'bad hand' (Mr Hands). Josh and Andre, written about here, have both appeared in *From Isolation to Intimacy*, in a detailed discussion of the problem of projected personalities reflected in positive and negative voices.[103]

Following some disturbed behaviour at school, Josh is put on a behavioural programme: he has to sit on a 'naughty chair' if he is deemed to have misbehaved. The outcome is disastrous. He stops talking to his mother and now only has conversations between Mr Pal and Mr Hands. For example, at bath time, he walks upstairs, Mr Pal saying cheerfully, '*I'm going to have a bath*', to which Mr Hands responds in an angry voice, '*I don't wanna have a bath*'. The distinction is quite clear between what his mother, or society, wants and what is expected of him, and how he feels about this.

At school Josh's behaviour deteriorates significantly. He will take himself to the naughty chair for any supposed activity, sit on it, cry and beat his head. At this stage, I suggest his mother starts using his non-verbal language to interact with him. Each time he bellows, she responds with an empathetic sound, confirming that she understands how he feels. Within three weeks Mr Pal and Mr Hands have disappeared and he is back talking to his mother. Occasionally he will actually enlist her help to defend himself against a negative feeling, saying, '*Mum, Mr Hands is bullying me again*'.

Andre lives independently.[104] In the evenings he goes to the pub. If the noise and bustle get too much, he responds to the onset of sensory overload by spilling a little of his drink on the table and doodling in it. He describes himself as looking for 'local coherence', which I take to mean an activity which his brain recognises when it is becoming disturbed. If this strategy does not calm him, he takes out his secondary defence from his pocket, two puppets, the equivalent of Mr Pal and Mr Hands. Although Andre is capable of conversation when he is speaking as himself, and can tolerate interruptions in his flow, when the puppets are speaking, he becomes extremely angry if they are interrupted.

It is vitally important to listen to the *quality* of verbal language and non-verbal sounds, since any sign of splitting into positive and negative utterances is a psychological red alert that the autistic adult or child is losing the connection between themselves and the feelings that determine their sense of self.

103 Caldwell P (2007) *From Isolation to Intimacy: Making friends without words*. London: Jessica Kingsley Publishers.

104 Nazeer K (2006) *Send in the Idiots*. London: Bloomsbury Publishing.

At this stage we need to try and pull together (1) our voice as a way of reflecting how we feel and who we feel we are and (2) interoception – the messages as they are interpreted in our partner's brain. The final stage of the interoceptive pathway is to map out a sense of identity, the state of which is reflected in the way we speak at any particular time.

How we obtain our sense of self is in large part due to how we feel our emotions. If the reality of these is being denied, it is going to have an impact on our ability to build a strong sense of self. 'If you reject the anger or hurt that I feel, perhaps how I feel is not real, so maybe the self that I feel is not real. The consequence is that I either project my negative feelings, or I project them onto something outside myself – and incidentally, something for which I am no longer responsible.'

And these feelings can run deep. People with autism often feel depressed and quite frequently express their feelings in such phrases as, 'I want to hit you' or 'I want to kill myself'. Rather than accepting that this is how they actually feel, our focus on social acceptability leads us to discourage them from expressing their emotions: 'You can't say that' or 'You don't really feel that'. In ignoring or reproving them for how they feel, we are denying our partner's feelings, with the implication that these are not real and not to be trusted as indicators of what and who they are, contributing to their self-doubt.

Although it may feel counterintuitive, we need to respond to and validate their negative feelings: 'You do sound as if you want to hit me'. The outcome of valuing their negative affect is almost always a sigh of relief accompanied by relaxation. If they swear at us, passive acceptance is more effective than reproof or ignoring them.[105] This is particularly so, if the swearing is personally directed and not just a habitual adjective. If someone says to me, 'Fuck off', and I reply, 'You sound really fucked off', they almost always respond, 'Oh yes I am'. But having had how they feel validated, their outwardly directed or self-directed aggression melts away.

At the risk of repeating myself; because it is so important, if we fail to confirm our communication partner's negative feelings, we are giving them the message that how they feel does not reflect reality, or that their feelings do not matter, with the implication that they themselves do not matter.

In order for this strategy to be effective, we have to respond by using their actual words, exactly as they have. It is not enough to say, 'You must be feeling miserable today'. Our response must be one that is 'part of' their expression of the sensation that is weighing them down. It is absolutely essential that if we employ this approach, all who support the individual know exactly *how* and *why* it is being employed. It is not a case of swearing at the person but tuning it to how they feel and acknowledging the feeling is real.

105 See Caldwell P (2006) *Finding You Finding Me.* London: Jessica Kingsley pp75–80 for extensive examples.

In terms of sense of self, the reason why scientists and philosophers are becoming so excited about interoception is that it is a new point of view and one that is beginning to throw light on this mysterious question of how we obtain this sense of self, our quiddity, the feeling of 'who' we are. At the same time, it is becoming clear why, in terms of self-awareness, the cards are stacked against people with autism. Again we need to qualify this, because what we are talking about is 'some' people with autism, since every person on the spectrum is different.

How autistic people feel about themselves ranges from the extremely (almost aggressively) confident, 'I'm autistic; get used to it', to those who have internalised society's rejection of them as (literally) 'mad or bad' and have completely lost connection with – and confidence in – themselves.

As we have seen, loss of sense of self may be intrinsic, stemming from internal disruption in the affective pathway that channels bodily sensations to the insula, where they are built into the personal map of this particular individual's emotional state. But it may also be extrinsic, in that it is the outcome of society's efforts to 'normalise' behaviour (however well intentioned), particularly stopping autistic people from using repetitive behaviour which they are using to help themselves know what they are doing, or when they try to tell us how they feel, rejecting their negative emotions as socially unacceptable.

Joe tells us how his loss of sense of self was related to physical confusion.[106] Joe was taken to see a psychiatrist because he would not stop jumping. Joe was jumping because he was sensorily confused, but the psychiatrist did not understand the roots of his bizarre behaviour. She said, '*Never jump again after you leave this room*'. Being obedient, Joe stopped, but he says that at that moment, he lost his physical sense of self. He adds that subsequently he took up other repetitive behaviours in order to bring meaning to his world. Regular sessions on a trampoline would have allowed Joe to build a physical sense of self in a more 'normal' way by keeping contact with himself.

But alongside getting poor sensory feedback from the physical world, an autistic person's physical confusion between 'me' and 'not me', may relate directly to failure to develop a sense of boundary; the limits of where 'I stop' and 'you begin'.

They sometimes feel as though they are merging with other people, or do not know if a limb belongs to them or to someone else.[107] Donna Williams says she does not know if the hand that is flapping in front of her, belongs to her, or to her conversation partner. Tight clothes and weighted jackets can help to provide artificial boundaries, providing external support, helping those with boundary

106 Joe in *Being Autistic* by Autscape (now out of print).

107 In 2014 The Nobel Prize in Physiology or Medicine was awarded in one half to John O'Keefe and the other half jointly to May-Britt Moser and Edvard I Moser 'for their discoveries of cells that constitute a positioning system in the brain' (called Place cells).

issues to define themselves – where they stop and the world out there starts.[108] At the age of 16, John tells me that wearing a pressure vest stops him feeling *'as if his body is actively blowing itself apart'*. Ron, who has very severe proprioceptive hyposensitivity, only stops running round the house hitting himself on the walls when he is wrapped tightly in sheet Lycra.

Because they cannot interpret the sensory signals of people in movement, other autistic people with boundary issues are afraid and lash out if approached. But they want to communicate and are happy to tap to people on the other side of windows.

Gary lives outside. Even in winter he rarely comes in except to sleep or eat. He throws his food on the floor before eating it. He keeps away from people but taps the window when he passes the sitting room. If the staff look up, he laughs and runs away. He wants to communicate but feels invaded if people come near. Sitting inside, we tap on a sheet of transparent polycarbonate, so he can see us but feel the boundary between us. He understands at once, and runs in to be with us next time we call.

Reg hits anyone who comes near him. His support staff say the only time he relaxes is when they take him for a ride in the van. It turns out the van has a sheet of unbreakable polycarbonate between the driver and the back where Reg sits. I sit in the front, and every time he makes a sound, I tap back on the partition. He really enjoys this. So we modify his house, putting a transparent door between the staff room and his flat. Again, this enables him to communicate without feeling threatened and invaded.

In addition to interoceptive dysfunctions, there is the problem of society's expectations as to how people should behave in public. Autistic people are constantly seen as getting things wrong – and being corrected. Not only do they have to grapple with sensory confusion, but they feel psychologically crushed by society's expectations much of the time. In failing to acknowledge their feelings as real, we are also telling them they themselves are not real. It is extremely important that we support people's sense of self, especially the reality of their negative feelings.

Some people with Asperger's develop strategies to cope with their lost sense of self, since without a sense of self they are vulnerable, with nothing to fall back on to protect them from the onslaught of emotional overload. Either they retreat into the protection of an inner world (Donna Williams calls it a prison,[109] where she has all the relationships she should have with the world outside), or, in the interests of self-preservation and conforming to the demands of society, they develop a mask,

108 Such as the Squease Vest – an inflatable gilet where the pressure can be adjusted by pumping to the appropriate level.

109 Williams D (1995) *Jam-Jar.* Channel 4. Glasgow: Fresh Film and Television.

retreating behind a false self. With a photograph she describes her false smile, which she wore all the time, unconnected with how she felt inside.

She goes on to model herself on different characters, a cheerful, socially acceptable one and a fierce one who lives under her bed and frightens people away.

Some children learn to develop a mask at school to avoid being bullied[110] but others 'mask' in order to trick their own brains into thinking they are loved and valued.[111] Grace describes the process of needing to fit in:

*'For as long as I can remember, autism wasn't something to be proud of, the stigma became my identity. I was discriminated against for anything I did or said, from some family members, tutors, friends, colleagues and employers. My career was already expected for me to be a supermarket trolley pusher. But I want more than that, to find a meaning to my life. I wanted to be seen as more than a label, to have a choice, a chance to be heard, to exist. So I made up the idea of wearing a mask.'*

One of the signs of masking is that the child may be apparently coping at school (but under stress due to sensory issues) and having meltdowns at home, where they feel safe to do so. In this case, their parents may be blamed for poor parenting skills, when the root of the problem is the bright lights and overwhelming noise at school. Whatever its origin, the mask of social acceptability is worn at the cost of anxiety, of being disconnected from how one really feels, and hence from one's true self. This can be at the root of extreme anxiety and stress. The consequence of wearing the mask is that it is very exhausting, takes a lot of energy to keep it all together. As Grace says: *'It can make me unappreciate myself, question my worth or who I am: feel unconfident being myself around other people'*.

Andy says:

*'I wonder how different and how much happier I could be if I didn't mask and I was myself from the beginning, if I had friends who actually shared my interests and I didn't have to put on an act whenever I was with them. It's so lonely when you don't even know yourself. Nobody ever tells you that emptiness weighs the most.'*

Grace talks about the backlash when distress and pain finally overwhelm the defensive mask:

---

110 *When Looking Fine isn't the Same as being Fine.* Autism Consultancy International 2018.

111 Understanding Autistics (2018) *Autism and Loneliness (#TakeTheMaskOff)* [online]. Available at: https://understandingautistics.blog/2018/08/07/autism-and-loneliness-takethemaskoff/ (accessed March 2019).

*'Once the mask is off, all the problems I've had during the day come flooding out of control in revenge for being locked up so long. That's where I would suffer from panic attacks, break-downs, depression, the feeling of drowning in self-pity.'*

Some autistic people find it is too much and opt out.

## Summary

If we judge the sensory experiences of autistic people by those we obtain from our own non-autistic world, it can lead to total misunderstanding of the autistic condition. Critics may say that in seeking to reduce or remove the triggers to the pain and confusion caused by sensory overload, Responsive Communication is not helping autistic people to adapt to the non-autistic world in which they have to live. Such an objection totally misunderstands the level of anxiety, stress and pain which sensory issues inflict on them, some of which can be relieved or avoided.

While some people at the high end of the ability level of the spectrum may develop their own ways of coping with their distress, even for them their protective devices come at a cost of anxiety and stress. Using behavioural methods, sometimes the brain may be trained to cope with a certain level of stimulus; but for other autistic people, forcing them to live with acutely painful triggers is a form of abuse. The consequence is that they retreat from the world we share, develop behaviours that make them difficult to be near or live with, self-injure, become anorexic, or are even misdiagnosed and detained; some are hospitalised and medicated for schizophrenia.

*'A growing body of research evidence is showing that many autistic people at some point experience mental health problems, such as depression and anxiety ... Studies have shown high rates of suicidal thoughts (10.9%–66%), and suicidal behaviours (11%–30%) in adults and children with autism.'*[112]

We need to inform ourselves and society about the sensory issues which underpin behaviour that society sees as challenging – and currently still underlie misunderstanding in services that manage the autistic condition. Some still have no idea of the stress and anxiety that their disregard for the autistic reality is causing the people they are set up to help.

For example, John is an exceptionally gifted individual with Asperger's syndrome. He is in a state of acute anxiety in the days preceding a PIP assessment for a flat in supported living accommodation. He is physically sick and cannot sleep. On the day, the official responsible for making the assessment does not turn up for the interview. No one gets in touch with the family to explain his absence. When

112 Interactive Autism Network (2018) *Diagnosing Depression in Autism* [online]. Available at: https://iancommunity.org/diagnosing-depression-autism (accessed March 2019).

his mother contacts the department, they refuse to give details but eventually say that a charge of assault has been made against John, so they will not be going ahead with the assessment. He protests his innocence.

The accusation turns out to be false, arising from an administrative error made by the service: a letter referring to another young man has been wrongly placed in John's file. But the real damage is done, not so much by the department's failure to deal with their own error, but in failing to recognise the stress laid on a severely autistic young man as days pass and they fail to communicate (waiting can cause extreme distress for some autistic people). In an email, John tells me, *'What got to me the most is that they were totally thoughtless for just letting agreed times for the meeting simply 'slip by' and not even bother to tell any of us, especially given the seriousness of the crime which had been imposed onto my name'*.

While the department responsible has admitted its fault, traumatic damage had been done through their ignorance and insensitive handling of their own mistake. The stress caused is chemically written into John's experience.

Currently, management and administrative systems are being carried out by agents who are so unaware of their own deficiency that they do not even know they require training. Quite simply, they do not know what they are doing. The question any of us who are in contact with (or supporting) autistic people always need to ask ourselves is whether the approach we are offering is increasing or decreasing stress. If the person cannot express their anxiety verbally, is their body language relaxed; are there positive changes in behaviour? Are they more able to tolerate stimuli that were difficult before?

We have a choice between two approaches. We can opt for the direction of containment and social acceptability, supported if necessary by medication. Or we can open ourselves up to what it is that has meaning for the autistic individual, working from the language that their brain can grasp without causing a strain on the sensory processing systems. When we reduce the pressure, the brain operates more effectively, difficult to manage behaviour is reduced, and, as so many parents say, *'I've got a happy child now'*.

We have so much to learn from autistic people. Using Responsive Communication, the combination of sensitivity to the triggers of sensory overload and communicating through a person's own body language (one that does not require elaborate processing in the brain) can bring about remarkable change to the lives of people who are otherwise struggling to make sense of their environment.

Finally, I want to introduce Hope Lightowler, who we have already met. Hope is the author of the next chapter. I first met her about eighteen months ago, after she had been discharged from hospital where she had been sectioned.

Whatever mental health issues Hope may or may not have had, what had been missed was the fact that she was severely autistic. Sitting in a darkened room, watching her reactions to sound and observing her boundary difficulties and emotional hypersensitivity, it would have been obvious that she was on the spectrum. As it was, she had only been observed in a clinic with its bright lights and noise, where she was terrified and shut down. Unless we see people in their normal environments it is very easy to miss the sensory difficulties they are struggling with and hence miss the autism, especially in women. Hope has written a remarkable and moving account of what it is like to be at the sharp end of diagnostic overshadowing.

## References


Amaral DG and Corbett BA (2003) The amygdala, autism and anxiety. *Novartis Foundation Symposium* **251** 177–187.

ASAN (2019) *About Autism* [online]. Available at: www.autisticadvocacy.org/about-asan/about-autism (accessed March 2019).

Barratt LF and Simmons WK (2015) Interoceptive predictions in the brain. *Nature Reviews Neuroscience* **16** (7) 419–229.

Barron J and Barron S (1992) *There's a Boy in Here: Emerging from the bonds of autism.* Arlington, TX: Future Horizons.

Betancur C (2011) Etiological heterogeneity in autism spectrum disorders: more than 100 genetic and genomic disorders and still counting. *Brain Research* **1380** 41–77.

Bluestone J (2005) *The Fabric of Autism: Weaving threads into a cogent theory*. New York: The Handle Institute.

Brown L (2011) The Significance of Semantics: Person-First Language: Why It Matters [online]. Autistic Hoya. Available at: https://www.autistichoya.com/2011/08/significance-of-semantics-person-first.html (accessed March 2019).

Caldwell P (2006) *Finding You Finding Me*. London: Jessica Kingsley.

Caldwell P (2007) *From Isolation to Intimacy: Making friends without words*. London: Jessica Kingsley Publishers.

Caldwell P (2008) *Using Intensive Interaction and Sensory Integration*. London: Jessica Kingsley.

Caldwell P (2014) *The Anger Box: Sensory turmoil and pain in autism*. Brighton Pavilion Publishing & Media Ltd.

Caldwell P (2017) *Hall of Mirrors – Shards of Clarity: Autism, neuroscience and finding a sense of self*. Brighton: Pavilion Publishing & Media Ltd.

Carreiro JE (2009) *An Osteopathic Approach for Children* (2nd edition). Amsterdam: Elsevier.

Claxton G (1998) *Hare Brain, Tortoise Mind: Why intelligence increases when you think less.* New York: Harper Collins Publishers.

Coughlan S (2015) Dyslexia not linked to eyesight, says study [online]. *BBC News* **27 May**. Available at: https://www.bbc.co.uk/news/education-32836733 (accessed March 2019).

Craig AD (2003) Interoception: the sense of the physiological condition of the body. *Current Opinion in Neurobiology* **13** 500– 505.

Craig AD (Bud) (2015) *How Do You Feel? An interoceptive moment with your neurobiological self.* New Jersey: Princeton University Press.

Cytowic R (1998) *The Man who Tasted Shapes*. Cambridge, MA: The MIT Press.

Damasio A (2003) The person within. *Nature* **423** 227.

Eagleman D (2015) *The Brain: The story of you*. London: Canongate Books.

Earl RK, Peterson JL, Wallace AS, Fox E, Ma R, Pepper M and Haidar G (2017) *Autism Spectrum Disorder: A reference guide* [online]. Bernier Lab, University of Washington. Available at: http://depts.washington.edu/rablab/wordpress/wp-content/uploads/2017/07/Bernier-Lab-UW-Autism-Spectrum-Disorder-Reference-Guide-2017.pdf (accessed March 2019).

Endevelt-Shapira Y, Perl O, Ravia A, Amir D, Eisen A, Bezalel V, Rozenkrantz L, Mishor E, Pinchover L, Soroka T, Honigstein D and Sobel N (2017). Altered responses to social chemosignals in autism spectrum disorder. *Nature Neuroscience* **21** 111–119.

Garfinkel SN, Tiley C, O'Keeffe S, Harrison NA, Seth AK and Critchley HD (2016) Discrepancies between dimensions of interoception in autism: Implications for emotion and anxiety. *Biology Psychology* **114** 117–126.

Gerland G (2003) *A Real Person: Life on the outside.* London: Souvenir Press.

Gibbons K (2018) Noise-cancelling windows could be the next boom industry. *The Times* **1 May**.

Grandin T (2013) *The Autistic Brain*. Boston: Houghton Mifflin Harcourt.

Hazell W (2018) *Exclusions of autistic pupils up 60 percent* [online]. Tes. Available at: https://www.tes.com/news/exclusions-autistic-pupils-60-cent (accessed March 2019).

Igoe G (2018) *'I am not autistic when I am making. I am me: creative, imaginative.'* [online] Learning Disability Today. Available at: https://www.learningdisabilitytoday.co.uk/i-am-not-autistic-when-i-am-making-i-am-me-creative-imaginative (accessed March 2019).

Interactive Autism Network (2018) *Diagnosing Depression in Autism* [online]. Available at: https://iancommunity.org/diagnosing-depression-autism (accessed March 2019).

Johansson Iris (2012) *A Different Childhood*. Scottsdale, AZ: Inkwell Productions.

Kana RL, Libero LE and Moore MS (2011) Disrupted cortical connectivity theory as an explanatory model for autism spectrum disorders. *Physics of Life Reviews* **8** (4) 410–437.

Kanner L (1943) Autistic disturbances of affective contact. *The Nervous Child* **2** 217–250.

Lau YC, Hinkley LB, Bukshpun P, Strominger ZA, Wakahiro ML, Baron-Cohen S, Allison C, Auyeung B, Jeremy RJ, Nagarajan SS, Sherr EH and Marco EJ (2013). Autism traits in individuals with agenesis of the corpus callosum. *Journal of Autism and Developmental Disorders* **43** (5) 1106–1118.

Lenzen M (2005) Feeling our emotions. *Scientific America Mind.* **16** (1) 14–15.

Mahler K (2016) *Interoception: The eighth sensory system* [online]. Available at: https://autismawarenesscentre.com/what-is-interoception-and-how-does-it-impact-autism/ (accessed March 2019).

Musings of an Aspie (2013) *Acceptance as a Well-being Practice* [online]. Available at: https://musingsofanaspie.com/author/musingsofanaspie/ (accessed March 2019).

Nazeer K (2006) *Send in the Idiots*. London: Bloomsbury Publishing.

Newcastle University Press Office (2019) *Blue room for overcoming phobias in autism.* Available at: https://www.ncl.ac.uk/press/articles/.../2019/02blueroomforovercomingphobiasinautism/ (accessed March 2019).

Nind and Hewett (2001) *A Practical Guide to Intensive Interaction*. London: British Institute of Learning Disabilities.

Palmen SJMC, Engeland HV, Hof PR and Schmitz C (2004) Neuropathological findings in autism. *Brain* **127** (12) 2572–2583.

Panju S, Brian J, Dupuis A, Anagnostou E and Kushki A (2015) Atypical sympathetic arousal in children with autism spectrum disorder and its association with anxiety symptomatology. *Molecular Autism* **11** (6) 64.

Ramachandran VS (2012) *The Tell-tale Brain: Unlocking the mystery of human nature*. London: Windmill Books.

Seth AK (2017) *Ted Talk: Your brain hallucinates your conscious reality*.

Shah P, Hall R, Catmur C and Bird G (2016) Alexithymia, not autism, is associated with impaired interoception. *Cortex* **81** 215–220.

Smith B (2018) Ted Talk: *The Role of Smell in Consciousness*. Available at: https://www.youtube.com/watch?v=V34N9YJAMsY (accessed March 2019).

Stern DN (1985) *The Interpersonal World of the Infant*. New York: Basic Books Inc.

Sudarov A (2013) Defining the role of cerebellar Purkinje cells in autism spectrum disorders. *The Cerebellum* **12** (6) 950.

Tuff T (2018) Shutdowns: the invisible enemy. *Aukids* **39** 9.

Understanding Autistics (2018) *Autism and Loneliness* (#TakeThemMaskOff) [online]. Available at: https://understandingautistics.blog/2018/08/07/autism-and-loneliness-takethemaskoff/ (accessed March 2019).

Von Boehmer H (1990) Self recognition by the immune system. *European Journal of Biochemistry* **194** 693–698.

Weizmann Institute of Science (2017) *Autism and the Smell of Fear* [online] EurekAlert! Available at: https://www.eurekalert.org/pub_releases/2017-11/wios-aat112717.php (accessed March 2019).

Weizmann Institute of Science (2017) *Autism and the Smell of Fear* [online] EurekAlert! Available at: https://www.eurekalert.org/pub_releases/2017-11/wios-aat112717.php (accessed March 2019).

Williams D (1995) *Jam-Jar*. Channel 4. Glasgow: Fresh Film and Television.

Williams D (1998) *Nobody Nowhere: The remarkable autobiography of an autistic girl*. London: Jessica Kingsley Publishers.

Wolfensberger W (2000) A brief overview of social role valorization. *Mental Retardation* **38** 105–123.

Yi C and Zhou T (2017) Autism as infantile post trauma stress disorder: a hypothesis. *Journal of Mental Disorders and Treatment* **3** 142.

# Chapter 2: Unrecognised autism

Hope Lightowler

My name is Hope Lightowler and I am 19 years old. I was diagnosed with autism in January 2017 and got an NHS diagnosis on September 2017. My diagnoses are obsessive compulsive disorder (OCD), generalised anxiety disorder, depression, autism and Irlen syndrome, although my diagnoses of autism and Irlen syndrome are much more recent. I at first hated my diagnosis but at the same time I was also relieved. I was also embarrassed, which is strange because I have never been embarrassed by my brother's autism. I think I was embarrassed because I was worried about how people would see me now – and that people would see me as fragile or weak because I was disabled. I also didn't want people who said I was autistic previously to be right, especially my mum. It took me a couple of months to actually come to terms with my diagnosis, as I felt it meant that I wouldn't get better and would stay as ill as I was forever and would just be a burden to my family, friends and also the government. I have come to realise that none of these are true. My autism diagnosis has actually helped me to become better, as I now know what the problem is and so can now alter the support I receive.

Before my diagnosis, I had been with mental health services for a while. I first went to CAMHS in Year 9, when I was caught by a friend trying to unscrew a pencil sharpener to get a blade and explained my plans to kill myself by slashing my wrists. She told the members of staff who called my parents. I was diagnosed with OCD and was given a psychiatric nurse (CPN) and went through cognitive behavioural therapy (CBT). I was then discharged after a period of time. Then after about a year, as my GCSEs were coming up, I started to get ill. I wasn't sleeping and my anxiety and OCD and depression were getting worse. I was prescribed melatonin and given CBT and family therapy and then eventually put on sertraline and then sent to hospital. I had been through CBT several times and couldn't understand why it wasn't working. I was also made to feel it was my fault and told it just wasn't the right time. I now hope to do CBT again but hopefully this time because of my diagnosis it can be specialised to autism, so will hopefully it will be more affective. Before my diagnosis I always wore earphones and constantly was listening to something, as if I didn't have this input every little noise would affect me and make me feel on edge and would just build up like layers being added, until eventually it would boil over and I couldn't stand it. I couldn't understand why I was like this and nobody else was, and why nobody else was so affected by the noise, apart from my brother who is on the spectrum and also has a learning disability. Since my diagnosis I have found sensory aids like noise cancelling headphones which have helped so much. They have especially made things like eating out so much less anxiety provoking and enabled me to go out of the house without it causing me lots of anxiety. Although I still find leaving the house difficult and require assistance to leave the house.

I also used to get really bad headaches almost every day and they were especially intolerable during the bright summer months. I hated the summer months and would try and spend as much time in the house as possible with my curtains closed. I couldn't understand why everyone else was enjoying summer so much. People especially adults started to not believe me when I complained about headaches because they didn't think you could have headaches that often. I found reading and writing really tiring and it took me longer than most people my own age. Which was incredibly frustrating. Also, lots of lights and bright colours would cause this build-up of pressure in my head to the point I couldn't cope. Since my diagnosis of autism, I now understand why this happens and have been diagnosed with Irlen syndrome and have coloured lenses and overlays. I can now tolerate with my glasses being outside in the summer without getting headaches and also read and write without getting headaches. I can also be in a room with strip lighting without getting headaches and becoming irritable.

I didn't understand why I hated taking my coat off in uncomfortable situations and why I actually found uncomfortableness, such as being hot in a coat or having something sharp digging into me, comforting.

Fiddly and small or intricate things were always my nemesis. I am so clumsy and as people always say 'you're like a bull in a china shop'. It didn't matter how hard I try, I might as well have clubs for hands. It has always been so frustrating for me.

Being sensitive to touch has always made things difficult as it means I can't stand certain textures and I really can't stand being touched, which is a problem when you are walking in crowds or round school as people push and shove, but the sensation of being brushed past makes me so uncomfortable and awful. I didn't understand why I got so anxious before changing classes or even going to school. I would purposely pack up slowly or come up with some reason to talk to my teachers to avoid the noise and the rush and also limit the amount of lunch and break time I had. It has also made hugging a big issue. I couldn't understand why I couldn't enjoy it and why it made it feel like my skin is crawling to the point where it makes me feel like I want to rip my skin off. It made me feel like I was a psychopath or just a horrible person and this was not missed by anyone around me especially my mum.

She used to say how she couldn't understand why she felt me go stiff when she hugged me and why it felt like I didn't enjoy it and felt so uncomfortable. But now I understand it I don't feel as bad but still get anxious when family come around and know I'm going to have to give hugs. Or around friends. Now I'm a lot less anxious about it and me and my mum understand each other a lot more. I actually enjoy our hugs and ask for them when I need them to release pressure when I'm getting overloaded.

I also thought I was a psychopath as I couldn't stand other people when they got upset and couldn't understand why they were upset. Furthermore, I didn't understand why everyone else seemed to be able to understand each other and how they were feeling and how they themselves were feeling and I just couldn't. I thought for a while that I was intellectually challenged and that was why I didn't have this innate ability. Why I had constant foot in mouth syndrome and couldn't understand anyone around me and why I wasn't like my peers and they knew it and I knew it. I did try to fit in better. I tried to be popular as everyone else seemed to be trying to or was popular and so I changed how I looked and tried to imitate the popular girls. I thought I had made it when they pretended to be my friend. I was too naïve to see that they were getting me to do stuff to laugh at me. Everyone around me could see it other than me. Other people could see I was easily manipulated so quickly followed suit. I was and am still easily manipulated due to my inability to see the bad in people because in my mind it's very black and white; you are either all good or all bad. This also means that I either like or dislike people, there is no in between. This can cause problems, as once people are sorted into these categories it's hard for me to change my perception. This is the same for my opinions, although I have got better at learning to listen to other people's points of views and not always seeing issues as black and white and correct or incorrect. Also changing my opinion on things and learning that's okay. People used to think I was just being stubborn and purposely rude but now most people know I just think in black and white because of my autism. Which has led to less friction. I now myself understand why I'm so rigid with my thinking and don't get as frustrated with myself.

I have always loved food but also found it stressful to try new things or change my eating habits. I also go through phases where I go off and start to enjoy new foods. I can't stand certain textures and although I like the taste of certain foods I can't stand the smell. I find foods sometimes overwhelming when there's too many different textures or flavours in one dish especially when I'm eating out as I am already in a state of anxiety/overload due to the surroundings.

Another issue I have is I have low feeling in my hands and feet which often leaves my feeling restless and a want to compulsively itch or move my hands and feet. It also means I struggle to notice pain which means it's hard to identify. It also explains why I'm so clumsy and struggle so much with fine motor skills.

Since my diagnosis all of this has started to make sense and helps me to make sense of myself and also helped me to find solutions to deal with my autism and improve my life for the better. In addition, I used to be worried I had some sort of neurological disorder as I would get involuntary movements and I couldn't help but fidget and twitch and would try to suppress until they built up and got too much. I also held my hands weird and wanted to do these movements more when I am stressed or excited. I now know that these are just stims and now I know this I have things I can stim with, so I'm not tiring myself out trying to suppress or letting them build up. I find Chewigem chews and Tangle Toys the most useful and I can use them when I'm out without them being too noticeable. Now I understand them I don't get stressed about them and actually enjoy stimming and find it soothing.

Before my diagnosis it was confusing and it was like the world was a giant jigsaw puzzle and everyone was a piece, each piece being slightly different to the next, but my piece just didn't fit at all and it made me feel inadequate and like I didn't belong and I shouldn't be here. I still struggle with these feelings but now understand why and it's not just that I'm a mistake, an accident of nature or a weirdo.

To address my low proprioception and general low sense in my fingers and feet and skin I use a sensory swing which is better than a hug, it's like a safety net it helps to calm me and get over overload when I'm about to boil over. I also have a weighted blanket which helps me de-stress and helps me sleep at night, a time that I used to find the most stressful point of the day. It is now my favourite part of the day and I love sleeping too much probably.

I have always found it difficult to talk to people, especially new people, as it is scary to not know what the other person is thinking about what you're saying or being able to read their expression/emotion, so you can never tell whether they like or dislike what you're saying or even if you've offended them. It makes conversation tiring as you're always second guessing and trying to figure out the other person. It's like performing mental gymnastics fighting with yourself about whether you've upset them or not, trying to not show at the same time the anxiety rising within. Every twitch they make with their face or body makes you think they dislike you, that they think you are disgusting. Because when your mind doesn't have the answer it fills in the blanks; when you are depressed your mind fills it in with negatives all the time no matter what you do or how much you try to fight it. Fighting the negative thoughts and feelings is really tiring and eventually you are too tired to fight them. It's this that leads to self-harm and suicidality.

Before I went into hospital and thus before my diagnosis, I got so anxious I started to have severe panic attacks that led to me collapsing and my body going into spasm. I was only sleeping two or three hours a night. I was constantly on edge, constantly overwhelmed and overloaded. Any little thing could tip me into self-harm and I was self-harming several times a day. Self-harm had become a compulsion. It was like a ritual I just had to do it sometimes because I was commanded to and other times just because I felt like I had to or wanted to. My OCD was controlling me, I was no longer in control of it. I couldn't even blink without having to count to five. My everyday revolved around the number five and avoiding germs and making sure things were straight. I had a lot of intrusive thoughts and images and it scared me as it was always threatening to hurt, or showed my family members being harmed. I was paranoid all the time, thought people were talking about me and thought people were plotting to hurt me. I felt like I could hear people's thoughts and they were always negative about me, which just added to my paranoia. I had a constant commentary sounding like it was coming from outside my head in other people's voices commanding me to do things, and also saying negative things about me. I would also see shadows – and sometimes actual figures of people. This was terrifying when I was sleeping. I was lucid dreaming but I couldn't control it and I would walk around my house and see my family dead and other things but I would still be dreaming. This was very distressing. I was depressed. It was like all joy in my life had gone. I had been passively suicidal for a long time but these thoughts started to reoccur at lot more regularly and more detailed plans had started to be made. Sometimes I couldn't control the plans being made but other times I was the one forming them. For example, I would never throw myself in front of a car going at 30mph because I would probably survive. I had started to obsess over it. I was fascinated by death instead of scared of it. But at the same time, I was too depressed and had such low energy that I didn't have the energy to actually act on those plans.

I had to drop out of sixth form after I collapsed in an exam and was struggling to cope with getting through a single school day. After this I got even sicker. I was collapsing from panic attacks. I became a recluse. I wouldn't get out of bed as I didn't have enough energy. But I also wasn't sleeping. I had constant brain fog. I couldn't hold a conversation as I didn't have the energy and I was so paranoid my brain would twist it and the constant commentary made it hard to concentrate. I would get confused between what people were actually saying and the thoughts I thought I could hear, which led to arguments and generally mistrusting people. I wasn't doing anything, I would just stare off. I was like a zombie, I was having a complete shutdown. I was no longer functioning. I was in a catatonic state. When I was speaking it was slow or I would stammer and I would forget about what I was saying half way through a sentence. This still happens when I'm overloaded but mainly when I'm shutdown.

I had been seeing a community practice nurse and a psychiatrist for a long time before I had got this ill. I always saw them at a clinic. We as a family had been seeing a family therapist as they felt that my problems were with my family and my relationship with my parents, which was inaccurate, although home was chaotic at the time. Seeing them at a clinic was stressful as it was busy in a strange old building. The stressfulness made it harder to communicate and open up. It was the second time I had been referred to CAMHS in order to help. They put me on sertraline but it was not helping so they kept increasing it, it wasn't working and neither was the melatonin I had been on for a long time before this. I was on the highest dosage of both and neither were working. I had also previously been put on diazepam to try help to prevent my severe panic attacks but I didn't like the way it felt, as it felt like I was out of my head and I had no control: being not in control is a real fear of mine. My physiatrist wanted me to go into hospital in order to reduce my sertraline and try me on something else as well, as he was concerned about all the plans I had, and how low my mood was and the fact I couldn't hold conversations. He was also concerned as my Dad was away and so my Mum was looking after four kids, two of which had additional needs, so Mum couldn't give me one-to-one observation 24/7 which is what he thought I needed. I refused to go into hospital as I just didn't want to go and I just wanted to be left to die at that point. I thought if I went to hospital it would make it impossible for me to kill myself and I didn't want to be somewhere surrounded by strangers. At the time I couldn't talk not even to my Mum and so I couldn't verbalise this. So, my psychiatrist told me to go home and told me he was sending the mental health act assessment team to my house.

I went home and slept on the couch for a couple of hours whilst something played on the TV as I was so exhausted from the meeting and too worried to compute what was actually occurring. A male doctor and a female social worker came that day. I couldn't answer their questions and they felt I needed to be sectioned. Thus, I was sectioned under Section 2 of the Mental Health Act. The lady then began to ring around and try to find me a bed, she eventually came back into the room and told us that she was calling an ambulance to take me to hospital. The social worker stayed and the doctor left. My mum then asked me if I wanted a walk, so me and her took a short walk around the block. All I kept saying was I didn't want to go – but it was out of my mum's hands and mine. My twin sister helped me pack a bag, as at this point I couldn't think of what I needed to pack. I packed my blanket which gives me such comfort and my unicorn pillow. I also downloaded documentaries as doing that helps me keep calm. We had to wait for a couple more hours before the ambulance came. It didn't come till about 8 or 9 at night. It was two ladies. I had to say goodbye to my siblings which was traumatic for them. I then got in the ambulance with mum and we set off. I just sat there watching my documentary which was Stacey Dooley's documentary about the Pulse nightclub shooting called 'Hate in Orlando' I think. It wasn't until we were about half way into our journey that it hit me what was happening and my thoughts started to spiral and I started to panic and cry and say I wanted to go home and I didn't want to go. It had hit me so late as I was so overloaded and shutdown it took a while to hit me and I was also in shock. My mum and the ambulance technician, who was lovely, reassured me. There were road works and diversions, so we got to the hospital between 11 and 12pm. I remember the lights hurting and it being deathly silent. One of the female ambulance technicians spoke to the lady on reception and we waited in reception for a while, until a nurse and a doctor took us through the door into a visitor's room. They asked a couple of questions which mum answered and explained to me what was happening and they admitted me. Me and mum then had to say goodbye; this was incredibly hard. I was then taken into like a first aid room where a wand was passed over me. I was then patted down and my phone and bag were taken off me (as my bag needed to be searched). Being patted down was the hardest and worst part of the day. It made me feel unclean and so uncomfortable, it made my nerves feel like they were all on end to the point of being painful. I was then taken onto a psychiatric intensive care unit (PICU) ward. I held my unicorn pillow so tight and started to panic. As a walked onto the ward all the patients were sat with the sofas put together staring at me. It was terrifying. I was walked to the other end of the ward because I was having a panic attack. I was given phenergan. I was told someone had to watch me all the time and was showed my room. I went straight to bed. As they were searching and logging my things, I couldn't get changed. I woke up confused and feeling all fuzzy. Another member of staff (other than my one) made me some toast and passed it through a hatch. I then wanted to change my clothes. They were being held in what they called the cage. I picked the clothes I wanted and they put the rest back in the cage. I then got changed. It was awful having to ask for my things and being told what I could and couldn't have them, and not being even able to make your own drink. And not being able to open a door, having to wait for someone to do it and being followed and watched by a stranger all the time was unnerving to say the least. Being there made me feel like my life had spiralled out of control and I'd lost everything and I wasn't going to be anything, and I had no chance of getting better or getting out of hospital. I was also embarrassed of what people would think of me being in a mental hospital, especially my friends and people I'd been peers with, as my twin sister still went to school and there was also my family members and neighbours.

Whilst in hospital, I was constantly overloaded and overwhelmed. There were alarms being pulled and blaring all the time. It was all bright white strip lighting and staff not following the rules or constantly changing the rules, which was the hardest part for me. And not having any real routine as it kept on changing: we had quite substantial time slots when we had no routine and nothing to do. Although I did like having a timetable I also couldn't stand having no control. When other patients were acting unpredictable or unsettled then it made me feel unsettled and there would be a lot of screaming and shouting. Staff were unpredictable, you didn't know who would show up; often agency staff would fill in this unpredictability which just increased my anxiety. And not knowing when I'd be able to leave or get to go home or even when people were coming to visit. This would lead to emotional overload, where I would go from being almost manically happy (where it was way beyond elation and happiness and hyperness, where I had all the energy in the world), to severe lows, where I would self-harm and make attempts on my life, as my bad thoughts would just consume me. My energy would drain from me and my mood would hit rock bottom. These could happen in a couple of minutes and would happen several times a day. They were mistaking emotional overload for having an emotionally unstable personality disorder. They also often mistook my anxiety as being rude and impatient even though my mum explained I was just anxious, and that's why I would ask again and again and get really irritable. But when I made an attempts on my life or self-harmed, this would lead to alarms being pulled and staff pouring into my room and me being restrained. There was hardly ever if ever any de-escalation first, which I found incredibly unhelpful, as it just escalated things for me and other patients. Up to eight people would be pinning you down, which not only uncomfortable, I found it painful and would result in injuries and also would make me panic as I felt trapped. I couldn't move and breathe and would lead to me panicking and fighting to try get out. The staff would shout or talk to you sometimes not very nicely. So, it would be light and always under bright strip lights. I would try to cover my eyes with hair so I wasn't staring anyone in the eye, as I just couldn't and it made me feel physically uncomfortable, and I just couldn't do it and also to hide from the light. It would make me feel even worse and like all I had to do was fight to get away, they would also threaten to inject you with PRN (medicine given as needed) if you didn't calm down, which would just make me panic more. But I would agree to take it orally as given the two options I know which one I'd rather take. It was because of this emotional overload that they thought I had emotionally unstable personality disorder and also because they were mistaking my anxiety as irritability and abrasiveness. For example, they kept changing if I could go out on leave. They would tell me I had leave and then another nurse would come along and tell me I wasn't going out today and then I would go into a meltdown and someone would come and tell me I was actually going out that day; they would also change who was going out with me. When I was becoming overloaded I wanted to be in my room in the dark (although I didn't understand why), but I would also act on my urges as I was overloaded, so I would do something and staff would drag me into a bright noisy and busy communal space. So I would try to steal their keys and beg them to let me into my room, which would end in being restrained as they saw this as threatening and attacking staff, which it wasn't. Or they would leave me in the communal areas which really didn't help. It would lead to things building up until I was let into my room again and it would lead to hours of having an incident and being restrained – and then the same thing several times – which would lead to staff getting frustrated and upset with me. It would continue until I completely burned out and just couldn't do it as I didn't have any energy and would go to bed and sleep.

They would change things all the time like it was agreed with me and the ward manager that instead of pat downs I could change my clothes in front of them behind a towel or something, as this would cause a lot less stress. She promised she would pass this on. She did not. The next day I had a hospital appointment to have an MRI, so had this really stressful appointment/day and was overloaded, so I got back already dreading what was going to happen. But glad I was going to do clothes change instead. So, I got into the search room and they say they going to pat me down and wand me. I start saying that the ward manager said I could do clothes change the day before, after getting really stressed and upset about it the day before. So they go and check and come back and tell me she hasn't written anything down and so I have to have a pat down. I go into meltdown and start to refuse. Just as this was happening a nurse from the downstairs ward walks past and makes a snarky comment about she hopes they enjoy dealing with me which only upsets me further. After a while I just relent and allow a pat down, but I found this incredibly upsetting and degrading and unnecessarily stressful. I was also always on edge as I didn't know what was happening as they could do what they wanted and send me to where they wanted at any time – and also what was happening to the other patients, especially ones I had become friends with, which just added to the mistrust and anxiety. After a couple of days on the PICU ward when I was getting used to the other patients and staff they told me they had admitted me onto the wrong ward and that I was moving upstairs onto the general ward. This move was incredibly unsettling, and led to me feeling unsettled and having several incidents and being overloaded. But in general, I was starting to settle and make friends again and get used to the new timetable. I preferred how much more settled the ward was, and that I could make myself a drink and had proper plates and knife and forks rather than the plastic ones. There was more freedom. They had rabbits and my family could come onto the ward to visit. There also were not as many locked doors, you could walk around the ward.

I had been going to ward round and they hadn't mentioned anything noticeable just talked about leave and how I was doing. The occupational therapist from the downstairs ward came and asked me why I was upstairs, as she had been told I was moving back downstairs, which sent me spiralling as I didn't know anything about this. So, I asked members of staff who didn't know anything about it so I tried to calm down. Then another nurse and the doctor for that ward came to talk to me and said that this ward couldn't cope with my behaviour and so I was moving back downstairs. So, I went into meltdown and was very rude to the doctor and called her all sorts of swear words, which I know I shouldn't have but I was just overwhelmed with emotions and I was spiralling. I had been on this ward for two weeks and once again was finally getting settled, when they decided without warning me that I was moving. It later transpired they had been planning to move me to a different PICU in a different hospital, for most of the time I had been there. This led to greater mistrust of the staff especially the doctors. I then moved back downstairs where I stayed the rest of the time I was in hospital. But I also witnessed other patients being told on the day they were moved that they were moving to different hospitals on the other side of the country, something which only increased my anxiety further. After this, I was told that I was being assessed for a Section 3, which could mean I would be in hospital for up to another six months. And if I didn't get put on a Section 3, I would have to be moved to another hospital as the general ward upstairs was full and they wouldn't have me back upstairs, but that even if I was no longer sectioned I wasn't going home. I thought I would try to get home anyway, which didn't work and I was then put on a Section 3. Before I left hospital, they were planning on moving me to another hospital. We went and visited it but I knew it wasn't right, as you weren't allowed in your rooms during certain times and you were forced to be in communal areas. And things I knew I could use to self-harm were just left around. I knew the change would be too much for me and lead to me having more incidents and I was worried I would then be transferred to another PICU and it would be like I was right back at the beginning.

In this hospital when you had an incident you were sent home, which I thought also would lead to something serious happening at home and I couldn't cope with going back and forth. Also to go to this hospital you had to be having unescorted leave without anyone with you, which I couldn't do due to the anxiety and for safety reasons. Even now today I can't leave the house without support, so there was no way back then that was going to happen which made me feel even more that there was no way I was getting out.

I was also worried the entire time I was in hospital as I knew that I was on a countdown, as I was 17 and it was coming up to my 18th birthday which would have meant moving to adult care. So knew I had to get out somehow before then as I was worried if I went into an adult hospital there was no way I would get out. But knowing that they wanted to move me didn't help my anxiety, I just wanted to go home and not all for the right reasons.

One incident stands out more than most and shows the lack of understanding and misunderstanding of my behaviour. It's the reason I was removed from this ward and banned from returning. I went out with a member of staff on leave and I went to the shops where I was looking for an art book, which happened to have a metal binder. I was getting an art book as I was doing an art project, so in my mind I needed a proper art book and there was no budging on this. No person/member of staff had told me not to get the binder even when I was buying it, or they said I could keep it in education and I had told education of my plans. Nobody had told me not to, or told me it was against the rules. Other patients on the ward had art books and just normal notebooks with metal binders in their rooms which I knew wasn't going to happen, so I wanted to put it in my restricted cupboard or leave it in education, as that is where I would be working on it. So, I got back to the ward. The nurse is checking what I bought back to the ward says she not sure it is allowed and so she goes to get the ward manager. The ward manager came and she says that it's not allowed on the ward and it's going in the bin, as it's a ward rule. I start to wind myself up. I point out how surely if it was a blanket ward rule, then how come some of the other patients have a metal binder art book in their rooms and I just wanted to have it in my restricted cupboard. She says that it is on an individual basis and I'm a risk and that's why I can't have it. I point out how she said it wasn't allowed on the ward full stop and how I understand I'm a risk which is why I want it in my restricted cupboard (where they put your personal items that you're not allowed, it's a locked cupboard in your room), or to be left in education. She just repeats what she's said before; we keep going back and forth and I'm getting more and more wound up. She says I'm not allowed to have it and starts to walk off which frustrates me further. She then slams her office door in my face and ignores me.

Which is just like a red rag to a bull. I start to go into a meltdown which leads to a rage, so the ward manager gets a torrent of abuse from me verbally. I just couldn't understand and nobody was explaining; she just kept repeating herself. If only somebody had just explained to me why properly. Also, she was saying it was going in the bin and I had bought it myself and surely, I could just take it home. It was this that upset me the most. I just couldn't understand why she wouldn't explain to me and why she would put it in the bin as it wasn't hers and I had bought it – and it could have stayed in the office until my mum picked it up. In the end I was allowed to keep it in education and I used it to do my artwork when I was in education. When they were telling my mum about it they couldn't understand why I had got so irrationally upset. My mum tried to explain that I think in black and white and think literally and so that's why I got so upset.

I was in hospital for five months in total. I found it stressful. It didn't make me any better, it gave me more ideas on how to kill myself and self-harm and made me more anxious to be in the outside world. It made me distrust professionals and I found the whole experience traumatic, although I did make some good friends who have helped me as they are a lot more understanding and we have a lot in common. Furthermore, it made me mistrust professionals and mental health and support workers as everything I said was twisted and turned against me to say I was too sick to be home and I still needed to be sectioned. They also said that my home life was the trigger, which wouldn't explain why my self-harm and suicide attempts increased in hospital. On the other hand, it improved my relationship with my parents, especially my mum and twin sister and my siblings, as they understand how ill I was and that it wasn't attention seeking. My mum knew that hospital wasn't the right place and asked if I wanted to leave, which of course I said yes. She then got advice from a charity called Mind, and a friend of hers that worked in mental health and started to work on getting me out, despite the fact that the hospital and its staff had threatened to remove her as nearest relative if she tried to discharge me from hospital. Mum's friend who worked in the mental health field gave mum some telephone numbers that could help in our area. My mum then wrote the hospital a letter declaring that as her right as nearest relative she could demand my discharge from hospital if she felt I was well enough. This gives 72 hours to agree and discharge you or block it. The staff at the hospital didn't understand this process. They didn't know my mum's right as nearest relative. I found this exciting as I thought I was going home but I was really anxious as I didn't know what was going to happen: 72 hours is a long time when you're waiting for a decision. This ran out at 11am on Thursday and we didn't hear anything. But on this morning, just before the time ran out, the doctor came to see me to tell me she had already signed the paperwork to block this. Bearing in mind she hadn't seen me to assess me for two weeks before and she hadn't come to see me, or assess me before she'd signed the documents saying I wasn't allowed to leave. I was crushed. Also, I wasn't allowed to see my mum this day which made it even worse as I just really wanted to see her, plus I knew she had travelled all that way which made me feel really guilty.

When permission to leave is blocked, there are several things that happen, one of them being a hospital manager's meeting. This was scheduled for the week after. A hospital manager's meeting is where three people from different professionals from independent places come to sit on a panel and listen to all the professionals and the person's evidence and decide whether someone needs to be in hospital. They can also decide whether you need to be on a section. A social worker I'd never seen before saw me the day before the hospital manager's meeting to assess me. The doctor in charge of my care didn't come to see me/assess me until after the meeting was scheduled to begin. I was getting ready to be discharged after this panel, as I expected to be coming off my section and going home. My mum and a solicitor had come providing evidence even though mum had been told she didn't need a solicitor. I couldn't attend the whole panel as I get really anxious in a room with lots of people I don't know, especially when the stakes are so high and it was going to be quite a few people in a small room. There was my mum, the solicitor, my advocate, two doctors, social worker, a nurse, an occupational therapist and the people on the panel. My doctor explained she didn't think I should go home and why. My mum counter argued that she felt the safest place for me was home and I was hurting myself more in hospital, and it had been one thing after another whilst there. The nurses provided false evidence, which my mum and the solicitor protested. The nurse and doctors refused to check this evidence. In their evidence they had given false dates for my incidents, some of them being serious. My mum knew these were false, as the hospital has a policy that if you have an incident whether minor or major, you have to wait 24 hours or 48 hours before you were allowed on leave again – and when they said I had had these incidents I had been on home leave or leave out the next day. So, because of the falsely provided incidents, and the lack of community support upon my discharge, the panel decided I was safest in hospital. I was told the news. I was heartbroken. I felt like everything had been ripped away. Me and my mum had a visit. We knew the evidence was incorrect, so the nurse went and checked came back and said it was correct. So, then Mum showed when I had had leave – and when they were saying I had had these incidents. The nurse checked again and came down with another nurse and they informed us that we were correct, and that the incident dates in their evidence were incorrect.

I was inconsolable. I was so angry and upset my freedom had been denied because of false information and all I wanted to do was go home and this wasn't the first time the hospital had messed up. I was fed up of their incompetency and what it had cost me and left me little faith in their abilities to treat me and keep me safe. There were no hospital managers still at the hospital as it was so late and all the panel members had gone home. When she was on the way home, mum had a phone call from one of the hospital managers, asking what had happened. My mum explained and he agreed to meet my mum in the morning. My mum met with him and the consultant and mum said that my nurses had given inaccurate information. If they had given accurate evidence, I would have been released. They told mum I had to wait another week for another hospital panel meeting. Mum said that I needed leave every single day and have overnight leave, whilst waiting for this hospital manager's meeting. So this was arranged. I went on an overnight stay and it went well, so that afternoon I had a meeting with my consultant and she decided that I could be discharged the following day at 12am. So, I was released the next day into my mum's care and I got to go home. I was elated and got packed up and waited patiently until 12am and got to go home.

It was like a weight had been lifted off my shoulders. I was now free. It was a very emotionally overloading journey home but what a relief. But I now had the pressure of making sure I didn't end up back there and the fear that I would end up back there started to set in; still to this day I worry I'm going to end up in hospital. When I came out of hospital I was back to weekly appointments with my CPN at the clinic, with the added fear anything I said would lead to being hospitalised again.

Around about this time I had started to struggle with not being able to talk to people I didn't know – and sometimes even people I did know. I still struggle with this today. It takes me a while before I can talk to people I don't know so I use an app on my phone. But back then I didn't know about this app so was using a paper and pen, although sometimes I was too anxious to write things down. I'm so anxious it feels like someone gripping my throat/voice box or like someone's pressing my chest. Also, just the fear that everything I say is going to upset someone I don't know, or be wrong or lead to me being back in hospital.

I didn't have any routine when I was out of hospital and we couldn't find an educational placement so mum was trying to put things in place. I wasn't getting any better, as I was just left with my thoughts and plans. It was also coming up to Christmas, which I find a really hard time of the year. It is so stressful to make sure everyone has presents and everyone is happy. People just pop round without warning and people get louder and all my siblings were going to be home which makes it busy and noisy in our house. It's an unpredictable part of the year where there's a pressure to be happy and make sure everyone else is happy which only increases my depression, and everything else that was going on including my suicidal plans and thoughts. This led to me taking two overdoses a couple of weeks between each other. One of them led to me having to stay in hospital overnight. Which only increased my anxiety as A&E is busy and noisy and has bright lights and you have to wear a gown and be touched and prodded by random people, also there was the prospect of maybe being put back in hospital. Especially as it was a significant overdose and my second one in two weeks. And my CAMHS psychiatrist had visited me after the first one had recommended hospital, so I thought I was going into hospital and they were just waiting to resection me. This made me dread Christmas even more.

Before I was allowed to leave the hospital after this second overdose I had to be seen by a doctor and nurse from CAMHS. When my mum talked to them, they asked if she thought I needed to be in hospital, which she said no to. She and my dad explained how Christmas is stressful for me and she felt the waiting for the autism assessment was causing this anxiety as well, and they agreed and said if we had the means, to pursue a private diagnosis.

It was one of the worst Christmases I have ever had. It was like I wasn't even there. It was like I was floating outside of my body being controlled by my thoughts and impulses. I spent most of Christmas upstairs in my room avoiding people, which is what I do when family members come around, as I find it so much I just hide upstairs to avoid it until I am told to get downstairs. I was terrified I was going to be like this forever or as long as I lived, which I hoped wouldn't be much longer. I still struggle with this feeling today. Me and my mum were getting really fed up of nothing changing and we couldn't wait any longer for an autism assessment as we needed to know what we could do, so I could actually get better.

So, we met Phoebe Caldwell, who gave us a lot of advice although she told us she was not able to give me a diagnosis, as she is a science doctor, not a medical one, but because of my severe sensory difficulties she said that we should go ahead with trying to get a diagnosis of autism. Her advice was invaluable and led to me getting my sensory equipment aids and Irlen lenses.

I then met a lady who ran an autistic girls' group. She told us all about the group and I started to go but found it really stressful and stopped going. The lady very kindly has made changes and I have started going back, which I find incredibly helpful and nice to be with people who understand me and who I can sometimes relate to.

After seeing Phoebe, we then went down the route to get an autism diagnosis privately. Once we had made the decision we gave them the evidence we already had, and went to several appointments and it was eventually concluded I had autism. Unfortunately, education would not accept this diagnosis as it was not a multidisciplinary team. I waited two years in total for my NHS autism multidisciplinary assessment and subsequent diagnosis and they now accept I have autism. Because of my mental health needs, education did do an educational healthcare plan (EHCP). My mum then helped me to make a self-referral to specialist autism counselling. This has been invaluable for me in order to appreciate my diagnosis and also learn to deal with my thoughts and feelings and learning how to prevent overload and shutdown and what to do when it's happening. It has helped me to process events which I'm finding difficult to process and also gives me a good time to self-evaluate how I'm doing and what I can do different to stop being overloaded and having shutdown.

After my mum calling up social workers and explaining the situation I finally got a social worker who then did an assessment which has led to me getting the right support. I now get 40 hrs per week of carer's hours. This allows my mum to go to work and me to stay at home studying. It also allows me to get to college and also go out places. It gives my mum a needed break and me a needed break from her. More importantly it helps me be an independent young adult and go out places and do what I want to do it. It has increased my confidence and I now go out more than I would have been able to do before. I am now able to do things like walk the dog. Which doesn't sound like much, but before, I couldn't do this as I was getting too overloaded, panicking that there was going to be lots of people when we were out, and sometimes would start seeing people that weren't actually there. And there were all the different sounds and smells and colours and things to see were just too much and I would have panic attacks.

Also, my dog Cassie's behaviour towards other dogs and worrying she wouldn't come back to me if I let her off the lead. I have been training her and so she is much better behaved and I don't have to get as anxious. The sensory equipment and my growing confidence thanks to carers has enabled me to be able to do this sometimes. Thanks to my growing confidence due to carers has meant I'm now able to go into college more and hopefully build it up even more. I also get respite hours, which are essential to give my parents a break and give me a chance to relax somewhere quiet and calm. It lets me recharge: this is essential since due to my constant anxiety and getting overloaded and shutdown, I'm often running on very little to no energy, although sometimes respite can be just as anxiety provoking.

I also kept looking for educational placements as I knew I wanted to learn as I love to learn. I also knew that learning would give me something to concentrate on and look forward to and structure my day with. So, I sat through several meetings and got really close to being in a placement and then got knocked back more than once. One time I had even visited the place and got all my school equipment and then a week before the end of the school year I got a call to say that they weren't taking over 16 year olds anymore. But then luckily my local college contacted me and told me what support they could provide, which was a change as usually you had to fight for the support, not get given it and told it straight away. It turns out this was the best place for me. I now do two online A levels in sociology and history and am meant to be going into college starting in September for an hour a week, where I have a one-to-one tutorial once a week in college for three hours – and I am also doing a BTEC in applied science. I also go into college for three hours once a week to do independent study in the study area with help from a support assistant. Once I have finished doing my courses at college I hope to go to university and do a biology/biological sciences degree with a foundation year away from home. If I do go away to university I will be living with a family through a scheme called Shared Lives, as living on my own would be too much and I wouldn't be able to cope.

When I go into a panic attack/overload it feels like the world is crashing and spinning around me and everything hurts. It feels like I can't breathe/talk or even move. I get the worst ever pins and needles in my extremities. It's like I'm not in my body anymore, I can hardly feel any of my body, not even my face. It feels like I'm stuck in a glass box and can't seem to communicate with anyone but it also feels like everyone is staring at me and thinking bad things about me. Everything is really loud and bright and the slightest brush or touch sends a painful shiver to my brain and back like I'm being electrocuted. It's like my brain is on fire, especially when I'm in meltdown all my thoughts are racing and crashing and I can't grab one or think straight. Somebody could be talking to me but it's like nothing is getting through as I can't process anything anymore.

Panic attacks/meltdowns sometimes have a lot of build-up and then other times they almost come out of anywhere. I find using my sensory swing really helps when this starts to happen as the motion is soothing and the deep pressure helps to release some of the pressure that feels like it's building up in my head and chest and is also just generally soothing, this also works with my weighted blanket. A shutdown is where it's like a computer when you are doing too much on it and it can't take it anymore so it just shuts off until you can reboot it. So, I can't feel anything, I can't think about anything. It's like the world is separate to me and I'm not in it anymore. I'm stuck outside my body and I can't get back into it. I can't do a lot or anything at all as I have no energy. I can do menial tasks sometimes but it takes doubly as long. It feels like I'm being weighed down by an invisible weight.

Often, I find that I have visual hallucinations when I'm overloaded or going into overload. It's like my brain can't take it anymore and so starts to misfire as things are just being fired everywhere in my brain before it shutdowns and it is these misfires that lead to visual hallucinations. A prime example of this was when I was in hospital I had had a very stressful day/week and the ward had been unsettled this led to me being overloaded. I was so overloaded I had been head banging for over an hour. This led to me having flashbacks to when I was abused and thinking I was back in it and I also had the voices outside my head. But they were pretending to be my mum and my littlest brother – it also made me crazy paranoid. So, I thought the lady doing one-to-one observation was going to hurt me/kill me and so I was trying to get her out of my room which led to me being restrained and placed into a seclusion room.

My tinted Irlen lenses enable me to see in 3D. Before everything was flat until I put on the lenses and it was like everything was a pop-up card, it was hard to get used to. It has meant I'm a lot less clumsy. It has also reduced my anxiety as I can now see how far away people are, so I don't have to worry that they're going to touch me or brush past me. I also get overloaded less as everything isn't as bright, I don't get as many headaches and I'm not in as much pain all the time. It has made my concentration better and I find reading easier.

I can't filter out noise; not only do I hear things louder than everybody else, I hear everything as I can't filter out background noise. Which means it layers up until it gets too much. Just having the noise cancelling headphones on damps every sound in general and also helps to dull the background noise. With them switched on it cuts out even more and helps me to concentrate on the conversation and it stops overload as it cuts out some of the layers. And when everything is getting too much, I can just put them on and blast my music and cut out everything.

I listen to music most the time as it helps to keep me calm as it's distracting and it also helps to cut out background sound, although when things are getting too much documentaries seem to work better then music, as I don't know the words and can concentrate on the documentary and enjoy it. I love documentaries.

Coffee shops are the worst as you have the chatter of people, the noise of lights (or sometimes radiator), the coffee machine, the music and the door opening and closing. I used not to be able to stand coffee shops but now, thanks to the headphones I can actually sit in coffee shops most of the time. It is the same when eating out at restaurants. I used to have a squeeze vest which I used to wear all the time. It gave me the deep pressure I needed when I wanted/needed which helped me release the tension within me. But I didn't like the feeling of the squeeze vest against me and I couldn't take it off once I was wearing it as it was underneath my clothes. Also, the noise was quite irritating. I have found that lap weights work better. I have two; I need the extra pressure as with just one I can't really feel it because of my low feeling in my body parts. It helps me relax and also stops me from moving my legs relentlessly which annoys people and myself. I also can put them on my shoulders and my head when my head is starting to hurt or get too much. I also can take them off when I want and position them whichever way I want. In addition, I find my sensory toys and 'Chewigem' chew toy helpful as they help me to stim so it doesn't build up. I like going to the cinema now as it doesn't hurt and I can relax and enjoy the film; as long as it is isn't busy I love going with my carers now. I use my lap weights and my headphones and my glasses and my sensory toys so I can concentrate and enjoy the film.

As my brain is always so busy and going so fast, I have to do things in order to keep me distracted enough to concentrate; sensory toys are a great way to do that. This why I watch documentaries when studying as music I would get too distracted by and end up singing along. But with documentaries I am just distracted enough to concentrate.

Since being in hospital (and even before hospital), I have always found mental health services difficult, as they never seemed to know what was going on with me or how to help me. It always felt like they were in conflict with me and my family and like they were always trying to blame my parents and twist what I was saying to fit their agenda. This includes diagnoses that were incorrect, mainly when it felt that they were trying to prove I had emotionally unstable personality disorder which I was certain I didn't have, but they were determined to prove this. Luckily recently, they have started to understand that I have autism this means I don't have a personality disorder. It felt like my mum was always arguing on my behalf. I was fed up with getting upset. My first CPN in adults said that in a couple of months' time I would be able to get on the bus and go to college on my own which I don't do now. When I tried to explain this was unrealistic, she said that I needed to have a more positive mind set and that I wasn't taking part in my recovery and I was stopping my recovery. I went to the adult clinic twice. Both times did not go well. The first time it was a multi-disciplinary one which I tried to go in, but ended up being in there for less than five minutes. Before I even went in I was having a panic attack. Being in a room with so many people just worsened this, so me and my Dad had to go back to the car. I thought I was going to pass out. The second time it was meant to be a meeting with my CPN and my psychiatrist. Before we even went in, me and my mum had to sit outside the waiting area as the strip lighting and all the office noise was making me anxious and it was a relatively new place. I think this was the first time I was meeting my adult mental health services psychiatrist as well. So, I was already anxious and had been pacing outside the waiting room which led to people looking/staring at me which only added to my anxiety. My CPN told me to come in, so I followed her. When she opened the door there was another stranger in the room, which sent me into a full-on panic attack. My mum had to ask her to leave. It turns out it was a student doctor which they had failed to inform me about/ask me if it was okay that she was in the room. I eventually calmed down and went back in the room but felt so uncomfortable, as it was a tiny room with people in it that I didn't know and they were asking me if I had plans to kill myself and things like that. That appointment also didn't go well. After this they said that my CPN could come visit/have appointments in my home. My appointments with my psychiatrist are now at my local GP surgery which is a lot better as I know that place. But even after I was being seen in my home, my CPN was trying to push me to go on walks with her and she wanted to have our appointments in a coffee shop. I found this more anxiety provoking then it needed to be as I would wind myself up for days before she even came knowing she was going to make me go out the house, as I didn't feel comfortable enough with her to be going out just me and her. I also find appointments stressful enough without it being in the outside world. I now just have appointments at home which is so much less stressful, although there is a high turnover of CPNs. I am now getting my fourth new CPN since being in adult mental health services. This is incredibly stressful but can't be helped. It makes making relationships with new CPNs incredibly difficult as am always anxious they are going to leave soon, which is anxiety provoking. They would also say that my mum was manipulating everything I was saying and me in general, as she talked for me when in appointments. This was incredibly upsetting and didn't aid us having a good relationship.

I have also had many arguments about medication as my psychiatrist wanted me to stay on quetiapine but try fluoxetine, or come off quetiapine and just try fluoxetine. But I felt this wasn't going to work as I hated quetiapine. It made me feel like a zombie when I was on a high dose but it was stopping my mood swings, which can be almost intolerable sometimes. I had been decreasing quetiapine as I wasn't me anymore, I didn't really have a personality and didn't have a sense of humour, but on a lower dose I didn't see the point in being on it as it wasn't doing anything at all. I also didn't just want to be on fluoxetine, as it is an SSRI and so is sertraline and it had failed to work. So, me and my mum had to keep fighting until the psychiatrist decided to give me a choice. She gave me several leaflets of different medications. I chose to go on risperidone, although even once I had decided it felt like people were dragging their heels and it took a long time before it was sorted out. Within the space of a couple of weeks I had come completely off quetiapine whilst starting risperidone. At times this was difficult as it was causing panic attacks randomly at night, so we had to decrease some of the medication as I was clearly having too much medication. I was having really bad mood swings which were scary at times. I felt out of control and to be honest I was. I also had a week where I just felt nauseous and had headaches and felt dizzy all the time so we halved my medication in the morning. But risperidone has worked wonders. I am now a lot less anxious overall. It has also almost completely got rid of the constant commentary and other people's voices when they are not talking which makes life so much better. It has also decreased my anxiety. I have got my sense of humour back and my personality, and my mood swings aren't as frequent. It just goes to show that professionals aren't always right and sometimes you've got to just stick by your guns. There were also many times we argued I was autistic not having a personality disorder. Most of the arguments with mental health come down to the fact they have no autism training and so find it difficult to understand.

# Chapter 3: Us in a Bus and Intensive Interaction

Janet Gurney

Back in 1990, when Us in a Bus was just pulling away from the kerb, we thought our purpose was to engage people in leisure. We had been set up as a three year pilot project to address the fact that a great many people with profound learning disabilities and complex needs who were living in long-stay institutions were spending an awful lot of time on their wards. What could we do to make that time more interesting? It took a little while for us to realise that leisure doesn't happen in anyone's life unless there is a level of engagement with other people. If I meet a friend for lunch, I am hoping for more than food and drink; I am expecting connection, mutual reflection, an exchange of news and opinions in a shared language, as well as the food and drink. How to build meaningful engagement with people who could seem very isolated or actively averse to connection became our focus. We were incredibly lucky to come across an old leaflet – *Augmented Mothering,* written by Geraint Ephraim – which led us to the work of Phoebe Caldwell, and of Dave Hewett and Melanie Nind, who were all already working so creatively, with Geraint's guidance, to develop the approach which was now known as Intensive Interaction. We started to see how this could help us build bridges of connection without demands, to explore from the inside out, rather than imposing our own interpretation of 'leisure'.

Us in a Bus are lucky enough to have the opportunity to support people over long periods, visiting once a week for months and years. Over the years since 1990, Intensive Interaction has enabled us to be part of hundreds of journeys exploring engagement, connection, communication – and real pleasure. Under Phoebe Caldwell's guidance we have added an understanding of the sensory processing issues that are a daily reality for many of the people we support, enabling communication to become more and more meaningfully responsive. Here, I have described three of those journeys with three remarkable people (identifying details of those people have been changed, but the description of the journeys is accurate). With Gwen, our journey has been simple, persistent Intensive Interaction. With Robert, our relationship deepened significantly when we noticed and addressed his sensory processing issues and added that to our Intensive Interactions. With Joe, we had to start by trying to understand his sensory overload.

# Gwen

Gwen is a lady in her 50s who has a learning disability and limited mobility; she also has a lot of energy, sharp eyesight and a big voice. We have been visiting her for an hour each week and it has been a delight to be part of her process of understanding the positive connections she can build with other people.

When we first met Gwen, she was very focused (for long periods of time) on tearing tissues and paper into small strips, which she would throw around her. Often she would add her saliva to these strips and roll them into balls before throwing them. This was not traditionally seen as a sociable activity and, when combined with Gwen's tendency to yell loudly at people, meant that she spent a lot of time on her own. Because the paper spit-balls were seen as a problem, it was a behaviour that was being discouraged. When Gwen didn't have access to paper or tissue, she would simply use her saliva to occupy her fingers.

Using the principles of Intensive Interaction, we decided that Gwen's interest – what she was actually doing – had to be our starting point in building a relationship with her. It was clearly of great importance to her and we started to let her know that we had noticed her interest. We did this without language – Gwen was expressing herself through her fingers, not through words, so we acknowledged her by copying her finger play. To start with, we watched carefully what Gwen was doing, not just with her fingers, but her whole body. We saw there was a rhythm to her paper-rolling, she 'led' with her thumb, she put enough energy into her finger movements to make her shoulders roll a little, she watched what she was doing but regularly shot quick glances around her, when she added her saliva to the paper she made a gentle 'phut-phut' sound, when she threw her paper she tensed her toes (Gwen generally preferred to be barefoot) and the whole process was interspersed with irregular, loud exclamations of 'Oi!' So it was clear that there was a lot more to 'finger play' than we had thought at first.

Working on the idea that Gwen was creating a series of internal messages for herself, we looked at ways of using those same messages to let her know that we had noticed her and valued her need for those messages. We speculated that they gave her a sense of control, a sense of herself, a feeling of satisfaction and achievement. We suspended any judgement about the value of paper rolling or spit – that was irrelevant to the process of offering her validation and exploring early steps of intentional communication with her. Effectively, we wanted to use her internal 'language' to explore a conversation together.

At first we copied Gwen's actions and sounds quite precisely – with a lot of repetition. We believed Gwen needed the opportunity to assimilate the message that we were acting directly in response *to* her – rather than expecting a response *from* her. This process involved us sitting on the floor, so Gwen could see us without having to raise her head, maintaining a distance so she wouldn't feel we were invading her space or trying to stop her activity. We physically copied her finger movements and the rhythm of her shoulder rolls. When Gwen made a sound we echoed it back to her. Gradually, we began to move from precise copying to a more responsive low-key celebration of her actions – for example, we added a low sound to chime in with her thumb movement; when she made her loud 'Oi!' sound, we started to answer with a slightly questioning 'Oooh?'. When Gwen threw her paper and tensed her toes we slapped the floor and quietly cheered.

We stayed in this stage of our Intensive Interaction with Gwen for quite some time. We resisted the urge to 'lead' Gwen or to 'entertain' her. It was essential that Gwen had an unhurried opportunity to experience the sense of being positively in charge of our behaviour. We were deliberately fostering Gwen's sense of intentionality – the sense that a previously exclusively internal experience was having an external influence on others. It became clear to us, through her pauses and the way she watched us, that Gwen was indeed becoming confident that we were following her. This made us braver about moving closer and getting a bit more involved. Unfortunately we overstepped the boundaries of her tolerance (sense of safety?) when we picked up a piece of her paper and copied the way she threw it. She showed her displeasure; the paper was clearly 'hers'. We retreated a little and very deliberately and clearly only threw pretend paper. This was fine! A couple of visits later, we started to bring our own paper, tearing it and throwing it like she did. Gwen was definitely interested in our paper and her body language invited us to move closer and begin to share.

We now moved into a more reciprocal, turn-taking stage of our interaction. Rather than simply responding to Gwen, we were leaving longer pauses, then more flamboyantly embellishing or exaggerating her actions. Gwen began to smile and even laugh as she waited to see what we would do in response to a new movement or sound of hers. We were thrilled when Gwen reached out to touch us for the first time. Admittedly, it wasn't a gentle touch – and robust touch now became part of our exchanges. We would present a part of us – a shoulder or a foot – that she could grab or slap. We would respond quite dramatically, sharing the slapstick humour of the moment. To do this we had to get even closer – a proximity that Gwen would previously have found invasive. This gave us the chance to slap her chair in response to her touching our shoulder. The paper-rolling was becoming peripheral to our interaction; eye contact and shared laughter were becoming the norm.

Over time, Gwen has initiated new activities and joined in opportunities we have offered (like strumming a guitar) in a way we could not have imagined when we first met her. Her use of sounds has significantly expanded. Recently we have found that using Gwen's very conversational vocalisations to invent 'languages' and 'rhymes' (often using tunes that are familiar to her) appears to capture her interest and we have spent up to twenty minutes or so having 'conversations' with her in this way. When our vocalisations echo her sounds and we embellish them we have found Gwen seems to extend her own sounds, often watching us with a sideward glance and smiling. These conversations sometimes become very animated and Gwen shows her excitement by jiggling her legs and flapping her hands. Occasionally we mirror these movements in a similar fashion (perhaps jiggling Gwen's legs too) and the energy of the moment is very intense and joyful. The challenge for us at these times is to judge just how exuberant to be to be sure not to over-stimulate Gwen or worry her. Gwen's emotions sometimes move quickly from seeming happy to becoming upset so it is important that we observe her carefully to gauge how she seems moment to moment.

The use of Intensive Interaction throughout our time with Gwen has been continuous. It is a 'lifelong learning' experience which has enabled her to form positive and mutually rewarding relationships with her support team. Paper rolling and throwing (with and without spit) is still an important fall-back activity for Gwen; it is probably reassuring and comforting. But Gwen is now confident that social interaction is a rewarding option for her. She is noticeably more relaxed, more interested in the world – and happier. The impact that sustained Intensive Interaction has had on her emotional well-being has been a joy for everyone in her life, as well as Gwen herself.

## Postscript

I had been hearing from the Us in a Bus team who visit Gwen how much more she was experimenting with intentional vocalisations; I recently took the opportunity to witness this myself...

As we walked into Gwen's room, she noticed Nicky (my colleague) and looked towards her – there was not much *change* in facial expression, but a certain alertness. Nicky immediately dropped down to be at the same head level, and capitalised on Gwen's alertness with a very definite (but not loud or over-jolly) '*Hello* Gwen'. Gwen turned her head to Nicky and vocalised what I heard as 'Ggg'. Nicky said 'Was that "Hug"?' and put herself in an accessible, huggable position, maintaining enough distance for this not to be a demand. Gwen paused, assimilated, decided and turned towards Nicky (who hadn't moved an inch or altered her facial expression in the 20 or more seconds this took), then reached out and embraced her. Only once she was enveloped did Nicky respond by moving into Gwen's embrace and reciprocating the hug. What Nicky couldn't see, but I could, was the beautiful, relaxed happiness spreading over Gwen's face (much more than a smile). It was a moment of complete mutual connection – totally in Gwen's control and totally real. As soon as Gwen moved to end the hug, so did Nicky.

A photo might have captured the joyful moment of connection. It could not have conveyed the series of micro observations/interpretations/actions that was informing the conscious steps of Nicky's practice throughout. The fact that it *was* practice does not in any way imply that the connection was not genuine and mutual – but it was *practice* which allowed it to happen so smoothly and so much in Gwen's control. And it was a clear example of the need to p-a-u-s-e and 'hold the space' for someone else to fill as they wish.

## Robert

We first met Robert nine years ago – although he could not have made it clearer to us that any desire to meet was purely on our side, not his. He was sitting in his kitchen with a table pulled as close to his body as he could get it. He was steadfast in looking away from the door, where we were, instead looking down towards the wall away from us. In the tight space he had left himself, he was rocking rhythmically, so that his head was (gently) tapping the wall behind him and his lower chest was tapping the table in front of him. When a member of his support team told him we were there to meet him, he roared deeply and increased the intensity of his rocking, so his head was now banging against the wall. He did not look at us. He continued to roar until he was sure we had left.

We had been asked to work with Robert as his team were so concerned at his seeming lack of options; he would take up this position in the morning and would remain there for as long as possible. If left alone, he was relatively calm. If invited to share space or do something, the relative sense of calm quickly dissipated. His team wanted him to be happier and to explore the world beyond the kitchen table. Our first thoughts were, 'Is he ever going to let us get near?'. Our second thoughts were more helpful and focused on Robert's needs, rather than our own! Robert was clearly telling us that distance was important to him and we needed to let him know we respected that need; this was our starting point.

To begin with, our weekly visits involved us sitting quietly on the floor in the corridor outside Robert's kitchen, near enough to observe his movements and sounds but not near enough to distress him – we were very clearly not in his room, in his space. We quickly saw how much energy he was putting into maintaining rhythms. Apart from his rocking, we saw that he was pushing the fingers of one hand into the palm of his other. We could hear that he was also creating rhythms with his breathing, sometimes adding a small vocalisation to his out breath. Because of his steadfastness in not looking at us, we needed to reflect his rhythms audibly rather than visually. The easiest way to maintain this was through tapping the floor, trying to find a balance between loud enough for Robert to notice and not too loud to upset him. At this stage, we were intent on letting him know that we were there, that we were maintaining the distance he wanted us to, and were noticing the rhythms that seemed important to him – acknowledging him in his own internal 'language'. He tolerated this for short periods – maybe five minutes to start with.

We began to realise that we may be imposing an interpretation onto his actions which fitted with *our* experience of the world, rather than wondering what his actions were telling us about *his* experience of the world. Was he actually saying 'Keep your distance', or were his increased sounds and rhythms actively helping him to cope with our proximity? Maybe his apparent need to keep people at a distance, coupled with roaring when people spoke to him, could be to do with sensitivity to sound. If Robert was anxious that we would make sounds that might be confusing or overpowering, it would make sense for him to create a predictable auditory environment for himself, particularly if the noises he was making were ones that he could experience through other senses as well. The low vocalisations he was making were backed up by rocking (sense of movement and balance) as well as the sharp pushing of fingers into palm, head against wall and chest against table (proprioceptive signals). When he roared, he would be experiencing an internal vibration to match the sound. If we accepted this interpretation, it was less about us ('he doesn't like us') and more about him ('he needs to act in this way to prevent sensory overload – we need to consider how to let him know we will do our best to act within his sensory comfort-zone'). We decided to slap the floor and the door frame rather than just tapping, so he might experience our acknowledgement of his rhythms through senses other than sound. At this stage we were simply focused on making our selves 'processable' – noticeable in a way that wasn't threatening and didn't add to his possible sensory processing overload.

Looking back (and we have notes to help the process) it is noticeable how long we persisted in this process of making ourselves safe and acceptable and, gradually, interesting to Robert – months of weekly hour-long visits. We had a strong sense that we mustn't rush and that he would let us know when he was ready to explore. A key moment was when we realised that he was not always actively looking away from us; sometimes he looked straight ahead and we thought he might be using his peripheral vision to notice us. We looked at ways of making our rhythm more visual, settling for tying a strip of sparkly material to our wrist, which would catch the light as we slapped the ground.

The next key moment was not of our planning, nor, we suspect, of Robert's choice. We arrived one week to find that the kitchen table had disappeared and that Robert was sitting on the floor in 'our' corridor! We sat down further along the corridor and started our usual mirroring of his rhythms. Despite the drastic change of whereabouts, Robert seemed accepting of us being, for the first time, in the same space, without a doorway between us. Because Robert was in a different position, on the floor not on a chair, we noticed another way that he was creating a rhythm; he was 'bottom-rocking', squeezing right buttock then left so he was rocking from side to side. We copied, finding it quite difficult to master and ended up laughing out loud. Robert turned and looked at us directly and we stilled, expecting him to show discomfort at our unplanned noise – but instead he smiled broadly before looking away. We suddenly felt that we had been accepted. We also had our first experience of Robert's sense of the ridiculous.

For whatever reason, even when a new kitchen table appeared, our sessions together were now taking place in the corridor. There was a lack of barrier and a sense of sharing space. The bottom-rocking developed into little flurries of movement on our part. If we saw that he had glanced towards us, we would make a warning sound (an increasing 'whooa') and would slide towards Robert and back again, maintaining any rhythms he was using. If we overstepped the mark, he would let us know by roaring – which we echoed with a sympathetic/apologetic lower roar of our own as we moved away. He was frequently glancing at us now, nearly always through his eyelashes – maybe limiting the visual information he was taking in, but wanting it nonetheless. His confidence in looking at us and allowing us to be closer seemed directly proportional to his levels of anxiety: we had made ourselves 'safe' by relating to him in his internal language, which made him feel less anxious. When not anxious, he could allow in more sensory information (our proximity, our noise) without being overwhelmed by it.

Humour now became part of our relationship. Robert was increasingly experimenting with vocalisations and sounds, including blowing raspberries, adding these to his rhythms and sometimes he would produce a combination that reminded us of a refrain from a song – so we would add words as well as movements to our celebrations of his sounds. We remained very careful of following his lead – we were not singing to him, but responding musically to him. Robert clearly noticed when we got it 'wrong' and would laugh at us. All the while, he was becoming more tolerant of our proximity. To try to bridge the remaining gap, one of us untied the sparkly material that we were still using round our wrists to visually emphasise our movements, and skimmed it across the floor towards Robert. He was far from impressed; visually, we think it overwhelmed him, but also we had gone against our practice of letting him know that he was in charge. We had allowed our desire to 'bridge the gap' take precedence over his sense of sensory safety.

So what was our purpose here? We were still aware that his support team were keen to get Robert out and about. Without being able to tolerate the proximity of others, this was unobtainable for him, so we had been focusing on helping Robert to increase his interest and confidence in the social world. Trying to 'bridge the gap' within our own time frame was at cross purposes with Robert's needs as it interrupted the flow. We needed to stick to the clear purpose of confidence building through Intensive Interaction and attention to Robert's sensory needs.

Our time together in the corridor was a significant inconvenience for others in Robert's home. A new opportunity arose when his team persuaded Robert to try the new sofa in the lounge. It was high-backed, shiny and quite hard –

maybe providing a similar proprioceptive feedback to the floor and wall. It was also long enough to accommodate Robert at one end and one of us at the other, with a good gap in between. This meant that there was now a clearly defined limit to how far away we could be – two arms' length – and Robert was brave enough to accept this. At this distance, on the shared sofa, he could easily see and feel us copying his rhythms. We began to copy his hand play – the way he pushed the fingers of one hand into the palm of the other. To begin with we did this with our own hands, but then began to use the sofa, pushing our fingers into the empty space between us. Robert reached out to stop us. We paused, then resumed. After 30 seconds or so, he stopped us again. The next time, as his hand came down to stop ours, we turned our hand, caught his and squeezed it. He turned and looked straight at us, paused then laughed. This opened the gates to a whole series of games involving anticipation, touch, sound, surprise and humour. Robert was learning how to predict other people's (our) behaviour – a hugely important skill when navigating the social world.

Our shared games – or conversations – became more complex, ridiculous and fun. The confidence of Robert's support team grew as they watched this, learning that this approach is transferable. Significantly, over the years of working with Robert, there were a few changes to the Us in a Bus team who visited him. Because our approach was so deliberately consistent, the changes did not bother him. Our input with Robert has come to an end and we are hopeful that the confidence and understanding of his current support team will mean that he is able to continue his exploration of the pathways he has discovered.

## Joe

When we first met Joe, his world had shrunk to his bedroom, sometimes just to his small ensuite bathroom. Invitations to leave this safe space could result in such violent self-injury (smashing his head against his knee) that his mother realistically feared for his life. When he had moved into this shared residential care home, from school, his horizons had been broader. His response to the consequent changes to his environment and routines had been expressed through quiet but persistent rocking, ear-defending, high-pitched sounds and finally significant self-injury. His support team assumed they were offering the wrong things in the wrong ways so offered more variety. When this was met with what was interpreted as more anxiety, the solution had been to stop offering choices and to leave Joe in the sanctuary he seemed to crave. This extended to him eating alone in his room and not venturing out of it. However, once a fortnight, Joe would happily and willingly accompany his mother to her home and spend the weekend out and about with her, coping with situations (crowds, dogs, change) that seemed too much for him at any other time.

Us in a Bus were invited by his mother to work with Joe and his team to see if Intensive Interaction could help resolve this situation and re-open Joe's horizons. On meeting Joe and hearing more about him, we believed that we could not begin to build a trusting relationship with Joe without paying attention to what his actions might be telling us about his sensory processing needs – making any communication between us responsive to the way he may be experiencing his sensory world. Unless we viewed what Joe was doing as evidence of his sensory turmoil, and tried through our own actions to mitigate the impact of that turmoil, we believed that engagement and communication would remain elusive.

So our process together started with observation. The most obvious thing Joe was doing was putting his fingers in his ears and humming. He kept his ears blocked even when drinking, swiftly covering one ear with his shoulder as soon as he reached for a proffered drink. We experimented ourselves, using our fingers to block our own ears whilst humming, playing with pressure we were applying and the timbre of our humming. It was clear that Joe was imposing a sophisticated and variable level of control over his auditory environment, rather than just blocking out noise. This was good news, as it meant we could look for a way of showing Joe that we respected his need for auditory control by finding a way to tune in with his control settings.

Joe's mother gave us a starting point here; she had found that a rapid rhythm on a tape of meditation music had appealed to Joe. We started to get to know Joe at a distance, sat on the floor along the corridor from his bedroom, using a soft beater to create this rhythm on a drum. Joe could, if he chose, lean and look at us via a mirror on his wall (placed there to give him warning of who was approaching). We kept this up for 30 minutes, during which time he didn't choose to look at us. We repeated this on our weekly visits, and became aware that Joe would shoot quick glances at us whilst we beat the drum; we could see that his fingers were in his ears when he did so. This gave us the courage to move closer. Our purpose was not to entertain or to stimulate Joe with this rhythm; it was to provide a totally predictable auditory environment which he could notice visually as well as hear. We were making ourselves safe and predictable for him within the confines of his sensory processing issues. Within three visits Joe felt safe enough for one of us to be beating the drum whilst sat on his bedroom floor; the other was still sat in the corridor – but making herself visually predictable and familiar by copying Joe's stance of fingers in ears and rocking in his rhythm. We wanted Joe to know, as clearly as possible, that we would not add to his sensory distress and that he was in charge of our interactions.

The next stage of our relationship came with Joe appearing comfortable to have us both sitting on his floor, with our fingers in our ears – also copying his humming patterns which we were now close enough to hear. The drum was on the floor in front of us; if he glanced at it we took it as an instruction to recommence the beat. We realised that we could capitalise on what we all looked like with our fingers stuck in our ears – our elbows stuck out. My colleague and I started to occasionally deliberate touch each other – elbow to elbow – as we rocked and hummed. We could see that Joe noticed this so we embellished it by 'counting in', not with numbers but with humming. (This is an advantage of having two practitioners involved; we can model an interaction, firmly within Joe's 'language', giving him a chance to assimilate but with no pressure to join in.) We were quite sure by this stage that Joe was letting in a lot of sound and that his fingers were poised ready to block sound, rather than doing so all the time. It felt as if there was a mutual growth of courage and adventure between us, especially when we saw him smile when my colleague and I accidentally 'clashed' elbows rather than just touching.

The upshot of this courage and patience was that with use of photographs, visual timetables, objects of reference (the drum!) and lots of planning, Joe left his room and home and came to join our Bus Stop – a weekly open-to-all interactive session in his local town centre. We made it as predictable as possible for him but it couldn't but be different and unpredictable. It took persistence and determination to re-tread the steps that had been laid down in the safety of his room – but he managed it. Joe was able to join in the 'Elbow Game' he had inspired, passing touch from one group member to another. We began to do this to a familiar tune, making the touch correspond to the end of each line, gradually moving the auditory predictability away from Joe's own rhythm to a more external, shared one. The occasion when Joe first took his fingers out of his ears, threw his head back and squealed with delighted laughter was a memorable one – and marked a new stage in shared enjoyment. Another member of the group took up Joe's sound; Joe flapped his arms and jumped from one foot to the other. We copied this action and soon the group was dancing. Joe uttered a deep 'aaa haa' sound which reminded one of us of the opening bar to an aria from the opera Aida, which soon became our established marching/dancing song.

It would be great to end the story on this high, but things changed. There were changes in the support staff team and commitment to bringing Joe to the Bus Stop shifted. Routine was broken for a number of 'small' reasons and uncertainty and overload drifted back into Joe's life to the extent that self-injury became a stark reality again. Us in a Bus tried hard to keep interest and knowledge of Intensive Interaction a live issue at Joe's home, but with regular changes in management its use there dwindled to negligible. Joe's horizons collapsed along with his confident exploration of communication and sociability. Joe retreated to the sensory certainty of his bedroom and fear of his self-injury prevented his team from encouraging him out again. His future looked bleak – and we looked on helplessly from afar, funding for his weekly Bus Stop no longer available as 'he didn't want it'.

For us this proved once again that there are no quick fixes here. Yes, we had found that using Intensive Interaction with an understanding of the way

Joe needed to process the sensory world had enabled him to take confident strides into the social and communicative world. But it was not a course of physiotherapy that had cured a sprained ankle – the input needed to be on-going and present in all aspects of Joe's life. An hour a week had made a significant difference – what could a universal and consistent use of the approach mean to the quality of Joe's life? And why was it such hard work to convince his team that they could do it?

Joe's mother was indefatigable in her conviction that a better life was worth fighting for. Two years later, Joe is living in a different home, with a support team we have trained in Intensive Interaction and who understand his sensory processing needs. The team changes, but we have worked alongside them to create a culture where the approach gets passed on; this is not necessarily consistent or easy, but there is an underlying commitment – and support from senior management, who see maintaining this approach as important as maintaining someone's medical regime. Joe is back out and about, able to negotiate trips around London's transport system just for *fun* (a feat beyond most commuters). Recently he has been exploring the boundaries of the choices available to him – and encountering some immovable limits.

At moments of extreme excitement ('I'm *really* happy to be home with my mother!') or extreme frustration or upset ('Burger King is shut but this is the point in my trip when I *always* have a burger!') Joe's ability to accurately process proprioceptive feedback deserts him. He has to create increased proprioceptive messages to re-ground or centre himself. What this looks like is big motor movements – jumping, rocking dramatically from foot to foot, or waving his arms. If this doesn't work for him, he has to deepen the proprioceptive message further – by repeatedly banging his head hard against his knee. It is easy to see this action as simply an expression of the emotion he is feeling, but when we do that we miss out an important link. The strong emotion has impeded Joe's ability to process a particular sensory message; this results in him feeling physically unstable (as we all may do when we find ourselves at the edge of a steep drop, for example). He produces a major sensation which eventually (but painfully, dangerously) stabilises him. The good news here is that once we realise this, we can help Joe regularly pre-load himself with proprioceptive input, in an interactive way, which means that he doesn't have to self-regulate to such an extreme extent when he suddenly finds himself under the influence of a strong emotion.

We have been focusing with Joe and his team on finding acceptable, enjoyable, reciprocal ways of topping up this proprioceptive sense of safety. We notice that he often offers his head to people he feels safe with; when we respond by leaning our head towards him, he presses his forehead very firmly against ours, smiling and looking deeply into our eyes. It is very much at his pace and in his control. Firm shoulder presses have now developed into arm pulls; we offer our hands in a certain way, and if Joe wants an arm pull he stretches his arm towards us. We then firmly place our hands at the top of his arm and pull strongly down towards his hands, ending in a firm hand squeeze. This is becoming an established (and recorded) part of daily interaction between Joe and his support team. Everyone feels better – staff feel accepted, we think Joe feels understood, his proprioceptive bank is kept topped up. It also gives him access to immediate help when he needs it most. This final story illustrates this.

We were recently called to see if we could help in a particular situation. Joe had got 'stuck' outside a local supermarket. The boundary he was exploring was 'How long can I stay here looking at people's feet for?' Joe has always loved looking at feet – but he had been here for over three hours and it was getting late! The support worker he was with was new to him – and was worried; whenever he indicated to Joe that they needed to move on, Joe hit himself, hard. Two of the Us in a Bus team were able to join them and a confident and entwined use of Intensive Interaction and sensory understanding enabled Joe to release himself and move on. Nancy stood beside him and copied the way he was looking at feet. At first she did this by sweeping her hands at knee level, mirroring the speed that Joe was moving his head to watch feet. He was only looking down, so her movements needed to be low to be in his view. She was silent; the greeting was entirely in Joe's 'language', not Nancy's. After a while he glanced up at her, either recognising her or realising that his activity was becoming a shared one. Knowing that there was now a link, Nancy shifted her position to be more directly in his view, but not blocking him in any way. Her mirroring of his actions was now more at eye level and allowed for eye contact if Joe chose to make it. (At this point a helpful cab driver approached and offered the useful advice 'You've got no chance love, he's been here for hours!', – giving Nancy's colleague Tiw an opportunity to explain what was going on, and hopefully spread a little understanding!)

Joe's solitary, self-absorbed actions were now shifting into a shared social zone. Nancy was still silent but decided to offer the visual cue for an arm squeeze and Joe responded by offering his arm. Tiw now joined them and offered an arm squeeze from the other side. So as well as the shared activity (foot watching), Joe was receiving acceptable, recognisable, interactive proprioceptive input which was helping to relieve the anxiety he had been experiencing when his support worker was trying to get him to leave feet and come home. Nancy and Tiw now added some playful anticipation, taking a couple of steps back before offering an arm squeeze. Joe stepped towards them to accept it. Thus began a cheerful and relaxed journey home, now with spoken commentary – 'The next squeeze will be by that tree', with Tiw running ahead to take up position and Joe following to continue the game. Joe was not being tricked or manoeuvred – he was being supported in a way that acknowledged and included him. He was able to release himself from the 'stuckness' he was in and get home; the whole process had taken nearly 60 minutes. The support worker was impressed enough to ask for training and is now establishing a strong understanding with Joe, which, if maintained, will be another strong guide-rope in place for Joe to use when navigating the minefield of everyday life.

Embedding good interactive approaches alongside an understanding of sensory processing issues experienced by the people we support is the bedrock of our work at Us in a Bus – both in our own day-to-day practice (through the interactive sessions we facilitate) and in that of support teams and family carers who want to learn to do the same (through the training and coaching we provide). We are deeply grateful to all the people, like Gwen, Robert and Joe, who have allowed us into their lives and have helped us learn, and to Phoebe Caldwell for her continuing insight, inspiration and friendship. Find out more about our work at: www.usinabus.org.uk.

# Chapter 4: Addressing sensory issues and body language with autistic people: Responsive Communication from an occupational therapy perspective

Jennifer Heath

I am an occupational therapist working at a combined school and residential children's home for children and young people aged 5–20 years old, who have complex and special educational needs. The majority have autistic spectrum condition. Some have attention deficit hyperactivity disorder and/or learning difficulties and some have mental health needs. Some also have physical health needs, such as epilepsy. All of the young people present with behaviour difficulties that challenge the people who work around them.

Our school is in Cumbria, set in the grounds of a large country estate. We are surrounded by beautiful, rolling English countryside and supporting the young people to experience this great outdoors is central to much of our work.

Our health and therapy team currently comprises a speech and language therapist, two occupational therapists, two educational psychologists, a mental health practitioner, two learning disability nurses, a child and adolescent psychiatrist and two health and therapy assistants. We are a large team; our size reflects the complexity of the young peoples' needs.

I want to talk about my role as an occupational therapist at the school and discuss some of the challenges that have arisen for me when delivering occupational therapy for these young people and working in this kind of setting. As the title of the book describes, I will be focusing on work which addresses sensory issues, particularly where these are relevant to meaningful interaction. Within this discussion, I will be recounting some examples from work with one young person in particular from our school, Sophie. Sophie has severe learning difficulties, autism and Cornelia de Lange syndrome.

Occupational therapists are inherently concerned with occupation and its intricate connection to health and well-being.[1] My role at the school is about supporting the young people to do the things they need and want to do. We think about occupation in the widest sense of the word – what occupies you on a day-to-day basis? From having a glass of wine after work with colleagues to gardening, riding a bike, working, swimming, having a shower, driving a car; these are all our occupations.

Occupational therapists think about occupations in three domains: self-care, productivity and leisure. All occupations fall into one of these areas and for different people they may have different meanings. An occupational balance between the domains is needed in order to maintain health and well-being (too much work can make a person ill too much leisure can make a person bored, unsatisfied).

During an occupational therapy assessment, the therapist will try to find out about the person, how they currently manage or perform the occupation(s) and the context of the environment which they are carrying them out in.[2] We will investigate all the skills needed to do the occupation (e.g. for riding a bike you need: effective enough body awareness and coordination; road safety; balance; visual processing; motivation of some description; and other skills) and take an assessment of what parts the person can/cannot do. We use the person's strengths in order to uplift or improve their difficulties and develop their skills.[3] In the bike riding scenario, we would use someone's keen motivation and good road safety awareness in order to help them to improve their coordination and balance. We would practice coordination and balance activities to build a more effective foundation and practice actually learning to ride a bike also. Especially with the young people at our school, practicing the actual skill is essential; it would not be enough to simply practice coordination and balance activities and hope that the bike riding improves on its own.

Working as an occupational therapist at our school, I use mostly two frames of reference to guide my work with young people who have learning disabilities (although others do come into the process also), compensatory and

1 Wilcox AA (2009) *An Occupational Perspective of Health, 2nd ed*. Thorofare, NJ: Slack Incorporated.

2 Law M (1996) The person-environment-occupation model: a transactive approach to occupational performance. *Canadian Journal of Occupational Therapy* **63** (1) 9–23.

3 Koenig K (2018) *Harnessing Strengths of Autism for Successful Adulthood – Everyday Evidence Podcast* [online]. Available at: https://www.aota.org/Practice/Researchers/Evidence-Podcast/autism-strengths-success-adulthood.aspx (accessed March 2019).

developmental.[4] Briefly, a compensatory frame of reference is where, because of the young person's difficulties, the likelihood of them learning a particular skill effectively is slim; therefore we provide them with some sort of helping hand (usually in the form of equipment) so that they can complete the activity with greater independence. A developmental frame of reference describes how the young person can progress and is likely to; therefore we scaffold the teaching process as much as appropriate in order that the young person learns to complete the activity with greater independence. When thinking about addressing sensory issues and enabling interaction, often both these frames of reference are in operation. Sometimes we may use equipment to aid someone's ability to maintain a balanced arousal level (compensatory). In addition, we may expect that perhaps they will learn to choose this as an option for themselves and manage this independently (developmental). I raise this here, as I attempt over the next few pages to offer and reflect on how we as occupational therapists work with sensory issues for autistic young people. I find it useful to consider the theoretical structures which help guide what I do at work.

Occupational therapists often have a dilemma when speaking about their work and tailoring this to meet the needs of their audience. It is important to make what we are saying accessible so that people can understand what we mean, without the use of jargon or special terminology.[5] In doing this however, it is possible for the richness and intricacy of occupational therapy intervention to be dumbed down. Occupational therapy intervention is a dynamic and complex process between client, therapist, occupation and environment.[6] I mention this here because, when working with young people who present with complex behaviour which challenges the people who work with them, it is a simplistic perspective to think that as things improve, we people who are working with the young person have merely got better at managing their needs. This discredits or devalues any process the young person themselves may be engaged with and can appear to place us in a hierarchical position. It seems a one dimensional conclusion to come to, when underneath is a complex tapestry of interwoven personalities, developing young person, attitudes, environments and knowledge.

The process of improvement or progress for young people with complex needs is an intricate and multifaceted procedure,[7] which is frequently measured by a reduction in incidences of seemingly distressed or what we perceive as agitated or frustrated behaviour. However, a young person may continue to communicate their anger and sadness in ways which are challenging to us but

4 HOTheory (2018) *Frames of Reference* [online]. Available at: https://ottheory.com/model-type/frame-reference (accessed March 2019).

5 Pentland D, Kantartzis S, Giatsi Clausen M and Witemyre K (2018) *Occupational Therapy & Complexity: Defining and describing practice*. London: Royal College of Occupational Therapists.

6 Lillywhite A and Haines D (2010) *Occupational Therapy and People with Learning Disabilities*. London: College of Occupational Therapy.

7 Imary P and Hinchcliffle V (2014) *Curricula for Teaching Children and Young People with Severe or Profound and Multiple Learning Difficulties.* New York: Routledge.

actually be making great progress in participation in activities of daily living, e.g. eating with greater independence, making more choices etc.

The process of progress or change in occupational therapy intervention (or any intervention) is complex. It is an ever changing, flowing process which involves the young person, for example: their self-confidence and perception of self; their family interactions and social networks; their willingness and motivation to work with the therapist or people around them; their hopes for the future, their capacity and ability for engagement in occupation performance (participation in activities and the skills needed for this, e.g. memory, processing, attention etc.); their personal, social and physical environmental context having an impact on them.

It also involves the therapist: their abilities in communication, humour, listening and compassion; their reasoning, judgement and reflexive skills; their use of thinking tools; their previous experience and knowledge about mechanisms of impact and evidence around the young person's condition. The environment impacts crucially on progress too: physical, social, cultural, political; available resources and funding; policy/organisational expectations. The skills and experience of the therapist or people around the young person in using assistive equipment or environmental adaptation, in changing activities, in passing on information about the young person's condition and theory for techniques and prioritisation and goal setting; all of this continuously changing and evolving context (and more) influences and impacts on outcomes.

This is significant when considering working with addressing sensory issues in order to facilitate interaction. It is a specific area for intervention which happens within the whole context of person, occupation and environment (including therapist); the impact of this whole context is taken into account when assessing, planning or looking at outcomes.

One of the difficulties for an occupational therapist working in the community can be the limited access one normally has to the person in following up interventions. The beauty of working as a therapist at this school is that we work with the young people within the context of their environments. Therefore, when things become difficult for them, we are well placed to unpick with other staff where and what might have been different, in that instance. We do not have the restriction of being bound by organisation policy on duration and frequency of sessions. If a young person's needs are such that they require our support daily for a period of time, we are able to provide this.

For the purpose of this chapter I am going to focus on talking about one young person I work with. This young person (Sophie) is part of a group of young people at our school who have the most significant disabilities, for example, students whose autism is part of conditions such as Cornelia de Lange, Lennox Gestalt or Fragile X. All are diagnosed with more than one condition.

Guidance from the Royal College of Occupational Therapy indicates that our focus when working with people with learning disabilities is on enabling meaningful occupation – a person-centred approach which focuses on what motivates and interests the person.[8] An occupational therapist from this document quotes:

*'The way we look at sensory things is quite unique ... we would look at the sensory base as for why someone's doing a behaviour which might be troublesome to others. And also the way we look at finding activities for people that ... help meet their sensory needs is quite unique.'*[9]

When working with autistic young people:

*'Occupational therapists support learning and engagement with their understanding of sensory processing, emotional and behaviour regulation, oral / fine / gross motor development, and task analysis; recommend modifications to the environment which support people to be able to participate more in their chosen and needed occupations; supporting people to have intimate relationships and advise on sexuality; supporting clients and families through education, consultation and advocacy.'*[10]

Research, guidance and intuition tells us that our most important questions when beginning a piece of work with someone should be: what is meaningful for this particular young person? Meaningful occupation is unique to each person and is in itself a subject for debate. What is meaningful? Do occupations need to be psychologically rewarding in order to be meaningful?[11] These questions seem particularly relevant when working with a young person who is severely autistic. Due to the nature of the difficulties the young people we work with experience, meaningful and psychologically rewarding occupation seems to be most possible when three key areas are experienced effectively, sensory processing and integration, communication and interaction, routines and predictability. Therefore, I see my job as doing whatever I can to improve the flow in these areas for the young person and the staff around them.

# Sophie

Sophie is sixteen years old and has been at the school since she was eleven. Sophie has a diagnosis of autistic spectrum condition, Cornelia de Lange Syndrome, severe learning difficulties and communication needs. Sophie

8 Lillywhite A and Haines D (2010) *Occupational Therapy and People with Learning Disabilities*. London: College of Occupational Therapy.

9 *Ibid* Lillywhite and Haines.

10 Canadian Association of Occupational Therapists (no date) *Occupational Therapists and Autistic Spectrum Disorder.* Canada: Canadian Association of Occupational Therapists.

11 Ikiugu MN, Hoyme AK, Muelle BA and Reinke RR (2015) Meaningful occupation clarified: thoughts about the relationship between meaningful and psychologically rewarding occupations. *South African Journal of Occupational Therapy* **45**.

does not use speech and has a significantly low level of cognitive ability. She currently uses a combination of physical prompts, gestures and behaviours to communicate her needs; she has some success at using objects of reference, particularly with places that are especially meaningful for her i.e. the sensory room and the dining hall. Occupational therapy with Sophie over the years has looked at many areas: access to activities off site (improved by providing a wheelchair); a 'getting going' dance and sensory sessions supporting her transition to and from her bungalow home to her class in the morning and after lunch; advice and facilitation of team discussions as to how we can adapt the environment to support Sophie to engage and to potentially feel more regulated. Finally, a sensory profile for Sophie suggests activities that support her to maintain a more balanced arousal level throughout the day.

When Sophie first arrived, she was fed by another person or she grabbed food herself. She did not sit at a table but spent a lot of time standing up, holding onto something and rocking back and forth. While she was doing this, she engaged in rhythmical breathing which was audible, often emitting a high pitched but quiet sound: the breathing was very shallow and almost seemed as if she was trying to hyperventilate. She would also seem to press her throat with her hand while she was engaging in this behaviour. She still uses this behaviour frequently to regulate herself. Sophie also preferred to be by herself, needing a classroom space designated to her due to the risk of her attacking other children. Sophie pulled out her hair, singularly or in handfuls, and she would also grab other people and attempt to pull their hair too. She struggled with all areas of self-care, including needing full support for dressing and undressing, bathing etc, and disliked brushing her teeth.

As with all new young people, initially we completed an occupational therapy assessment. Standardised occupational therapy assessment tools for people with complex needs, severe autism and low cognitive ability have been difficult to find in my experience, and almost always include some kind of adaptation in order to make it meaningful and beneficial to the young person. At this school we use the Short Child Occupational Profile (SCOPE)[12] assessment tool from the Model of Human Occupation,[13] which gives an overall perspective of the young person's occupational performance to inform further assessment of the young person's current areas of strengths and difficulties. I find the SCOPE useful for children and young people with severe learning difficulties partly because it includes an assessment of the environment, in connection with the person and occupation. The SCOPE includes a parent/carer and teacher questionnaire. We also use the Roll Evaluation of Activities of Daily Living.[14] This assessment gathers

12 Bowyer PL (2008) *The Short Child Occupational Profile (SCOPE)*.University of Illinois, Chicago: Model of Human Occupation Clearinghouse.

13 Kielhofner G (2008) *Model of Human Occupation (4th edition)*. Philadelphia: Lippincott Williams & Wilkins.

14 Roll K and Roll W (2013) *The Roll Evaluation of Activities of Life.* USA: PsychCorp.

information, via a caregiver, about the young person's abilities to engage in all areas of domestic living skills (e.g. getting dressed, undressed, bathing, toileting and eating) and community living skills (abilities to use phones, be organised for school, use money etc). We and staff also like this assessment because it gives a baseline of young people's abilities in these areas. However, for some of our children, the concluding scores are meaningless because they score so significantly low. They score low because they will most likely always need support for dressing, bathing etc. and are likely to always have someone with them, at all times and for all of their life.

When assessing sensory processing, if this has been identified as an issue through assessment of occupational performance we would observe the young person's behaviour in different environments, observing play and daily routines, conduct parent/carer/teacher interview, gain a sensory history and complete one of the sensory questionnaires appropriate to that person (e.g. the Sensory Profile,[15] the Sensory Processing Measure[16] or the Sensory Inventory[17] This layered approach is recommended by Schaff & Roley (2006).[18] The Data Drive Driven Decision Making Model is recommended for therapists assessing and using sensory integration as a best practice.[19] We work towards this as a standard but would openly admit that we do not meet it for every assessment and intervention plan. In assessment we consider the following sensory integrative functions: interoception (tells the person about information from inside the body); proprioception (tells the person information about gravity and movement) and exteroception (tells the person about sensory information from outside of the body).[20] We also analyse the person's ability to register sensory sensation and modulate (capacity to adapt and organise responses to different durations and intensities of sensation) and discriminate (information and interpretation of the qualities and details) sensory information.[21]

The questionnaire which seemed to suit Sophie's needs most was the Sensory Processing Inventory.[22] This assessment takes one through different sensory systems (proprioceptive, vestibular, tactile) and includes parts analysing self-injurious behaviours. The inventory is limited as

15 Dunn W (1999) *Sensory Profile*. USA: The Psychological Corporation.

16 Parham D and Ecker C (2007) *Sensory Processing Measure.* USA: Western Psychological Services.

17 Reisman JE and Hanschu B (1992) *The Sensory Integration Inventory – Revised.* Minnesota: Pileated Press.

18 Schaaf RC and Roley SS (2006) *Sensory Integration: Applying clinical reasoning to practice with diverse populations*. Austin, Texas: PRO-ED.

19 Bogdashina O (2003) *Sensory Perceptual Issues in Autism and Asperger Syndrome.* London: Jessica Kingsley Publishers.

20 Mailloux Z (2001) Sensory integrative principles in intervention with children with autistic disorder. In: S Smith Roley, EI Blanche, RC Schaaf (Eds) *Understanding the Nature of Sensory Integration with Diverse Populations* (pp365-382). USA: Harcourt Health Sciences Company.

21 *Ibid* Schaaf and Roley.

22 Kathyn Smith's additions to the SPI (unpublished course notes).

it does not include reference to the auditory, visual, gustatory, olfactory or interoceptive sensory systems. However, I use Kathryn Smith's[23] unpublished additions for these systems (does not include interoceptive however) to include some measure of these. I do frequently find when analysing the assessment that my results for this particular client group are so variable that it can be an almost meaningless conclusion. That is, the young person demonstrates equal amounts of under- and over-responsive behaviours in proprioception, vestibular and tactile sensory systems. Children with autism commonly fluctuate between over and under responding, particularly in the tactile system.[24,25] The assessment does however give therapists evidence to back up conclusions from observations, utilising a published and validated assessment.

The limitations of all the occupational therapy assessment tools for this client group are that they are mostly subjective by necessity, relying on the therapist's skill, knowledge and expertise in observing and analysing the young person and talking to the people that work with them (or family). For any of the questionnaires, the skill is in eliciting the right kind of information from the people who know the young person intimately in order to make some meaningful (and accurate) conclusions.

My working hypothesis, following assessment, was that Sophie had poor sensory processing, poor motor planning and poor organisation of behaviour which impacted significantly on her ability to participate in daily life activities and to socially relate to others. Her sensory processing issues included: under responsivity to proprioceptive, vestibular and tactile sensory stimuli; excessive seeking of vestibular and proprioceptive stimuli; under responsivity to visual and auditory sensory stimuli. We also questioned Sophie's capacity to process and respond to interoceptive sensory stimuli, given the excessive breathing behaviour (perhaps seeking this type of sensation?) and possibly her constant desire for food.

One of the other issues considered was that it is estimated that 85% of people with Cornelia de Lange experience gastroesophageal reflux (GERD).[26] This was bought to our attention by Phoebe Caldwell in a visit to our school. The pain that accompanies GERD can make eating unpleasant and cause behaviour difficulties. Following a doctor's advice,

---

23 *Ibid* Smith.

24 Mailloux Z (2001) Sensory integrative principles in intervention with children with autistic disorder. In: S Smith Roley, EI Blanche, RC Schaaf (Eds) *Understanding the Nature of Sensory Integration with Diverse Populations* (pp365–382). USA: Harcourt Health Sciences Company.

25 Bogdashina O (2003) *Sensory Perceptual Issues in Autism and Asperger Syndrome* London: Jessica Kingsley Publishers.

26 Cornelia de Lange Syndrome Foundation (2017) *Characteristics of CdLS* [online] Available at: http://www.cdlsusa.org/professional-education/characteristics-of-cdls.htm (accessed March 2019).

Sophie started on a course of anti-reflux medication, to see if this eased any symptoms for her. There were no immediately noticeable effects but as Sophie's presentation is so complex and different on a day-to-day basis, it is difficult to tell; we continue to monitor this. The following sensory profile demonstrates my hypothesis for Sophie's sensory processing and integration in a table created for easy access, for staff at our school to reference the strategies and use through the day.

## Sensory profile for Sophie

| Sensory processing presentation | Presenting behaviour | Strategies |
| --- | --- | --- |
| I do things which suggest I seek vestibular and proprioceptive sensory input.<br><br>This is to help regulate my under responsivity to this kind of sensory information. | ✔ I rock on the floor/in chairs during and in between activities.<br>✔ I twirl or spin myself regularly throughout the day.<br>✔ I seek out all types of movement activities e.g. playground equipment (merry go round, swing, trampoline) more than other children.<br>✔ I seek all kinds of movement and this does sometimes interfere with daily routines.<br>✔ I seek opportunities to fall to the ground without regard to personal safety<br>✔ I'm not very good at coordinating the two sides of my body (bilateral integration)<br>✔ I have difficulty motor planning and performing motor sequences.<br>✔ I have poor coordination of head and eye movements. | ✔ Encourage me to jump on the spot. Star jumps, jump in different directions, run, hop, skip, spin, twirl. If possible support me to use a mini trampoline.<br>✔ Support me to practice swaying, holding my arms.<br>✔ When out and about, play with me on playground equipment (see saws, swings, merry go rounds, balance beams, trampolines).<br>✔ Find me an exercise ball to lie on my tummy and help me to lie upside down on.<br>✔ Play spinning with me; checking for safety issues first, hold my hands, lean backwards and spin around as fast as you can (this is a very alerting activity so don't do it just before bed!).<br>✔ Help me to rock, back and forth whilst holding onto your hands.<br>✔ Play push/pull games with me, whilst holding onto my hands.<br>✔ Think about getting me a rocking chair for my class or bungalow.<br>✔ Support me to participate in swimming. |

| Sensory processing presentation | Presenting behaviour | Strategies |
|---|---|---|
| I do things which suggest I seek tactile input.<br><br>This is to increase my tactile input, as I seem to be under responsive in this sensory system. | ✔ I enjoy getting hands messy or don't seem to mind when they are.<br>✔ I don't always like having my hair washed, cut, washing generally or having my teeth brushed.<br>✔ I frequently like to go barefoot.<br>✔ I really enjoy water play.<br>✔ I am always touching interesting toys, surfaces or textures.<br>✔ I really like to put things in my mouth. | ✔ Provide a variety of tactile experiences in class. Introduce games and activities that enable tactile input to me such as: brushing different parts of body (arms, legs) with different textures, rolling on a texture mat, dress up, 'pretend' paint, tactile dominoes, shape and object feely bags.<br>✔ Increase tactile contrasts between items, objects and tasks. For example use items or objects that are soft/hard, fluffy/coarse, warm/cool, smooth/rough, heavy/light. Cover different objects with rough textures such as sandpaper or tacky textures.<br>✔ Perform warm-up activities that have a strong tactile focus. For example patting rhythms on each other's backs, clapping and jumping songs, body slapping songs.<br>✔ Use a variety of different objects and textures such as: feather, ruler, wood, glass, ice cubes, cotton wool, sponge, dough, metal, rigid plastic, pottery, polished board, plastic cup, sandpaper, bark, paper, lamb's wool, velvet. Some of these could be used to create a texture display board for the class room or home.<br>✔ See OT advice re. hair washing.<br>✔ Play resistance games with me using my hands.<br>✔ Play 'hand sandwich' with me.<br>✔ Play tug of war using hands or an object.<br>✔ Encourage me to lie on the sofa and have a ball rolled on my back.<br>✔ Make blankets (see OT for weighted blankets) available to me. I like to sit with one over my lap. |

| Sensory processing presentation | Sensory processing presentation | Sensory processing presentation |
|---|---|---|
| I do things which suggest I seek tactile input.<br><br>This is to increase my tactile input, as I seem to be under responsive in this sensory system.<br>(Cont.) | | ✔ Give me a hand massage (encourage me to massage your hand) (see OT for massage advice).<br>✔ Make sure my chew toys are available at all times.<br>✔ Make me a little den (I really like the cave in the sensory room) to hide in.<br>✔ Give me bear hugs.<br>✔ After swimming or a bath, provide firm towel rubbing.<br>✔ When giving me instructions; provide firm pressure through my shoulders at the same time to keep me focused.<br>✔ Make sure fidget items are available for me to hold in my hands (textured ball, squeezey toys). Put these in a bag so I can choose my toy.<br>✔ Use vibration; try a vibrating toothbrush. These can be easier to tolerate. |
| I do things which suggest I process auditory information differently to other young people. | ✔ I have difficulties with speech and language.<br>✔ I enjoy making unusual noises/seeks to make noise for noise's sake. | ✔ Give me cues to gain my attention and to signify beginnings/ends of activities. For example, clap, ring a bell, blow a whistle (to gain attention not startle).<br>✔ Provide me with nonverbal cues to supplement verbal directions and instructions.<br>✔ Give me a break sometimes from verbal interaction. Create occasional times during the day when there is no verbal-word interaction. |
| I seem to be under responsive to the visual sensory. I seem to seek out visual sensory input. | ✔ I sometimes look very carefully or intently at objects, or people.<br>✔ I frequently enjoys bright lights.<br>✔ I really enjoy visual sensory items. | ✔ Use strong visual cues to draw my attention to what you want me to look at. Use highlighters, outlines, stickers, draw arrows.<br>✔ Provide distinguishing visual characteristics for items. This helps identify objects with clear characteristics, e.g. colour code things for different subjects or for different rooms/ activities. |

| Sensory processing presentation | Sensory processing presentation | Sensory processing presentation |
|---|---|---|
| I seem to be under responsive to the visual sensory. I seem to seek out visual sensory input. (Cont.) | | ✔ Provide strong contrasts between work materials and the working surface. Use a coloured mat, brightly coloured rectangle of paper, rectangle of different textured material under work. |

Initially, as Sophie's sensory processing needs were significant we held individual therapy sessions, with a teaching assistant also present we also shaped her day to include sensory experiences in the context of her natural environment. We also made alterations and adjustments to these environments to support her in maintaining a more balanced arousal level.

In our school and children's houses, we use sensory strategies or sensory activities throughout the day to support young people in maintaining more of a balanced arousal level. This type of approach is frequently called a sensory diet. (In order to support my understanding of these needs I have completed modules one, two and three from the Sensory Integration network. We are working towards all therapists having completed at least level one.)

We do not purport to be facilitating Ayres Sensory Integration Therapy (ASI) at Underley Garden, where I work. In order to enable this, we would need to verify each component on the ASI fidelity measure[27] during our therapy sessions. There is growing evidence to suggest that ASI provides improvement in sensorimotor skills[28] and achievement of individualised goals.[29,30] However, the evidence for sensory strategies or sensory activities to facilitate increased participation in occupation or modify behaviour however is limited, and what information there is often reports that these do not work.[31] This has been reported to be because the studies on these

27 Parham LD, Cohn ES, Spitzer S, Koomar JA, Miller LJ, Burke JP, Brett-Green B, Mailloux Z, May-Benson TA, Roley SS, Schaaf RC, Schoen SA and Summers CA (2007) Fidelity in sensory integration intervention research. *American Journal of Occupational Therapy* **61** (2) 216–227.

28 May-Benson TA and Koomar JA (2010) Systematic review of the research evidence examining the effectiveness of interventions using a sensory integrative approach for children. *American Journal of Occupational Therapy* **64** (3) 403–414.

29 Pfeiffer BA, Koenig K, Kinnealey M, Sheppard M and Henderson L (2011) Effectiveness of sensory integration interventions with children with autistic spectrum disorders: a pilot study. *American Journal of Occupational Therapy* **65** (1) 76–85.

30 Schaaf RC, Benevides T, Mailloux Z, Faller P, Hunt J, van Hooydonk E, Freeman R, Leiby B, Sendecki J and Kelly D (2014) An intervention for sensory difficulties in children with autism: a randomized trial. *Journal of Autism and Developmental Disorders* **44** (7) 1493–1506.

31 Case-Smith J, Weaver LL and Fristad MA (2014) A systematic review of sensory processing interventions for children with autism spectrum disorders. *Autism* **19** (2) 133–148.

do not follow treatment protocols, or target specific sensory processing problems.[32] It is not necessarily that the strategies don't work; anecdotally, from talking to many autistic people and therapists/carers working with them, we know these approaches (things like weighted vests/blankets, or sensory strategies through the day) do work for many people (not all, but many). The current problem lies in measuring and researching in a rigorous enough manner in order to prove their efficacy.

However, evidence does indicate that proprioception has a regulatory effect over other sensory systems and arousal levels in general.[33] One of the most frequently used sensory strategies is to increase proprioception throughout the day. Proprioception is what happens when we move our muscles. If we move our muscles against a weight or against gravity, the amount of proprioceptive input we receive increases.[34]

Deep tactile pressure is another frequently used sensory strategy. Deep pressure is defined as the 'sensation produced when an individual is hugged, squeezed or held firmly'.[35] It was purported by Jean Ayres to be calming and organising for the nervous system. There is growing evidence to continue to support Ayres's postulate. Particularly since the film about Temple Grandin's life[36] which explicitly explains her squeeze machine and the benefits she felt from this, wider interest in deep tactile pressure and its benefits for autistic people who struggle with tactile sensory processing difficulties has increased. Although a small study (only 13 participants) Bestbier and Williams (2017) found positive benefits for all 13 participants, although they caution against a generalised approach to applying deep pressure and emphasise the use of individual approaches in using these techniques.[37] I mention it here because of its direct relevance to the client group we work with at our school.

32 Ouellet B, Carreau E, Dion V, Rouat A, Tremblay E and Voisin JA (2018) Efficacy of sensory interventions on school participation of children with sensory processing disorders. *American Journal of Lifestyle Medicine*. Published online ahead of print.

33 Blanche EI and Schaaf RC (2001) Proprioception: a cornerstone of sensory integrative intervention. In: S Smith Roley, EI Blanche, RC Schaaf (Eds) *Understanding the Nature of Sensory Integration with Diverse Populations* (pp365-382). USA: Harcourt Health Sciences Company.

34 Mailloux Z (2001) Sensory integrative principles in intervention with children with autistic disorder. In: S Smith Roley, EI Blanche, RC Schaaf (Eds) Understanding the Nature of Sensory Integration with Diverse Populations (pp365-382). USA: Harcourt Health Sciences Company.

35 Ayres AJ (1972) *Sensory Integration and Learning Disorders*. Los Angeles: Western Psychological Services.

36 HBO Films (2010) *Temple Grandin*. Film directed by Mick Jackson. Produced by HBO films, Ruby Films, Gerson Saines Productions.

37 Bestbier L and Williams TI (2017) The immediate effects of deep pressure on young people with autism and severe intellectual difficulties: demonstrating individual differences [online]. *Occupational Therapy International* **2017**. Available at: https://www.hindawi.com/journals/oti/2017/7534972/ (accessed March 2019).

An analysis of the neurology behind why deep pressure is known to be calming and organising for the nervous system is unfortunately beyond the scope of this chapter. Suffice to say firm touch and light touch are processed along different neural pathways, activating different parts of the brain. Light touch is more alerting and arousing (e.g. tickle) whereas firm or deep pressure is known to be more calming and to lower the arousal level.[38]

As we all got to know Sophie better, it was clear that she really enjoyed social interaction, particularly with adults. We noticed that if she was well regulated (I am using the term here in reference to sensory regulation – the ability to regulate one's response to sensory input) and in a calm and alert state, then interactions with her were full of humour, laughter, turn taking, Sophie being fully attentive to the 'conversation' and requesting different types of physical interactions e.g. tickles (light touch activating the anterolateral pathway, triggering higher state of arousal). If Sophie was not well regulated, then she made her choice to not interact very clear by pushing people away, moving away herself and, if people did not notice her choice straight away, grabbing or pulling their hair and moving on to biting if people had still not got the message. In this instance, it was a case of giving her the space and time to regulate by herself (most frequently by her rocking and breathing behaviour); removing or modifying the environment (e.g. turning on music, turning on/off lights or fans) and continuing every now and again to join her.

Sophie demonstrated behaviour which indicated she had a strong and central need for vestibular and proprioceptive input. She liked to start her day with a good half hour on our rotary, bolster swing, with loud repetitive music playing. I would use this activity for opportunities to interact, as the better regulated she became, the more likely she was to engage in this. I would hold the swing, stopping her from going immediately until we had used 'ready, steady, go' in order to give salient cues about the start of the activity. Sophie preferred to swing rotary; however I would start the session with some back and forth (linear vestibular input) in order to offer this sensation, which is known to be calming and organising for the nervous system.[39,40] Following this, I would stop the swing from time to time, in order to prohibit her from becoming too aroused and to encourage her to request more (she would do this by physically gesturing or grabbing or sitting on the swing). Rapid, sudden, jolt type sensory input can have an excitatory influence to the nervous system, thus resulting in a more

38 Reeves GD and Cermak SA (2001) From neuron to behaviour: regulation, arousal and attention as important substrates for the process of sensory integration. In: S Smith Roley, EI Blanche RC Schaaf (2001) *Understanding the Nature of Sensory Integration with Diverse Populations* (pp89–106). USA: Harcourt Health Sciences Company.

39 Cornelia de Lange Syndrome Foundation (2017) *Characteristics of CdLS* [online] Available at: http://www.cdlsusa.org/professional-education/characteristics-of-cdls.htm (accessed March 2019).

40 Mailloux Z (2001) Sensory integrative principles in intervention with children with autistic disorder. In: S Smith Roley, EI Blanche, RC Schaaf (Eds) *Understanding the Nature of Sensory Integration with Diverse Populations* (pp365-382). USA: Harcourt Health Sciences Company.

alert state, potentially facilitating further interaction.[41] Sophie would often seem to find the 'stop' funny, smiling and laughing out loud (demonstrating this more alert state). Sophie could spend several times through the day on the swing, smiling and laughing; yet there were other times that she appeared not to want this at all. Staff became experts in reading her cues as to what type of input she was seeking and then using this to enable meaningful interaction.

There were always other sensory items around for her to engage with, e.g. vibrating gadgets which she frequently enjoyed. These gadgets afford deep tactile pressure, to which Sophie appeared to respond positively. Sophie also enjoyed flapping a piece of card in front of her; again, this was one of her regulating strategies. This activity affords visual stimuli, proprioceptive input as you move your wrist (especially if you do it as fast as Sophie did) and also the feeling of air moving on your skin. It was possible to join her in these activities in order to facilitate an exchange or interaction. Staff could do this either by copying her actions or doing something which was similar but not quite the same. However, at times, if staff sat next to her (in front always seemed too direct or to annoy her), unless she was well regulated, the interaction would seem to annoy her. She would become aggressive, attempting to grab our clothing or hair and clearly communicating that the interaction was not wanted at that time or maybe that people had got how they were interacting with her wrong somehow.

Other times, if we got it right, often when there was loud, repetitive music playing, we could join Sophie and before we knew it, we would be in the 'flow'[42] of a simultaneous conversation. This would start off by paying careful attention to her body language (is she looking or engaged in a repetitive behaviour, appearing as if trying to avoid people or stimuli, or is she looking more aware of the room around her, receptive to a conversation?); then sitting down next to her; waiting for her to take your hand, perhaps tapping your own hand to the beat of the music on your own leg. Sophie would invariably take your hand and place it on her shoulder or back and indicate how she wanted you to press (and how hard), tap or tickle in time to the music. If, as with the swinging sessions, you stopped, she would again indicate where to start once more. Frequently the conversation became a turn taking exchange, with Sophie and you taking it in turns to lead the conversation, in terms of which physical interactions together, where and for how long.

The transactions between us and Sophie that I am describing, using body language to communicate in this way, are commonly known as Intensive Interaction. At the same time, we were looking at the sensory feedback Sophie was giving herself (e.g. wanting more swinging, seeking more pressing, or head

41 Mailloux Z (2001) Sensory integrative principles in intervention with children with autistic disorder. In: S Smith Roley, EI Blanche, RC Schaaf (Eds) Understanding the Nature of Sensory Integration with Diverse Populations (pp365-382). USA: Harcourt Health Sciences Company.

42 Csikszentmihalyi M (1997) *The Masterminds Series. Finding Flow: The psychology of engagement with everyday life.* New York: Basic Books.

pressure or tickles) or seeking from us which indicated to us she needed more proprioception and/or tactile/vestibular sensory input. This awareness and readiness to recognise and meet the sensory need, and communicate using this and body language, is Responsive Communication.

If our attention got drawn into communicating with someone else in the room, Sophie would quickly and clearly tell us that she was annoyed with us for allowing ourselves to be distracted and not giving her our full attention whilst conversing. She would communicate this by pulling our clothes and grabbing our skin or hair.

We developed the dance/sensory sessions in order to facilitate and encourage this kind of responsive interaction for Sophie and also to afford more daily sensory experiences to support Sophie's arousal level. At the start of this intervention, we used a basic arousal level scale to measure Sophie's arousal level at beginning and end of session. We also recorded whether she had engaged in shared attention, taking turns, responding and initiating interaction. The music selection we used included all her favourite tunes; the moves were things we knew she enjoyed (tapping, light touch, strokes, pressing, bouncing on therapy balls, using different sizes and textures of balls to facilitate different touch). We included some challenges for different moves to see if we could introduce some new movement strategies for her.

It was clear that on some days she did not want to participate; she seemed engaged in her own movement and her rhythm with the music, not wanting to switch or change from this. On other days, she would positively interact with all moves and some lovely 'flow' interaction was possible. We started and ended with the same tune every day to indicate a clear start and finish to the session.

Following the dance/sensory sessions the expectation for Sophie was that she engaged in some kind of functional task, e.g. making a snack. We wanted to see if the activities impacted positively on her ability to engage immediately following the session. Her willingness to engage in putting some bread in the toaster, pressing it on and then spreading with butter improved on some days. On others, however, it seemed to make no difference at all. Perhaps our activities were not right on that day for her; perhaps on some days she did not want a snack (unusual for Sophie). It has frequently been my experience that, with this group of young people with complex needs and severe learning disabilities, on some days, some things work – on others they don't. We are always re-jigging and amending, looking for something else to add to what we do or change, in order to try and meet the young people's needs.

Another activity which Sophie particularly enjoyed was massage. When Sophie was unsettled she would often seek to bang her head against a wall; also she would commonly seek to press her head against or between your legs, seeking this kind of intense pressure to the head. Pressure to the head is commonly sought by children who are severely autistic.[43] Recommendations are to be extremely careful with pressure to anyone's head for risk of injury or damage. It is not known currently how much pressure is needed to cause injury[44] especially with this particular client group who already experience brain structures which are different to neurotypical. However, I would argue that if a young person seeks this pressure out (by placing an adult's hands on their head and pressing or by the other means listed previously), it is safer that we support her in gaining this kind of input in a safe way by offering head massage than allow her to bang her head against a wall. Head massage and/or deep pressure is an activity in which I facilitate training for staff first; people learn some very basic techniques and gain an awareness of how hard they typically press, becoming more aware of the pressure they are giving someone else from their own muscle sensation. One person's idea of deep pressure can be very different to the next person. Offering hands to the front and back of the head (where the bone is denser) is recommended to be safer. Being guided by the young person and them indicating the pressure they wish to receive is also a safer and less intrusive way to facilitate this. It was clear to see from Sophie's facial expressions and her behaviour that she enjoyed this activity greatly; it also frequently went on to facilitate further meaningful interaction between Sophie and staff. The hypothesis was that the deep pressure lowered Sophie's arousal level and therefore enabled a flow of interaction. As we communicated and interacted with Sophie, we adapted our response to include the type of sensory input we could see she was seeking.

During the five years that Sophie has been at our school, I think it is fair to say she has made significant progress. One of the most notable things for her is that she is able to interact and be in a room with other young people and staff. This has an impact on the number of places she can go and be in and the activities available to her. Sophie's capacity for interaction with people has dramatically increased since she first arrived. She seeks out interaction with familiar and unfamiliar staff and will also interact with young people some of the time. Sophie is able to be in places which would formerly have caused her to become extremely agitated, e.g. the supermarket, school disco, school community events, library or swimming pool. Sophie is currently able to undress independently (and dress mostly when in the right arousal level). She eats independently using a spoon or fork. Sophie is able to use simple objects of reference to communicate to staff what or where she would like to go next, e.g. to lunch or the sensory room.

Sophie's progress is made up of deeper engagement in occupations that seem to be meaningful/psychologically rewarding for her, and meaningful to her

---

43 Summers Shahrami A, Cali S, D'Mello C, Kako M, Palikucin-Reljin A, Savage M, Shaw O and Lunsky Y (2017) Self-injury in autism spectrum disorder and intellectual disability: exploring the role of reactivity to pain and sensory input. *Brain Science* **7** (11).

44 BrainInjury.com (2018) *Brain Injury, Head Injury, Injury to the Brain* [online] Available at: https://www.braininjury.com/brain-injury.shtml (accessed March 2019).

family and the people who work/care for her. How her progress came about seems a rich and complex tapestry (the process as discussed and reflected on in earlier paragraphs). I have attempted to describe part of the physical, social, therapeutic environment which has been a piece of this tapestry. Ultimately the centre of the process of progress is Sophie! In this chapter, I have described an aspect of our work as occupational therapists at the school/children's home where I work. I have discussed my thoughts on what occupational therapy is and what this transcribes to doing at our setting. I have looked briefly at the differing assessments for this group of young people, to support my explanation of work with Sophie. I have described our working hypothesis for her sensory processing and integration and some of our interventions which seemed to hold the most meaning for her. I have attempted to describe Responsive Communication interactions with Sophie and how this transpired. I feel extremely aware, all the way through, that I have been discussing a person who does not speak herself and I would like to acknowledge Sophie at this point, for giving us the chances and possibilities to try and understand more. I hope I have been true to her nature! I have frequently heard people describe working with young people of this complex nature (or any young people for that matter!) as an on-going jigsaw which is never completely solved. We continue to fit pieces here and there (frequently getting it wrong), occasionally getting a better or more beneficial view of the whole picture.

I would like to finish this chapter by raising awareness for the #IAMchallengingbehaviour campaign[45] and in doing this, add my support for this cause, which is changing the way people (particularly professionals) talk about the people they work with. The campaign talks about how people who are labelled as having challenging behaviour are displaying the emotions which all of us feel, e.g. anger, fear, anxiety and sadness. It is the extremes of the ways in which some young people do this (e.g. slapping or pinching themselves or others, banging their heads against walls, smearing faeces, making themselves vomit), which can be challenging for us, who care and work with them. But the label of challenging behaviour can influence people's first impressions of the young person and could give the impression of something which is perceived as negative. Distressed behaviour can be a more useful term, since almost all behaviour which is construed as negative is frequently due to problems processing the world around us.

*Thank you very much to Sophie and her family (who have given consent for me to talk about her in this chapter). Also to the enthusiastic and inspiring young people and committed staff at Underley Garden, Kirkby Lonsdale, Cumbria.*

45 Sly S and Crosby N (2017) *I AM Challenging Behaviour* [online]. Available at: https://www.facebook.com/pages/biz/I-AM-Challenging-Behaviour-1728074550828176/ (accessed March 2019).

## References

Ayres AJ (1972) *Sensory Integration and Learning Disorders*. Los Angeles: Western Psychological Services.

Bestbier L and Williams TI (2017) The immediate effects of deep pressure on young people with autism and severe intellectual difficulties: demonstrating individual differences [online]. *Occupational Therapy International* **2017**. Available at: https://www.hindawi.com/journals/oti/2017/7534972/ (accessed March 2019).

Blanche EI and Schaaf RC (2001) Proprioception: a cornerstone of sensory integrative intervention. In: S Smith Roley, EI Blanche, RC Schaaf (Eds) *Understanding the Nature of Sensory Integration with Diverse Populations* (pp365-382). USA: Harcourt Health Sciences Company.

Bogdashina O (2003) *Sensory Perceptual Issues in Autism and Asperger Syndrome*. London: Jessica Kingsley Publishers.

Bowyer PL (2008) *The Short Child Occupational Profile (SCOPE)*. University of Illinois, Chicago: Model of Human Occupation Clearinghouse.

BrainInjury.com (2018) *Brain Injury, Head Injury, Injury to the Brain* [online] Available at: https://www.braininjury.com/brain-injury.shtml (accessed March 2019).

Canadian Association of Occupational Therapists (no date) *Occupational Therapists and Autistic Spectrum Disorder*. Canada: Canadian Association of Occupational Therapists.

Case-Smith J, Weaver LL and Fristad MA (2014) A systematic review of sensory processing interventions for children with autism spectrum disorders. *Autism* **19** (2) 133–148.

Cornelia de Lange Syndrome Foundation (2017) *Characteristics of CdLS* [online] Available at: http://www.cdlsusa.org/professional-education/characteristics-of-cdls.htm (accessed March 2019).

Csikszentmihalyi M (1997) *The Masterminds Series. Finding Flow: The psychology of engagement with everyday life*. New York: Basic Books.

Dunn W (1999) *Sensory Profile*. USA: The Psychological Corporation.

HOTheory (2018) *Frames of Reference* [online]. Available at: https://ottheory.com/model-type/frame-reference (accessed March 2019).

Ikiugu MN, Hoyme AK, Muelle BA and Reinke RR (2015) Meaningful occupation clarified: thoughts about the relationship between meaningful and psychologically rewarding occupations. *South African Journal of Occupational Therapy* **45**.

Imary P and Hinchcliffle V (2014) *Curricula for Teaching Children and Young People with Severe or Profound and Multiple Learning Difficulties*. New York: Routledge.

Kielhofner G (2008) *Model of Human Occupation (4th ed)*. Philadelphia: Lippincott Williams & Wilkins.

Koenig K (2018) *Harnessing Strengths of Autism for Successful Adulthood – Everyday Evidence Podcast* [online]. Available at: https://www.aota.org/Practice/Researchers/Evidence-Podcast/autism-strengths-success-adulthood.aspx (accessed March 2019).

Law M (1996) The person-environment-occupation model: a transactive approach to occupational performance. *Canadian Journal of Occupational Therapy* **63** (1) 9–23.

Lillywhite A and Haines D (2010) *Occupational Therapy and People with Learning Disabilities*. London: College of Occupational Therapy.

Mailloux Z (2001) Sensory integrative principles in intervention with children with autistic disorder. In: S Smith Roley, EI Blanche, RC Schaaf (Eds) *Understanding the Nature of Sensory Integration with Diverse Populations* (pp365–382). USA: Harcourt Health Sciences Company.

May-Benson TA and Koomar JA (2010) Systematic review of the research evidence examining the effectiveness of interventions using a sensory integrative approach for children. *American Journal of Occupational Therapy* **64** (3) 403–414.

Ouellet B, Carreau E, Dion V, Rouat A, Tremblay E and Voisin JA (2018) Efficacy of sensory interventions on school participation of children with sensory processing disorders. *American Journal of Lifestyle Medicine*. Published online ahead of print.

Parham D and Ecker C (2007) *Sensory Processing Measure*. USA: Western Psychological Services.

Parham LD, Cohn ES, Spitzer S, Koomar JA, Miller LJ, Burke JP, Brett-Green B, Mailloux Z, May-Benson TA, Roley SS, Schaaf RC, Schoen SA and Summers CA (2007) Fidelity in sensory integration intervention research. *American Journal of Occupational Therapy* **61** (2) 216–227.

Pentland D, Kantartzis S, Giatsi Clausen M and Witemyre K (2018) *Occupational Therapy & Complexity: Defining and describing practice*. London: Royal College of Occupational Therapists.

Pfeiffer BA, Koenig K, Kinnealey M, Sheppard M and Henderson L (2011) Effectiveness of sensory integration interventions with children with autistic spectrum disorders: a pilot study. *American Journal of Occupational Therapy* **65** (1) 76–85.

Reeves GD and Cermak SA (2001) From neuron to behaviour: regulation, arousal and attention as important substrates for the process of sensory integration. In: S Smith Roley, EI Blanche and RC Schaaf (2001) *Understanding the Nature of Sensory Integration with Diverse Populations* (pp89 – 106). USA: Harcourt Health Sciences Company.

Reisman JE and Hanschu B (1992) *The Sensory Integration Inventory – Revised*. Minnesota: Pileated Press.

Roll K and Roll W (2013) *The Roll Evaluation of Activities of Life*. USA: PsychCorp.

Schaaf RC, Benevides T, Mailloux Z, Faller P, Hunt J, van Hooydonk E, Freeman R, Leiby B, Sendecki J and Kelly D (2014) An intervention for sensory difficulties in children with autism: a randomized trial. *Journal of Autism and Developmental Disorders* **44** (7) 1493–1506.

Schaaf RC and Roley SS (2006) *Sensory Integration: Applying clinical reasoning to practice with diverse populations.* Austin, Texas: PRO-ED.

Sly S and Crosby N (2017) *I AM Challenging Behaviour* [online]. Available at: https://www.facebook.com/pages/biz/I-AM-Challenging-Behaviour-1728074550828176/ (accessed March 2019).

Summers Shahrami A, Cali S, D'Mello C, Kako M, Palikucin-Reljin A, Savage M, Shaw O and Lunsky Y (2017) Self-injury in autism spectrum disorder and intellectual disability: exploring the role of reactivity to pain and sensory input. *Brain Science* **7** (11).

*Temple Grandin* (2010) Film directed by Mick Jackson. Produced by HBO films, Ruby Films, Gerson Saines Productions.

Wilcox AA (2009) *An Occupational Perspective of Health (2nd edition).* Thorofare, NJ: Slack Incorporated.

# Chapter 5: Autism support in Cumbria: understanding behaviour and supporting change

Jemma Swales

*'You can't judge a person by their looks. But once you know the other person's inner self, both of you can be that much closer'*

(Naoki Higashida, *The Reason I Jump: One boy's voice from the silence of autism*)

My name is Jemma Swales and I am an autism practitioner working in Cumbria. After completing a degree in psychology I have spent the past thirteen years working with autistic people in a range of settings. I moved back to the Furness peninsula after a few years away studying and working in both Leicester and London. On my return, I decided to become self-employed and began to open the door on the local autism community. I found a great number of families and individuals in the area needing support, so much so that soon my books were filling up. As well as my one-to-one work, I am a director of Autus Cumbria Ltd: a not-for-profit organisation running term-time youth groups, holiday activity sessions and training for parents, teachers, support workers and local businesses.

In both my one-to-one work and the work we do at Autus, I am engaging with both verbal and non-verbal autistic people and supporting a range of ages. In this chapter, I shall focus on work with those individuals who use verbal language to communicate, those who are in mainstream education and those who can explain how they are thinking or feeling. The purpose of this chapter is to lift the lid on what long term support looks like, why it helps and why it is so incredibly important if we want to truly engage with autistic people. How can we explore what it takes to really help someone to overcome trauma, to change the way they do things, to understand how they learn and how they can develop a confident, true sense of self.

Over the past thirteen years I have seen just how much time and support needs to go into helping autistic people and, despite the presence of a range of support teams, groups and individuals out there, we need to do more, listen more – and spend more time learning from those who need help.

## The factor of time

In his book *The Body Keeps the Score*, Bessel van der Kolk remembers the time one of his professors, Elvin Semrad, remarked: '*There is only one real text-book: our patients*'.

I only began to really learn about autism when I started to spend time with autistic people. On my very first day working as a support worker at a day service in north London, I was tasked with the job of massaging an elderly man's hands. It was the part of the day where individuals could choose what they wanted to do, and this man particularly liked the sensory feedback of having his hands massaged. I was twenty-two years old, fresh out of university and only had a smattering of autism knowledge. The gentleman was in his 70s, did not use verbal language to communicate and we had just met. What followed was a wonderful 30 minutes where we were both present in the moment and had a wonderful conversation through his hands. We were both relaxed and I knew then that I was privileged to be there to learn what communication meant to different people.

Since that moment, I have kept learning from those around me, and each time I can have a conversation in the language of an autistic person it adds to my understanding and I am humbled by it. When I first start the journey of working with someone, I speak to either them or their family about the factor of time. The work is slow because in order for behaviour to shift and change, the neural pathways in the brain need time to rewire. This is particularly difficult when dealing with the autistic brain as it is holding onto past trauma. To let go of this is no easy task.

I liken it to a diet plan. If someone undertakes a 'lose weight fast' diet by cutting out certain food groups they will see quick results; however that isn't sustainable, so soon enough the weight will go back on. If someone decides to take the time to work out what their food and exercise difficulties are and plan a manageable routine and takes months or even years to change, the change will be hard-wired in and they are more likely to succeed in their weight-loss mission in a healthy way.

I view my work in much the same way: it's only through time, patience and a lot of hard work that we see changes. For the people I work with who are verbal and cognitively able to discuss their autism, it takes a huge leap of faith on their part to change. I am suggesting to them that there are easier ways to do things, different ways to process and understand the world, which is why it takes time. For our brains to trust that doing things a different way might be better for us, we need to take a leap of faith, so that we *experience* it being better.

## Consistency and trust

Why is it important to have consistency, to have one person to work with? I asked this question to Andrew, a highly intelligent young man I have worked with for the past five years. He thought and gave me this response:

*'The world is made up of lot and lots and lots of patterns, like a giant tapestry made by 7 billion people. Some people are better weavers than others, some people go over other's work etc. If you can stick with one weaver, it gives you one path to follow. You don't have to worry about the other weavers. Once you have one pattern, it makes it easier to hop on to other ones so you can learn ... Every time a new person becomes involved, not only do they bring their own difficulties to process, they also add complexity to interacting with those that are already involved. Following a person is like one of those "find the right string" challenges except it's constantly moving. Even on a good day, managing with just one person can be a daunting challenge so each additional person you add, adds another challenge at the same time as the original, making it exponentially harder.'*

Andrew has imaginative ways of describing how it feels to think and feel the way he does and he went on to talk about how working with the same person for long periods of time 'provides security and consistency', tools that are paramount for building trust. He talked about control and that to 'give it up' so that someone can help him 'requires a huge amount of trust', further highlighting the need for consistency.

Julia, another highly intelligent young lady I work with, talked about not feeling like she can trust anyone, saying '*You just kind of assume that everyone is lying to you*'. I asked her why she thought this was and she talked about how right from the beginning of school, she was unsure of what to say to adults in case they shouted or told her off. 'What do they want me to say' and 'What is socially acceptable to say' are thoughts that go through Julia's mind every time she is faced with an interaction. Adults have lied; for example, a doctor saying, 'this won't hurt' (when giving an injection), with 'yes it does!' being the response (Julia is hypersensitive to pain). A teacher saying, 'I won't be cross, just tell me what happened' and then, in Julia's experience, they still get cross. She now sees all adults as the same, so to open up and trust is something completely alien to Julia and 'not worth the risk' in case she is embarrassed, hurt, frightened or upset. Whilst this method keeps Julia feeling safe, it also blocks her brain from experiencing positive interactions and keeps her nervous system in constant 'alert' mode, which is exhausting for her and means that she'd rather stay in the comfort of her home than be out in the world. When she does venture out, her system becomes overloaded very easily and she is prone to shutting down to the point where her whole body cannot respond to outside stimuli no matter how hard she tries.

By taking the time to understand an individual's past story and experiences, I am better able to help in the present; it helps me to navigate my way around their fears and anxieties. It is not enough to tell a person 'I know you've been hurt by adults in the past but I'm different, I won't shout at you or tell you you're making it up' or 'to just get over it'. Until enough time has passed in our working relationship for that individual to actually see and *feel* and know that what I say is true, they shouldn't be expected to trust me. In the same vein, it is hugely important that if we do 'mess up' (this could be being late for an appointment, saying something that an individual takes literally which we hadn't picked up on, etc.), we apologise. This might sound so simple and obvious, but it astounds me how little it happens, especially when the dynamic is adult–child. It is as if our adult egos get in the way of admitting we messed up. I have seen the power in saying 'sorry' to someone and giving them the space to explain how they feel. It strengthens our working relationship and shows them that I am human so will get things wrong sometimes, but I will acknowledge that and validate how they feel.

## Realistic working

The individual stories I will describe here are ones of hard work, setbacks, frustration, care and a lot of patience. Throughout my work I must constantly re-evaluate what I'm doing and if it is serving a person. I have days where it all seems to be for nothing and days where I feel burnt out. These feelings are ones I see in families and carers of autistic people too; however, I am very aware that I get to go home at the end of the day, shut the door and recharge, which most families and individuals cannot do. A big part of supporting an autistic individual is to support the unit around them too, whether that be a single parent or a large family with many siblings. This is another reason why the work needs to be slow and manageable as I need to be mindful of the family setup and what each member can give to the process. There is no point asking a parent to change their whole way of working with their child if they are currently surviving on three hours' sleep a night and have done for the past six years. We need to work on helping the sleep first so that everyone has more energy before moving on to other areas. If I ask families to change a lot too quickly and they are unable to do so, guilt, frustration and even anger will arise and become part of the relationship, which is not helpful for anyone involved. Processes of change will require hard work and commitment from the unit around the individual, that is part of the deal. I do work hard to tailor the work in a way that is achievable, which will encourage people to keep going.

Whoever I am working with, I am in the moment with that person, working on our relationship right then and there. This means that I tailor the support they need from what they tell or show me through their words or actions. I show them I value their world and what is most important to them rather than leading my agenda and 'outcomes' of my work. This approach is a difficult one for the systems we currently have in place which are mostly 'outcome based'. What changes are we seeing, how quickly is someone progressing, are they engaging in the 'therapy' are all the top priorities, rather than how a person is in any given moment. When starting to work with an autistic person it is of course useful to have an understanding of what they and/or their family want, their aims and aspirations, so we can all be working together to ensure that a person can develop and reach their goals. However, I am careful not to let those goals become the main focus of the work as we can quickly forget that people are allowed to change their minds, or through the process it might become clear that they will need a lot longer to reach those aims than originally thought. I agree that having a goal is important (we all have things we want to achieve, be it in work, education, our personal life, travel and so on), and by talking about our goals we invite support from people around us to enable us to succeed, I believe that autistic people deserve the same. However, how many of us are doing the things now that we saw as goals when we were younger? Some of us, maybe, but I wouldn't be surprised if most of us are not. I certainly haven't reached the goals I set for myself at twenty years old. I have a very different set of circumstances that I am grateful for, but if I focused on what I hadn't achieved, I might be feeling frustrated and upset with myself. By allowing myself to change and evolve what I wanted out of life, I have found new avenues and embraced my new circumstances.

'Won't engage in the service' is a statement I often hear or read when working in this field. Most people I have worked with over the years fall into two categories; those who are desperate to understand their autism, want to learn and change things, and those who 'won't engage in the service'. For those individuals I work with who are in the latter category (of which there are many), if I had given up in those early days I wouldn't have a job. If someone is not engaging, then it is a clear signal to me that I haven't got it right yet. I need to try other routes, have more patience, adapt my strategies and listen. If I set out a way of working and expect every autistic person I work with to accept it and use that way of working to engage, learn and develop, then I am in the wrong profession.

At the beginning of my one-to-one work, I made the decision to work with people in their home environments to help them feel as relaxed as possible and to change the dynamic that so many people are used to of going to visit a professional at a clinic or hospital. Whenever an individual leaves their home, they have to work hard to process their sensory environment and their anxiety will rise as they are in the social world which is often challenging. By working in the home environment, I am taking away some of the variables which cause this anxiety, which is useful as speaking to a new person is anxiety-inducing enough.

Every time I begin a new working relationship with an individual I have to foster an environment where they can feel safe and not rushed into a working relationship with me, taking into consideration their past and their present. I use my theory of mind to put myself in the position of someone I am working with. How might it feel to have a stranger come into your home and take an interest in you? We need to take our time to build up trust and help an individual feel safe. As Andrew says: *'Have you ever had to talk to a random person about what you think is the worst part of you?'*

If I enter someone's home and start asking them to discuss their difficulties straight away, their anxieties may heighten and they may shut down. I start any working relationship by getting to know what they like, be it Pokémon, wrestling, skateboarding (yes, I have 'tried' to learn to skateboard!) or types of hoover. Whatever it is, I want to hear about it and help them feel that I am interested in what makes them feel relaxed and valued. This means having lots of discussions about topics I may or may not be interested in myself, but by putting my agenda aside, I can enter their world and I get to see them at their most animated or relaxed or confident. Positive, self-affirming conversations are such an important way to start.

If we face the issues head on, we run the risk of the individual completely shutting down or heading into the fight or flight response as their body feels under attack. Many autistic people I have met and worked with have usually seen a range of professionals; from speech and language therapists to educational psychologists, psychiatrists and so on. They have had a range of tests and observations, and may have had a lot of questioning. By the time I arrive on the scene, I am another new face who they think will probably only be there for a short while before going again, so their barriers are up and understandably so.

## Trauma

*'Being traumatized means continuing to organise your life as if the trauma were still going on.'*
(Bessel van der Kolk, *The Body Keeps the Score: Mind, brain and body in the transformation of trauma*)

We think of trauma as something monumental which changes the shape of our lives, like being in a war zone, death, abuse, illness etc. However, trauma can be an accumulation of smaller events, or even, for an autistic person, a single event (to a non-autistic person, a somewhat forgettable event), that sticks out and encourages new behavioural patterns to form. I have had numerous conversations with the people I work with, such as 'that time a teacher first shouted at me to stop talking', which resulted in a voice literally being silenced for fear of being shouted at again. Or 'I was told to stop eating sugar by the dentist when I had my brace fitted', leading to an eating disorder, refusing to eat anything in case it contained sugar. These stories are not rare – in fact they are the norm. Most autistic people have experienced trauma at various points in their lives, which has caused such emotional and physical backlash that they will do anything they can to avoid it happening again.

The trauma stays in their system and, as van der Kolk says, they continue to organise their lives around it. Many people I have spoken to have said that they have been told numerous times to 'get over it' or 'forget about it' as it is in the past and is finished now. Whilst that statement is true, it is virtually impossible for them to do that, as their whole body is responding to fear that it might happen again on a daily basis and forms a foundation on which new experiences are moulded.

For example, a man I work with has had many experiences where he has been bullied, laughed at and told off. He was diagnosed quite early on in his childhood; however his autism was never explained to him in a way he could understand so he spent most of his school life feeling like an outsider, being misunderstood and frustrated. Early trauma means that he is now on constant 'alert' when out in the community. He describes how it can feel when walking down the street if he passes people who are laughing:

*'The first fear can be that people are laughing at me, however, it can also be a matter of not knowing what they're laughing at even if it's not me. The unknown can be a "threat" at worst or a persistent worry. Sometimes, the first thought/instinct isn't always a case of feeling like I'm a target but could be an afterthought or unclear conclusion after the event happened. There are times it can be a sense of irritation because at worst, it plays with my senses or I get jumpy so sometimes, the challenge is more coping with the sudden shock or overwhelming assault on my senses (e.g. someone is laughing suddenly and loudly near me). Often, I need to understand the situation or context before my mind gives it the go ahead to "stand easy".'*

He can spend hours, sometimes days, churning over why they were laughing, his own behaviour etc, often leading to a downward spiral of emotion.

People laugh all the time and most of us wouldn't think anything of it; we would simply think they were sharing a joke between themselves and we would move on with our day. It is so important that we don't brush off the intense feelings an autistic person may experience when they talk about these incidents, using our own feelings as a marker, because there is no comparison. The simple act of listening and understanding that the trauma is real for that person instantly makes them feel valued, listened to and understood, which forms the basis for change. It is important that we keep in mind previous trauma when supporting autistic people, as I often hear people describe behaviour as having 'come out of nowhere' when in reality, it may have been an accumulation of experiences, anxiety, fear, shame and embarrassment. When we couple that with all the sensory feedback those emotions can bring with them, the individual may have finally become overwhelmed by something in their environment (which may have been very small) which acted as the catalyst for the behaviour.

## Validation of feelings

Delivering autism training is a big part of my work and one I really enjoy. For understanding to grow around how best to support an autistic person, we have to keep sharing ideas, challenging the way we work and listening to autistic people themselves. A key part of my training is highlighting the importance of validating an individual's feelings. Phoebe Caldwell taught me this simple yet remarkably effective tool a few years ago and I have used it ever since, producing some amazing results. To use this simple tool all that is required is for us to listen and repeat back the **exact** words an individual is using, this allows them to feel heard and their feelings validated.

A wonderful example of this comes from when I was working at a youth group one Monday night. One young lady was being quite vocal about having to wait her turn to make some sausage rolls. She was shouting and raising her fists to the support worker who was working with another individual. She shouted, '*If I can't make sausage rolls now then nobody can make sausage rolls!*' The response from the support worker (who was new to the group) was to remind her that she had to wait her turn. She became even more furious and said it again. By this time, I had quietly moved in between her and the support worker so on her next round of shouting I answered calmly '*You sound like if you can't make sausage rolls now then nobody can make sausage rolls*'. What happened next was incredibly powerful. She lowered her arms, relaxed her tight, angry face and said, sadly, '*No one plays with me at school*'.

A bad day at school was fuelling her anger and her tolerance for waiting was gone. It was the last straw, but when her feelings were validated, she felt listened to and understood. We could then go and have a chat about her school day that made her feel calmer, by which time it was her turn to make the sausage rolls.

To some people that may seem like I allowed her to 'get away' with bad behaviour, shouting at an adult etc. What I saw was the opportunity to listen, as she was telling me, in the only way she knew how, that she was hurting. She'd had a bad day and needed someone to initiate the conversation about it because she was unable to. How could she possibly learn new ways to communicate if she is met with hostility when she tries (albeit in ways which may not be the best)? What she needed at that time was understanding and support, and once she was feeling more relaxed, we could then talk about better ways of letting people know when she was feeling sad or upset etc, without the expectation that she would always be able to do it. We need to allow room for error. We do it for ourselves, so why not for those who have valid reasons for why they might get something 'wrong'?

## Attention seeking

A statement I hear a lot in my work is that an individual is 'attention seeking'. This statement has negative connotations and is often used to brush off behaviour and boil it down to these two words, putting the individual to blame. It is up to them to stop 'attention seeking'.

So let's dig a little deeper and ask, 'Why are they seeking attention?' Let's look at the biggest attention seeking platform of the 21st century: Facebook. As adults, we are very quick to judge children's behaviour as attention seeking; however, it has become socially acceptable for us to use a social media platform to do exactly that. We post pictures of us looking our best, with our partners, on our great holidays, or we describe bad events that we've suffered, all to gain attention. We feel better when people offer support, 'like' our pictures and give us positive comments. Why do we do this? Maybe we are feeling lonely, insecure, sad or excited about life and we want to share it with others, it comes from a place of emotion and is valid. But when it comes to behaviours that challenge us, we boil it down to 'attention seeking' in its negative form.

All behaviour has a purpose to communicate some form of emotion or sensation, so when we spend the time working out what that emotion is then we can help, and the behaviour truly changes. By changing our approach, we are also showing the person the possibility of a new response. So many autistic people have negative responses to their behaviours which heightens their anxieties and lowers their self-worth, thus engraining the behaviours even more.

Whenever I find myself becoming frustrated at a person's behaviour, I take that as a warning sign that I need to go back to the metaphorical drawing board and start again – look at their behaviour, and mine, and see what I can do differently. This might have to happen a few times until something works and changes but that is okay.

## Learning to be quiet

It is too easy to become too focused on 'doing' and forget 'being', and one of the greatest gifts we have when supporting autistic people is the gift of silence. I like to talk, I really do; however I have found a place of silence, which feels comfortable and even essential at times. Being with someone means focusing on how you feel, how they feel and letting the gaps between the words or sounds do the work.

All too often I am reminded of how important it is to be quiet when people I work with talk about how they shut down when a teacher repeatedly asked them a question, or they ended up being physically or verbally aggressive when constantly talked at by a parent or support worker. They are then the ones who end up with the blame and label of 'aggressive', 'rude' or 'stubborn'.

The autistic mind can all too easily become overwhelmed with words and noise; therefore, giving a person the mind space to think whilst you are with them will automatically help them feel less anxious, which will aid any work being done. The use of sounds and gestures, as discussed in other chapters in this book, show just how powerful the connection is when used, and alongside that are the gaps between those interactions. I watched my two-year-old nephew look to me for confirmation of how to respond after he fell over the other day. It was a small fall and one I knew wasn't serious. He immediately looked to me for confirmation and I sat quietly with a calm look on my face. In that moment he worked out for himself what he felt and when I didn't seem worried, it validated him. He got up and went back to playing. It then led me to think about the people I support and how important even a few seconds' thinking time is to allow us to process what is happening in our minds and bodies. When we are quietly supportive, it gives the brain more space to think about what is happening and how that individual feels. A five-year-old boy, who currently uses limited verbal communication, often experiences moments of frustration and anger when things aren't feeling right. Due to his limited vocabulary, it must be highly frustrating when things don't feel right in his mind or body. As he has grown and developed, I can see just how powerful it is when he becomes upset and I give him quiet support. I am in the room with him but let him work it out and connect with his body, rather than immediately trying to make it okay for him again. I want to give him the space to *feel*.

## Working examples

During my working life, working alongside autistic people, I have learnt a huge amount and have had the time to develop these ways of working I have discussed. I have asked permission from some of the people I work with to share their journey with you as working examples of why time, consistency, trust, support, hard work, care and patience work. Mark's story is one of patience and time, George's is one of adapting the working dynamic in order to teach and learn and Stuart's speaks of the importance of finding ways to communicate when an individual might not be ready to work on their sensory needs.

### Mark

One of the most complex situations I was asked to give my support to ended up being one of the most rewarding, challenging and educational.

Mark was a twelve-year-old boy who had recently begun to struggle to get to secondary school. He was becoming 'stuck'; his body had shut down so he was unable to get up or dressed to make it to school on time which was, as each day passed, becoming increasingly difficult for him. He was engaging in checking routines that had taken over even the simplest of tasks and his whole body was shutting down. On difficult days he was unable to get out of bed even to make it to the toilet. On other days, he would eventually make it out of bed (after sometimes hours of 'checking'), but getting dressed, personal care, even eating was too complex for him. I, like many other professionals involved, thought there must be something neurological happening to cause such a shutdown. However, numerous tests were performed and, over many, many months, he was given the all clear. Great for his health but leaving me scratching my head.

This shutdown continued for many further months until Mark started on a small dose of medication and we started to see a small change in him. He began talking in more detail about his checking and about wanting to make changes. This was what I thought was the beginning of our work. What I later realised was that our 'work' started months earlier when I would spend hours a week standing outside his bedroom listening to him talking about how he felt or putting my hand into the room to give him a focus point on the wall to look at to help with the checking. It was the hours we spent sitting on the stairs moving one step at a time, working on breathing and waiting whilst he had to start again and go back up to the top. All these small steps (although at the time it felt like we were getting nowhere) were actually building up our working relationship. I felt his frustration and freely gave my encouragement (if not verbally, through my actions). I gained an insight into just how tough each day was for him and how desperately he wanted things to be different. My patience was tested and tested but I wouldn't give up and Mark knew that. During that time, we would take one step forward and then a few back as each move forward was so exhausting for Mark it would often leave him bedbound for a few days which meant I had to learn how to pull back, wait and not rush him.

Mark wasn't able to process much feedback from his body so needed a guide during the early days. He spoke about how his body might have physically moved from his bedroom to the front room but he still felt like he was in the bedroom. He was experiencing some form of dissociation, so we looked at ways of helping him connect with his body through the use of tinted lenses in his glasses (these currently help him process walking up and down the stairs) and 'fidget' toys he could use to let him know when he was in a different room (a different toy for each room). When working on touching the front door, Mark would hold his breath which increased his anxiety. We had the idea to use a clicker (the type a doorman would use to know how many people had come into a venue) which I clicked to give him a guide of when to breath. This worked well as he followed each click and synced his breathing, bringing down his anxiety. These items gave him anchors to rely on until his confidence grew.

After finding the right medication Mark's anxiety was reduced just enough for the work we were doing to move forward. (N.B. I am not advocating the use of medication for all. For many people it is not the right pathway and for those where it is, it should not be used instead of one-to-one support; it should be used in conjunction with it.)

We started to build up a programme that Mark was in charge of and each session we worked on taking another step forward. I had to learn to be led by Mark and not put my own agenda on the metaphorical table. We spent hours talking about his interests to bring his anxiety levels down and helping him tidy his bedroom, working on letting go of old childhood toys he no longer needed so he could feel more like a young man, which boosted his self-confidence. We would use funny videos on YouTube to help relax him during difficult sessions, watching a video and then working on a task such as walking to the front door, video, then try again, and so on.

One of the most memorable days with Mark was the day he went out in the back garden. He had not been outside for nearly two years. We had spent weeks working on opening the back door without the need for checking routines and this day was the day he made the first steps outside. His anxiety was sky high but as soon as we opened the door and he smelt the outside air his whole body changed. He took a deep breath and relaxed his shoulders; a smile covered his face as the realisation that he had made it outside set in. I felt like I'd won the lottery.

To get to that point had taken three years of work, and what made it possible was that Mark knew he was safe with me but that it was him who was in charge. And now, any step forward is managed by Mark, so during the actual task we are subconsciously working on his self-esteem and sense of self. For Mark, feeling good enough is a big issue so it is paramount that he is able to take ownership of his achievements. He is more in tune with his body so can now communicate when he feels anxious and can tell me what sensations he is feeling, so we can work with them to help lower his anxiety.

## George

I was reminded of the power that can come with being open a few months ago when I was seeing George, a young lad I have been working with over six years. George is thirteen years old, very bright and inquisitive. I had recently gone through a breakup so was feeling a little less buoyant than usual. George picked up on this and asked me (somewhat uncharacteristically) if I was OK. The thought crossed my mind to give the tried and tested answer 'Yes' or 'I'm fine' but the sheer fact that he had asked me meant that he had picked up, possibly via subconscious transference, how I was feeling.

I went off script and told him that I was feeling a bit sad because my relationship had broken down. He looked worried and said 'I never know what to say when people tell me things like that', so we discussed how it was normal to feel like that and talked about possible answers he could give. We then went on to talk about other people's feelings and if we were responsible for them. I told him that he wasn't responsible for making me feel OK and that I was still there for him and that I would be OK once I had stopped feeling sad. It was a real turning point for George, as he was able to see that it was helpful to be honest about feelings and that I was a human being who got things wrong, felt strong emotions and had hard times too. He could relate and that made our working relationship stronger. If I had given my first answer of 'I'm fine' we would have missed out on that valuable learning experience for both of us. A few people I work with have talked about the confusion they experience when they pick up that someone might be feeling something only for them to report that they feel something completely different. This can leave them unsure of what they feel and mean they learn not to trust their instincts which can be damaging to self-esteem. It must be very confusing to try to understand and manage emotions in a world where many people try to cover them up.

A few weeks later he asked me '*Are you doing better now?*' to which I relied '*Yes, thank you for asking me*'. True understanding and care. Priceless.

Now, I'm not saying that this approach would be great for everyone. There are some people who would find my sadness incredibly overwhelming, so I would safeguard them from that as it wouldn't serve them to know. Again, adapting the way we interact and knowing intuitively what would best serve someone is key to gaining trust and being truly person centred.

## Stuart

I sat across the table from Stuart and looked at his tense body. For as long as I had known Stuart (around two years), he had always looked like this, uneasy in his body like he was just carrying it around and didn't really know what to do with it. Any attempt at talking about sensory needs was met with a blank response as he was unable to or didn't want to process what I was asking. Stuart has been experiencing periods of 'shutdown' for over six years and was currently unable to express why this was happening and what he was thinking about. He had many professionals working with him over the years and so far, they had been unable to find out what was going on for him.

Stuart had only been diagnosed as autistic after he had a breakdown when he was fourteen years old. Since that time he had stopped talking as much, eating had become a big problem and he needed prompting with most aspects of his daily routine. After working with him for a few weeks, I could see that talking therapy wasn't working, as he was finding processing my words too difficult (it was taking him sometimes as long as 15 minutes to answer a question and most answers were 'I don't know'). Over the two years I have worked with Stuart, we have tried many different approaches throughout his cycles as he is unable to talk when he is in a 'down' phase. So, we focus on practical activities such as cooking, baking or walking. Everyone involved in supporting Stuart just wants to know how to help him but as he is unable to vocalise his thoughts, we have to be patient and I have been working on building up our trust. Recently I have tried a new approach where we use an iPad to talk during our sessions, I type a question and Stuart answers in his own time. This is proving to be easier for him, and given the choice between typing and talking, he often chooses the former. I am hoping that over time he will be able to type out his thoughts and feelings, as he is an intelligent young man who seems to be fearful of the reactions of others, meaning that to vocalise thoughts can be incredibly frightening. Building up trust in me is key so he knows that whatever he says, he will not be judged by me.

One day during one of our regular sessions, something felt different. Stuart was in a good mood and his 'upward spiral' had been in effect for a few weeks. I said to him *'You look very tense in your body Stuart'*, and pointed to the area below my neck: *'you are breathing from here'*. I then took a deep breath and lifted my shoulders to my ears before dropping them down again as I exhaled, encouraging my body to go 'floppy'. I asked him if he could do that too. He thought about it silently, processed it and followed my actions perfectly. It was the first time I had seen his body relax and his face change. Simultaneously, tears sprang into my eyes as I felt such a feeling of relief. It wasn't relief that he had done what I had asked, it was more that I was feeling what he was feeling, which was wonderful. I held the tears in as I didn't want to overload Stuart with my emotions and take away from his moment, but they were there. This was a small drop in the ocean moving Stuart forward with his sensory understanding, but it was all he could do at that time.

It is clear to me that Stuart is struggling with his sensory system and has huge difficulties around knowing where his body is, gaining the appropriate feedback to carry out tasks (such as turning a tap on) and processing language.

Stuart is currently not in a place where he is able to process his sensory needs and to use the tools which could be of use to him to help his body relax. I must respect that and work hard to find ways to engage him which do not overload him, confuse him or make him feel pressured to change. Again, time and patience are key.

## Conclusion

As someone who spends a huge amount of time learning from autistic people, it is clear that if an individual is given time with a consistent support person who is there to support, learn and be patient, positive change will happen. We need to spend more time adapting our practices to meet the needs of an autistic person, rather than expecting them to fit into the services on offer. There needs to be a greater understanding of the amount of trauma so many autistic people are carrying and how that affects their ability to trust, change and learn. I have seen and felt first hand just what time and patience can give a person and why. Without it we will continue to see autistic children grow into autistic adults who have such ingrained and complex behaviours that they are unable to lead the lives they otherwise could do. The autism community deserves our time and patience. When those who can communicate to us what it feels like, looks like and thinks like are speaking we need to listen, because they hold the answers. We need to listen when someone tells us it hurts, or that they can't go outside, or that they are too scared to try out a new sensory support item that we know will help them. We need to continually keep evolving our practice to work with the high levels of anxiety caused by past trauma, so we can find new ways of supporting autistic people to try the things we think may help or to adapt their behaviours for them to lead lives that are not as exhausting.

Using our intuition when working alongside autistic people is incredibly powerful. By being quiet and calm and allowing space between words or actions, we are better able to work out what might best help someone. Spending time to help reduce an individual's anxiety and build their trust in us lays the foundation for learning and change. We can't learn and develop when we are in an anxious state. Spending time really getting to know a person, what their interests are, how they see the world and how they want to be a part of it creates a deeper understanding and allows us to see beyond the behaviours to the person, their experiences, beliefs and needs. What a privilege.

# Chapter 6: A one year Responsive Communication pilot project in Carmarthenshire

Kate Richardson

This chapter shares insights gained from providing a Responsive Communication service to autistic children and young people in rural south-west Wales. At the outset, the challenge was to design a way of working together with families that was sufficiently robust to hold the fluid, organic nature of Responsive Communication, yet flexible enough to support autistic individuals in the context of their family lives.

The key to getting this balance right was co-production – to work in partnership with the parents and children whom we wished to support. Specifically, co-production meant being receptive to and actively responding to the parents' ideas.

For the service to work, let alone be successful, we knew we had to take time to listen to parents' experiences, to work in partnership with families and to remain flexible throughout the pilot project. It was important that we listened to the families and gave priority to what they needed us to be, thereby building a trusting relationship that would allow us – practitioners, parents and children – to be equal partners in the service delivery process. For the service to have any chance of creating positive outcomes for autistic children and young people, it was essential that parents felt heard and felt safe enough to reflect openly on the communication and the dynamics within their family.

The service was provided by a project co-ordinator and two Responsive Communication practitioners – the author (a speech and language therapist) and Angela Lane (a parent practitioner). The partnership between the practitioners was fundamental to the success of the project. Angela shared with us her personal experience of being a parent of a child with disabilities. Cherry, Angela's thirty-year-old daughter, although not physically with us during the project, nonetheless had a significant presence. Over the course of their shared journey, Cherry and Angela have found their own way to Responsive Communication. Throughout the project, Angela shared numerous insights into her and Cherry's experience of using Responsive Communication. Angela offered parents in the project warmth, empathy, understanding, creativity and first-hand knowledge. Her experience of using a variety of services over the last thirty years was an important element in the design of our project – we were committed to creating a service delivery model that was different, something that 'fitted' families and recognised that families are all unique and all different.

Mainstream autism service provision typically takes an impairment-based approach – the practitioner looks at the difficulties the individual is having and focuses on those difficulties. Many interventions seek to 'change' the individual or to get the individual to do more or less of a given behaviour. Typical targets for an autistic child may include, for example, working towards increased eye contact or working towards increased joint attention skills.

Responsive Communication seeks neither to change the individual nor to modify their behaviour. Rather, it takes a holistic, systemic approach that aims to reduce the individual's distress and to support meaningful social and emotional engagement between the individual and those around them. Responsive Communication considers the autistic individual in their varied environments and seeks to modify those environments in order to maximise the individual's opportunities to flourish in all aspects of their relationships and wider life.

Stakeholder consultations confirmed our instinct that the most effective way to support autistic children and young people was to place the family at the heart of service delivery. Each unique child is part of their own unique family. Understanding and embracing the complexity and dynamic nature of the relationships and the circumstances of *that* family is crucial to supporting *that* child. When supporting an autistic child, we work with the family to create an environment in which the child and the other family members can connect with each other responsively, in a way that reduces distressed behaviour and creates opportunities for improved well-being for everybody. When you take a systemic approach, you support the family to make choices and changes that feel achievable within the context of the dynamics and capacity of that particular family, at that particular time. You are responding to the lived reality of that family.

A child may respond well to a given approach, but if the approach does not sit comfortably within the structure and context of the child's family, then it is unlikely to become embedded in the culture of the family. We did not want to simply 'provide a service' to families – there one day, gone the next. Rather, we wanted to meet the family and to engage with them as individuals. We wanted the family to *own* the Responsive Communication approach, to explore it in their own context and to feel confident and empowered enough in the approach to advocate for its use across contexts.

Equally, we did not want Responsive Communication to be 'yet another approach' the family had tried and then felt they had failed at. If a particular approach is not adopted by a child or their family, then it is simply not the right approach for them. Over the course of our project in Carmarthenshire, several parents told us they felt judged or responsible when there were difficulties with their child's communication or behaviour management. We had a number of parents on the project who were trying so hard to stimulate their child's language development that the child at times would become overwhelmed and go into 'shutdown' or 'meltdown' as a consequence. By supporting the parent to accept that is it *okay* simply to be a mum or dad, that they do not need to be teacher, therapist and parent all rolled in to one, you give back to the parent some of the power to trust their own intuition and judgement once more. We supported parents to recognise that 'pauses' and 'silences' are good, that they create opportunities for their child to regulate and find their own voice.

An infant's ability to self-regulate is influenced by interactions with their caregivers, and vice versa, a process known as co-regulation. By the same token, all of us, autistic and neurotypical alike, affect and are affected by the regulatory state of those around us. We wanted our project to nurture and support parents, given that a reduction in parental distress would in turn positively influence the child's regulation. Knowledge and understanding of their child's sensory and communicative behaviours is a key part of this. If the parent is supported to understand sensory processing and the way that their child's sensory distress can express itself via the child's behaviour, then the parent begins to have the capacity to respond to their child's behaviours with greater empathy and compassion. With this knowledge and understanding of sensory processes, the parent is able to reflect on the possible causes of their child's distress. In turn, the parent feels more confident to identify and experiment with ways of addressing the triggers for the behaviour or, alternatively, to offer more appropriate support. One parent on our project commented: '*I feel closer to him as I try to look for reasons behind behaviours. I feel more tolerant and accepting of his actions. I want to be with him more.*'

Responsive Communication supports co-regulation in a number of ways: by attending to and supporting sensory regulation, by responding to the child by staying with them in the moment, by empathising with the child non-verbally using the child's own 'language', and by accepting and validating the child's emotional expression. The significance of responding empathetically cannot be overestimated.

The importance of co-regulation was highlighted by a number of parents in their post-project evaluations, completed around two months after service delivery. Parents reported positive changes in their own regulation, some explicitly making the link between their own well-being and the associated impact on the child. Parents commented:

'[the project] *has given us more understanding of [our son's] needs which has made us more relaxed which is definitely reflected in him*';

'[it] *has made our home life calmer which has enabled her to be calmer*';

'[the project] *has had a big impact because if [my son] is calm and relaxed, that affects everyone else in the family*'.

Likewise, a reduction in distressed behaviours in the child has a positive influence on the parent's well-being. One parent wrote: '[he] *is happier, then I am less worried*'.

The majority of the families we supported experienced some degree of isolation in their daily lives – not just the autistic child or their parents, but the whole family. Autistic children may experience isolation for a number of reasons, whether because of their distressed behaviours, sensory processing difficulties, reduced communication skills or their reduced ability to connect with or tolerate being with others in their immediate family, or indeed beyond it. Parents often feel alone in their situation; they feel different to other parents who have neurotypically developing children. Parents feel judged by professionals as well as by their community and wider society. Working parents, typically fathers, often feel too little involved in caring for and making decisions regarding their child, not least because the parent is often unable to attend appointments with services or professionals. Single parents, being the sole carer for their autistic child, often feel isolated and alone. Siblings feel different to and isolated from their peer groups, often because they are informal carers or because they feel responsible for their parents' well-being. Grandparents, at a time in their lives when they may have their own health concerns, often provide childcare when parents separate or when there is unexpected change such as a bereavement or loss of household income, or simply because the parents are unable to cope.

In addition to recognising the impact of isolation, we also needed to account for the complexity of people's lives. The families we worked with on our project in Carmarthenshire were extremely varied – we supported undiagnosed and diagnosed autistic parents, parents who had more than one child with autism, parents and children with complex epilepsy, mental health difficulties, self-injurious behaviours and additional health needs. We supported parents who lack literacy skills and struggled to access information about their child's condition and needs; we supported families experiencing poverty and families experiencing relationship breakdown and bereavement. By taking an open, holistic approach to working with families, we create a space in which such complexity can be articulated and accounted for and the associated emotional experiences validated.

For families and individuals, our model of service delivery had to be flexible, meaningful and effective. For us as service providers, it had to be affordable as well as logistically manageable. As practitioners and as an organisation, we wanted to be able to acknowledge the impact of isolation and the complexity of participants' lives. We wanted to provide meaningful support to families as a whole, as well as to the autistic family member.

The service delivery model we designed following consultation with parents and professionals took the form of working with six autistic children per month over the course of a three-day weekend. Over the project's one-year duration, we therefore aimed to support six different families each month. On the first day of service delivery, we brought together six parents of autistic children.[1] This day included getting to know each other and introducing the parents to the key features of Responsive Communication. Over the next day and a half, each family received a half-day home visit from either Angela or the author, in order to spend time with the child and the wider family and to explore using Responsive Communication. The parents were lent a camera to record interactions with their child. On the final afternoon, we came together as a group again and the parents shared the films they had recorded over the weekend.

We worked hard to ensure that compassion, acceptance and responsiveness were at the heart of both project design and delivery. We were acutely aware of the negative experiences a number of our families had had in their attempts to engage with services. As such, we wanted to ensure that when a parent took the leap of faith to participate in our project, we nurtured them and created a space where they felt acknowledged, supported and safe. We wanted the parents and their children to feel seen and heard and for their emotional experiences to be acknowledged and validated. One parent wrote:

'*I feel more "connected" with* [my daughter] *and have a better understanding of her behaviour. I also feel I have been listened to and although there is no magic wand, practical and useful suggestions have been made which are realistic to implement and so I feel I am doing something to help* [my daughter].'

For many parents, it was no small thing to be invited to 'open up' their lives to us by talking about their child and their family situation, to have a practitioner in their home, to film interactions with their child and for these recordings to be shared and discussed with other parents. Therefore it was essential that we as practitioners created and 'held' a safe space for this kind of service to be delivered safely and effectively. One parent wrote: '*Participating in the project means opening up and leaving yourself very vulnerable with other people you don't know initially. I think our group gelled and was facilitated really well*'.

1 When there was more than one child with autism in the family, the group was smaller as that parent was representing more than one of their children.

Towards creating a nurturing and safe environment, we ensured that the first day of service delivery had a relaxed pace and that there was space for each caregiver to introduce themselves and to talk freely and openly about their autistic child and what life was like in the family home. Taking the time to find out about each other, having an informal atmosphere and sharing meals together all played a significant part in creating the safe space, a 'pause' in the participants' life in which they were given the opportunity to step back and reflect and to reach out to others who could empathise with aspects of their situation.

Diversity was a feature of each group and, through careful facilitation, this diversity became a strength. Whatever their background and circumstances, each parent felt heard and able to contribute. Each month there were animated reflections and exchanges of ideas. The unifying effect of being part of a shared experience, and parents supporting and accepting each other despite their disparate backgrounds were, together, very powerful. Parents made open, candid revelations and shared experiences of joy as well as of pain, confusion and loss. Without exception, parents reported that being part of the group was a positive experience. Parents offered each other mutual support, advice, comfort and care. There were many tears in the groups but often even more laughter as individuals shared and reflected on their experiences. One parent wrote, *'invaluable experience being able to talk with parents who understand, and not having to constantly explain yourself was refreshing'*.

Sharing film clips with the other parents in their group and accepting each other's observations and reflections gave participants increased confidence in using Responsive Communication and also affirmed and strengthened their perception of themselves as capable, loving parents. Deep connections were made between individuals in groups. Some connections have carried over beyond the confines of the group as well as between groups, whether by arranging to meet up or via the closed social media groups that we set up for participants.

Although working professionally, Angela and I were very much ourselves. We both felt it was important for these families to meet someone they could connect with and trust. Autistic children are often 'open to' a number of professionals whom the parent might see on short, infrequent visits, if at all. Parents often report feeling 'invisible' to services. We wanted to be present and accessible to parents and for them to trust us enough to let us see their family in all its complexity. One of the greatest strengths of this project has been the development of these positive working relationships between parents and practitioners.

On the morning of day one of the service delivery, during the introductions that each parent gave about their child and their family life, Angela and I listened, but did not offer any comments or suggestions. This was important in many ways, in particular to ensure that the parent felt held and heard by the group. Our 'holding stance' allowed parents to share their ideas and experiences and offer support to each other. After these extended and often emotional introductions, Angela and I presented the concepts underpinning Responsive Communication. It was during this 'teaching' phase that parents began to ask questions about the approach in relation to their own child. This was hugely significant. The parent, rather than the practitioner, was more often than not the one to say, 'Do you think that might be why my child does this?'. It was during these times that Angela and I could respond and offer further interpretations or hypotheses of why their child may present in a certain way, or support the parent to explore these. Working in this way means that the parents are not passive recipients of information, nor are they having yet another 'professional' telling them what to do. Working responsively places the parent firmly in the driving seat in using this new lens through which to observe and begin to understand and interpret their child's behaviours and the family context in which they occur.

When we use Responsive Communication, we explicitly acknowledge that the parent is the one who knows their child best – the parent is the expert. We start from the premise that the parent needs to 'own' understanding and interpreting their child's communicative invitations and behaviours. When the parent then goes on to share their learning with other significant people in the child's life, the parent 'owns' these ideas and interpretations and has intuited them themselves at first hand. The parent understands and can explain what they are advocating for their child and they impart this knowledge with greater confidence and conviction than if a professional had simply told them the information. One parent commented:

'*We are a unique unit in the home, as it is just my daughter and I, so things are very* [my daughter] *friendly. It* [the project] *has improved my awareness which has added to our relationship. She will say "you understand me Mummy, other people don't". The wider family have benefitted from my knowledge which has had a positive impact on* [my daughter].'

Working in this way supports the parent to have more confidence in their own intuition and ideas. In so many of the cases we worked with over the course of the project, parents had felt not listened to, dismissed, blamed for their child's behaviour or simply not believed. Parents who participated in our project told us that, after the service delivery, they felt bolder and more empowered to take the next step in the journey, inspired anew to support their child. Similarly, a head teacher commented to me how she noticed a change in the parents who had participated in the project.

Conceptualising Responsive Communication as a disposition, a way of being and responding, rather than a set of learnt techniques, created space for the flexible interpretation that was necessary in order to meet each child's and family's needs during the pilot project. We offered parents an alternative paradigm through which to view and understand their child's behaviours and motivations.

As an approach, Responsive Communication is dynamic and flexible enough to be used with children of widely differing presentations and capacities. Indeed, the strength of Responsive Communication lies in its flexibility and its capacity to respond to individual circumstances and the way that these change over time. Despite our initial idea to work solely with non-verbal or minimally verbal children, it soon became apparent that there were children 'across the spectrum' who might benefit from the service we were providing. Parents of autistic children who are proficient in using speech to communicate tend to find it difficult to access any statutory support as their child does not have a learning disability in addition to their autism. In this way, more able autistic children may fall between two stools and receive little or no support at all. The principles of Responsive Communication are to acknowledge and respond to the individual's sensory experience (by removing or reducing sources of sensory stress whilst increasing those sensory inputs that are experienced as positive), and to respond to the individual using their 'own language' (their body language and/or verbal or organic utterances), all the time acknowledging and responding to the emotional affect behind the communication or physical expression.

Through participation in our project, parents have developed skills to 'read' their child's 'own language', however that may be expressed – whether as silence, self-imposed isolation, loudly and physically, as self-harm or in the need to be in close and constant contact with their caregiver (to name but a few). This 'reading' of their child's body language may not provide all the answers, but nonetheless the parents are now analysing their child's behaviour and looking for the motivations behind it, rather than simply responding to a behaviour, as may have been the case previously.

In order to illustrate this further, I should like to introduce Linda and Nia. Nia was thirteen when she took part in the project. She has Down's syndrome and a diagnosis of autism and is a non-verbal communicator. Nia finds it challenging to be directed, to concentrate and to complete tasks. She can get frustrated and upset and can show distressed behaviours. As she is non-verbal, Nia uses behaviour as a means of communication. Services working with Nia can find it difficult to figure out how best to support her.

After the initial morning of introductions and the Responsive Communication exposition, Linda and I went to her home to spend time with Nia. As Nia does not respond well to direction but loves dressing up, I hid my sensory resources (Squease pressure vest, vibrating hand massager, wobble cushion etc) under a pile of dressing up clothes. When Nia discovered the hand massager, I showed her how to switch it on. I used Responsive Communication throughout our interaction, responding to Nia's vocalisations and validating her emotional affect. At one point, having first sought her permission by the use of gesture, I placed the vibrating hand massager on Nia's foot and she looked pleasantly surprised by the sensation. Nia explored applying the vibration on other parts of her body. After applying the massager to her foot again, Nia then indicated for her mother to take her boots off. Then Nia took her mother's socks off and applied the massager to her mother's feet. As I was the one who had initially placed the massager on Nia's foot, Nia then wanted me to place the massager on her mother's foot. It was clear that Nia had experienced something that was meaningful to her and had enjoyed it and she wanted her mother to have exactly the same experience.

Linda and I discussed this exchange later. During the exchange, Linda had thought to herself, 'well done Nia, lovely turn-taking' (turn-taking being a skill that is supposedly under-developed in autistic people and that professionals often look for and seek to promote). However, by instinctively and understandably homing in on the turn-taking aspect of the exchange, as professionals will tend to do, Linda missed the opportunity to consider other, more holistic interpretations of the exchange. When we considered the exchange again, I proposed a possible alternative interpretation, namely that Nia was showing empathy towards her mother. The following day (day three of the service delivery, the reflection and evaluation workshop), Linda shared with the other parents in the group her belief that Nia had shown more than empathy: it was an expression of love. Nia had had this meaningful experience which she wanted her mother, the one she loves, to experience in the exact same way as she had done. Linda reflected on several previous interactions with Nia and now intuited an emotional content to these interactions which she had previously not discerned.

Another example of Nia's desire to share her experience occurred later in the home visit. Nia, who was exploring wearing a swimsuit, on top of a floaty fluorescent pink top, on top of her trousers and jumper, was enjoying the sensation of the tight clothes as she bent herself double and looked at her feet and touched the grass. After experiencing this fun sensation herself, Nia clearly wanted her mother and me to experience it too. So, full of laughter, she consciously and deliberately linked arms with us and we all bent double repeatedly.

Nia kept the swimsuit on over her clothes for at least thirty minutes, then it was removed for her to take a comfort break, but she wanted to put it on again straight afterwards. Nia appeared to enjoy having the pressure sensation of the tight swimming costume worn over her clothes. This tightness would have provided her with a meaningful proprioceptive input, in the form of deep pressure, in much the same way as a pressure vest does.

The children we supported over the course of the project consistently provided us with clues or pointers regarding their sensory and emotional needs. What is important is that we 'see' and reflect on the child's behaviours and then offer hypotheses as to the motivation behind these behaviours. When we look at Nia's behaviours through a sensory processing lens, we see that there are many instances when she is doing the best she can to regulate herself by seeking proprioceptive inputs, for example by stamping her feet, pushing into other people's bodies, leaning on family members whilst pulling their arms around her, hitting out or pushing over heavy dustbins. Whilst it is undoubtedly the case that Nia uses some of these behaviours in order to communicate a need, they also clearly provide her with meaningful sensory input that contributes to Nia feeling more regulated and more embodied.

To illustrate this, I noticed during my home visit that Nia often spits. This type of behaviour is typically interpreted as being directed at the person on the receiving end, i.e. as having a primarily communicative motivation. However, when Nia is alone in her tent in the living room, she continues to spit, which supports the interpretation that Nia spits primarily to meet a sensory need rather than as a means of communication. When you spit in the way that Nia does, it provides increased proprioceptive sensation in your lips and cheeks but also in your chest and diaphragm. As a result of providing Nia with opportunities to experience increased proprioceptive input orally (using sensory chews or sucking drink through a straw, for example), she now spits less frequently. Similarly, wearing a compression top, for example, will give Nia increased proprioceptive input to her chest and diaphragm. During the home visit, Nia's mother and I discussed how providing a variety of opportunities for proprioceptive inputs throughout the day would support Nia to experience longer periods of sensory 'peace'.

When we take an 'autism from the inside-out'[2] stance and begin to consider behaviour from the perspective of the autistic child, a variety of different interpretations become available to us as practitioners and as parents. Equally, an 'autism from the inside-out' stance will foreground the child's skills rather than any putative 'deficits'. For example, think of Nia enjoying the foot massage. Her desire to share that experience with her mother and then making it happen required Nia to undertake significant and complex ideation and planning. Nia had to indicate what she wanted to do to her mother, to manipulate her mother's foot and begin to take off her mother's boots and then her socks. Nia had to apply the massager to her mother's foot and then get me to apply the massager in her stead. Nia needed to consider her mother's and my perspectives in order to orchestrate our involvement in her plan.

Trusting that the child knows what they are doing and that the child is doing their best to cope was a core concept during the project. When viewing their child's behaviour in terms of how 'deviant' it is from 'the norm', parents can struggle to see or appreciate any logic behind the child's behaviour. It is not necessarily logic on a conscious level; rather the child is doing what they need

2 Williams D (1996) *Autism – An Inside Out Approach*. London: Jessica Kingsley Publishers.

to do to be 'okay' in a given situation. For example, one child we worked with always straps his body in several belts. He would not be able to tell us his reasons for doing this any more than he could explain his drive to continuously bounce on the sofas – nonetheless in both cases he is not being 'naughty', he is simply doing his best to gain the sensory inputs he needs in order to regulate himself. By participating in the project, both he and his parents were able to understand the physiological need that drove him to do these things. We addressed this boy's need for proprioceptive stimuli by giving him the Squease pressure vest to put on, at which point he simply said he felt 'safe'.

Another boy, Lucas, showed me most clearly how movement, the need to move and obtain active proprioceptive input, can have a direct impact on cognition and the ability to complete a task. Lucas was eight when he and his mother, Sara, took part in our project. Lucas was minimally verbal and attended an autism unit attached to a mainstream primary school. At the time of referral, Sara described their feelings of '*helplessness as a family unit*', given the distress which Lucas was experiencing because of his communication difficulties.

Lucas is highly motivated by his Lego and is very good at following the often complicated instructions that come with his Lego kits. During my home visit, I observed that Lucas was unable to concentrate on his Lego for more than a minute before he would run off, making vocalisations and bouncing. When he returned to the Lego, he remained very still and concentrated intensely for a short period of time before he needed to run, bounce and vocalise again. Lucas's mother reported that he regularly ran circuits between the kitchen and living areas and the interconnecting spaces. Whilst on the move, Lucas does present in a heightened state of arousal. However, there is a marked change in his state of arousal when he stops moving and returns to his Lego. He becomes calm and alert and is able to focus and follow the next instructions.

This account graphically illustrates the relationship between, on the one hand, Lucas's physiological need to see sensory stimulus, and, on the other, his ability to focus on the Lego that he is motivated to build. It shows clearly the role that proprioception plays in supporting cognition and emotional and sensory regulation. When she considered Lucas's behaviours in these terms, Sara saw his running, bouncing and vocalising in a different light and so was able to respond accordingly. Similarly, viewing Lucas's repetitive behaviours through a sensory lens, Sara stated '*I am not so desperate to stop them. Lucas recognises this and is less frustrated with me*'. Sara reported that there has been a reduction in Lucas's distressed behaviours because she 'understands more' and so is 'calmer and less demanding'.

Lucas had high anxiety levels, in part because he was trying to respond to parental demands. Sara was trying so hard to support Lucas to develop speech that she was not allowing herself to simply be with Lucas. On the recommendation of professionals, she had been trying to stimulate Lucas's language. However, prior to taking part in our project, Sara had not understood the impact that her attempts to stimulate his language were having on Lucas. Just as Lucas needed to regulate himself through movement and vocalisation in order to be able to follow the relatively complex Lego instructions, he also needed to regulate himself to be able to process his mother's spoken language and understand her task demands. It was difficult for Sara to reduce the amount of spoken language she was using with Lucas, a common theme for many of the parents we supported. Parents are anxious to avoid any silences and, in their sustained attempts to teach their child and to support the child's learning and development, parents are often unwilling to 'take their foot off the pedal' in case the child stalls in their learning or, worse, regresses. It took courage on Sara's part to let go of her expectations of Lucas and to allow for silences and to respond to Lucas's non-verbal communication by using his 'own language'.

When Sara returned for the reflection and evaluation workshop on day three of the service delivery, she brought with her the film she had recorded and was excited to show it to the group. In the film, Sara succeeds, silently and calmly, in using Lucas's 'own language' and in responding to the emotional affect behind his presentation. Lucas is calm and better able to attend. He actively takes his mother's hand and pulls it towards him to invite her to continue playing with him. One year on from the service delivery, Lucas has blossomed, he is calmer, less distressed and has begun to use language to communicate. Sara reports that the project has had *'a huge impact on our well-being as a family –* [we] *are able to enjoy and relax more'*.

By reducing the use of spoken language, reducing demands and expectations on the child, and by using non-verbal communication, we go some way towards taking take the pressure out of interactions. In turn, this opens up opportunities for acceptance, connection and joy. One parent reported, '[my daughter] *seems a lot happier to share her space and let you join in with her*', whilst another commented *'I find that* [my daughter] *is interacting more and is a lot happier when interacting*'. The received wisdom that autistic individuals do not want to communicate can blind us to the interactive intent underpinning many children's behaviours.

When we broaden our understanding of what communication is so as to encompass the rich variety of non-verbal expression, we begin to notice more and more invitations to connect. It may be a small gesture, barely noticeable. A look, a flick of a finger, leaning in towards someone. One parent reported that, since taking part in the project, '[my son] *is trying harder to communicate*'. One girl on the project was lying under an upturned chair when I arrived, and she stayed there. Interpreting this as her telling me she was not ready to interact or to acknowledge my presence yet, I spoke instead to her mother. The girl tapped the chair. I responded using her rhythm, tapping the chair in return, while continuing to chat with her mother. The girl and I exchanged a series of taps and, when she was ready, she came out from under the chair and began to openly interact with me. On a different home visit, a boy, hidden under a blanket from head to toe, was using an app on his iPad to make animal noises. Much to his and his mother's amusement, I responded to the animal sounds as if they were an invitation to communicate with him. After a while, the blanket was slowly removed and the boy began to interact with me directly rather than via his iPad.

By using Responsive Communication and acknowledging and responding to the gamut of communication invitations offered by the autistic child, the parent confirms and validates that expression. When we are validated and feel 'seen' and 'heard' by our communication partners, this feeds into our sense of self and has a positive impact on our well-being. One parent reported, '*I think he feels that he is not on his own. That someone "gets him"*'.

In addition, Responsive Communication can bring about a change in how the parent views their child and how they view spending time with their child, especially with a non-verbal child. Responsive Communication offers the parent a way in, a means of connecting with their child in a way that they may not have been able to do for a long time, if ever. One parent wrote:

*'It's made me look at him and his quirks with fresh eyes. It has made me revisit ideas I've had in the past and made me want to 'try again' […]. Overall, it's made me feel closer to him and I generally feel more loving towards him.'*

Responsive Communication has been understood, embraced and adapted by each family to meet their own particular needs. The approach has yielded positive outcomes for every child and family that participated in the project. For some parents, it entailed nothing more than a shift in perception leading to greater understanding and tolerance. For others, it has transformed the way in which family members interact, leading to improvements in well-being for the autistic child as well as for their siblings and parents. A year on from the relatively short, three-day input that the pilot project provided, the families continue to benefit from having taken part. Phoebe Caldwell describes Responsive Communication as like planting a seed, in that positive outcomes for the individual and their family continue to grow and multiply. One mother reported:

*'Once you learn a better way of communicating with your child and reinforcing your child's form of communication, there is no turning back. It strengthens the bond. Even though my daughter is verbal, I still benefitted hugely from this course'*.

Nia's mother, Linda, describes her family's participation in the Responsive Communication pilot project as 'pivotal in our relationship and really helped me develop a closer bond and understanding of Nia'. Sara describes herself as '*genuinely a different person*' having taken part in the project. Gaining knowledge and understanding of sensory processing has equipped parents with the tools to reflect on and better understand their child's behaviour. Many parents have deepened their understanding by reading and researching, building on the foundations that the project gave them. Parents, more self-confident and benefitting from peer support, are better able to advocate for their child's sensory needs. One mother of an autistic toddler wrote, '*I feel more confident about taking* [my daughter] *out and about in public places, as I feel more confident in dealing with her "meltdowns"*'. By embracing the principles of Responsive Communication, parents have found the confidence to trust their instincts and to respond intuitively and creatively to their child's communication rather than relying solely on speech.

# Chapter: 7: A psychiatrist's perspective on Responsive Communication

Dr Elspeth Bradley

## Introduction (including some words about terminology)

I am a psychiatrist and my specialty is in understanding, assessing and treating mental distress in individuals with intellectual and developmental disabilities and autism (for short I refer to intellectual and developmental disabilities as IDD and autism as ASD). As a medical doctor and psychiatrist (often working as one member of the mental health team), I am asked to evaluate what may be giving rise to such distress; in particular whether the cause may be a medical or psychiatric condition, a combination of both, or something completely different.

People with IDD or ASD suffer broadly the same range of medical and mental health problems during their lives as those without; and like anyone else when referred to medical and psychiatric services for assessment and treatment, they become known as patients. Unfortunately, in the past many with IDD or ASD lived in institutions and were referred to as patients even though they did not have any medical or psychiatric concerns. This was wrong. An additional confusion is that developmental conditions such as IDD or ASD continue to be included within current classifications of mental disorders (e.g. ICD-11, DSM-5). This is problematic on several counts: from a service perspective there are fundamental differences between atypicalities in development and psychiatric disorders; many with IDD and ASD understandably also find this inclusion inappropriate and unacceptable. Individuals with IDD or ASD, as for those without IDD or ASD, may or may not have mental distress, or diagnosable psychiatric disorder and may or may not have other medical conditions. In the context of being a physician providing medical/psychiatric care to patients, and in the spirit of inclusion, participation and equal rights, in this chapter I refer to individuals with IDD or ASD as being 'patients' only when referencing those with health conditions accessing health services.

## Boxes to support text

In order to maintain clarity and the gentle flow of ideas in my writing in this chapter, I have confined more complex, technical or difficult (in so far as the science is still being worked out) information to boxes; some readers may find this additional detail helpful as it supports content and concepts described.

# Responsive Communication

Responsive Communication involves three interlocking fundamentals. First, the use of body language and non-verbal articulations to engage with the affective state of another person (an approach known as Intensive Interaction), second, attention to sensory issues and third, supporting an environment for that individual that minimises the negative impact of any sensory concerns.[1] Importantly, Responsive Communication gives voice to the success of combining the use of body language to communicate, with attention to sensory difficulties. Finding optimal ways of engaging with individuals suffering mental distress and attending to the impact of environments on their mental well-being are also central to good psychiatric practice. These three fundamentals of Responsive Communication will now be explored further from this clinical practice perspective, working with people with IDD and ASD.

## Intensive Interaction and the use of body language to engage affectively

### Intensive Interaction and the therapeutic relationship

Intensive Interaction is a way of working with, and supporting, individuals who are nonverbal but also those who are fully verbal but find it difficult to keep up with the flow of conversation. For example, Donna Williams, a very accomplished adult with autism who spoke four languages, still said that she found it hard to keep up with the give and take of dialogue and that when she heard one of her own non-verbal sounds, it was like being thrown a life-belt in a stormy sea. Highlighting emotional engagement through body language, Intensive Interaction offers psychiatrists a way to align themselves with the affective state of individuals with IDD or ASD, thus optimising the therapeutic relationship with patients who may otherwise be hard to reach. The emotional valence (Box 1) of this engagement, whether warm or more distant, provides the psychiatrist with a measure of the patient's affect – i.e. their emotions communicated through body language – in the absence of the patient being able to speak directly about their feelings and emotions.

1 The Caldwell Autism Foundation (2019) *Responsive Communication* [online]. Available at http://thecaldwellautismfoundation.org.uk/index.php/responsive-communication/ (accessed March 2019).

We are born into the world seeking social and emotional connection with others.[2,3,4,5] Before verbal language develops, infants spontaneously engage in reciprocal conversations in the language of babble and body movements with their primary care provider and with each other.[6] The baby sets up expectations in this dialogue and when mother stops her involvement by withdrawing contingent vocalisations and facial expressions, instead remaining quiet and flat faced, the baby becomes exceptionally distressed (Beebe's 'chase and dodge').[7] In observing, as well as listening to these dialogues, it is clear that the baby's behaviour and physiological state are being co-regulated with that of the mother's. Through these early and ongoing exchanges, the baby is learning how to self-regulate in the presence of the calming other, as well as learning about specific facial expressions and vocal tones that will be recognised as calming (or otherwise) in later relationships. These baby observations can inform the therapeutic work of psychiatrists supporting patients for whom communication based on language or symbolic representations may be absent or significantly diminished.

Rhythm and pattern, key elements in body language, are recognised early in infants, perhaps related to the plethora and integration of sounds, vibrations, and rhythms experienced by the baby in utero, linked to their own and their mother's physiological homeostatic regulation (such as heart beat, respiration and respiratory heart beat regulation). We may not always be consciously aware of our heart beat or breathing patterns, and are totally unaware of the phasic pulsations continuously permeating our body tissues, but all are contributing to our felt physiological state, our felt sense of self. Tuning into the physiology of our bodies, for example tuning into our breathing pattern and those of our patients, as a portal to bring down heightened states of arousal (which are typically accompanied by increases in breathing and heart rate), may help the patient back into their recognised comfort zone (physiological homeostasis) and with this their felt sense of safety (Box 2).

Essentially the same approach (although using alternative titles, 'Adaptive Interaction' and 'Validation Therapy'), Intensive Interaction has been used

2 Stern DN (1985) *The Interpersonal World of the Infant: A view from psychoanalysis and developmental psychology.* Basic Books: New York.

3 Trevarthen C (2016) Pre-birth to three: Professor Colwyn Trevarthen – Relationships. Available at: https://www.youtube.com/watch?v=2kJI6G35TNk (accessed March 2019).

4 Trevarthen C and Delafield-Butt JT (2017) Intersubjectivity in the imagination and feelings of the infant: Implications for education in the infant. In: EJ White and C Dalli (Eds) *Under-Three Year Olds in Policy and Practice* (pp.17–39). New York: Springer.

5 Zeedyk MS (2008) *Promoting Social Interaction for Individuals with Communicative Impairments: Making contact.* London: Jessica Kingsley Publishers.

6 Talking Twin Babies. Available at: https://www.youtube.com/watch?v=_JmA2ClUvUY (accessed March 2019).

7 Beebe B (2014) My journey in infant research and psychoanalysis: microanalysis, a social microscope. *Psychoanalytic Psychology* **31** (1) 4–25.

with adults with dementia who no longer have speech.[8,9,10] Ellis and Astell identified the unique communicative repertoire of adults with late stage dementia and no functional speech by observing the details of their eye contact, facial expressions, speech, sounds made, gesture, imitation and turn taking, at baseline. In subsequent planned encounters with the researchers, these movements, patterns and sounds were mirrored back to the adult when they occurred. These mirrored patterns were recognised by the adults, but now experienced them coming from the outside (rather than generated internally by them), therefore engaging their attention with the researcher and opening up further opportunities for reciprocal interactions. The study demonstrated that an Adaptive Interaction approach supported and promoted shared communication in adults who had lost speech consequent to dementia, and also demonstrated their continued desire to communicate (increased eye contact, laughter, and other vocalisations during the planned encounters compared to baseline) when given the opportunity.

Davies *et al* trained young volunteers to use Intensive Interaction in their work with severely deprived children in a Romanian orphanage.[11] All volunteers reported positive changes in their engagement with the children under their care, including increase in child attention to them, increased positive affect displayed by the child, and increased flexibility and ease in interactions; the latter permitted spontaneous creation of new games and routines. All but one of the 12 volunteers spontaneously reported on the ways Intensive Interaction had positively changed their relationship with the children; volunteers' motivation and commitment intensified once they felt they had established a bond with the children.

Residential care givers trained in Adaptive Interaction working in dementia services also reported mutual benefit when they used this approach with the adults with dementia in their care and families spontaneously commented on the positive changes they noticed in their family member.[12]

We are learning from these research studies and baby observations that verbal language and symbolic representation are not essential for communication and emotional connectedness, either before language develops or even after it has

8 Ellis M, Astell A and Scott S (2018) *Adaptive Interaction and Dementia: How to communicate without speech*. London: Jessica Kingsley Publishers.

9 Gladys Wilson and Naomi Feil (2009) Available at: https://www.youtube.com/watch?v=CrZXz10FcVM (accessed March 2019).

10 Feil N (2015) TEDx Talk: *Validation, communication through empathy.* Available at https://www.youtube.com/watch?v=ESqfW_kyZq8 (accessed March 2019).

11 Davies CE, Zeedyk MS, Walls S, Betts N and Parry S (2008) Using imitation to establish channels of communication with institutionalised children in Romania: bridging the gap. In: MS Zeedyk (Ed) *Promoting Social Interaction for Individuals with Communicative Impairments: Making contact* (pp. 84–101). London: Jessica Kingsley Publishers.

12 Ellis M, Astell A and Scott S (2018) *Adaptive Interaction and Dementia: How to communicate without speech*. London: Jessica Kingsley Publishers.

been lost. We are born with capacities to recognise sensory patterns (visual, auditory, olfactory) and other aspects of body language. Emotional connection and the regulation of physiological state can occur with an attuned other through these nonverbal communications; good or bad feelings in the presence of the other (positive or negative valence – Box 1) reflects the physiological state of our bodies.

### Psychiatric evaluation and Intensive Interaction

Individuals with IDD and coexisting ASD are often referred to the psychiatrist because of what are seen as difficult to manage behaviours. It is important to note here that if the psychiatrist sees the individual in a typical outpatient clinic, any difficult behaviours displayed in this setting may be triggered by different circumstances than those triggered in their usual living environment. The former is more likely triggered by general stress due to anxiety of being in a strange place, while the latter triggered by unique circumstances of their living environment, such as specific sensory issues. Seeing the individual in their usual living environment is often essential in identifying situations that may be distressing to the individual and triggering these difficult to manage behaviours.

Wherever the psychiatrist meets with the patient, these difficult behaviours are nevertheless part of the patient's body language and communicative repertoire; working with these behaviours through an Intensive Interaction approach informs the psychiatrist about the patient's mental state and contributes to the psychiatrist's assessment of: affect, engagement, initiative, orientation, responsiveness to the social and physical environment, responses to a broad range of sensory stimuli, and whether the patient has specific sensory issues. When assessing patients who have little or no verbal language, an Intensive Interaction approach offers a more comprehensive psychiatric assessment and robust diagnosis. Indeed, this way of working marks the beginning of the therapeutic relationship and alliance necessary for optimal treatment outcomes.

Where medication may be needed to treat a specific psychiatric disorder, care givers using Intensive Interaction with their clients between appointments are more attuned to client's emotional responses, which in turn enhances staff/care provider skills in monitoring target behaviours to assess benefits (or otherwise) and side effects of any medication started. The psychiatrist using Intensive Interaction at follow up appointments is creating a reproducible clinical encounter, comfortable and familiar to the patient, that provides for the psychiatrist a reliable and systematic way to measure changes in the patient's affect and observe for side effects, consequent to starting medication.

## Attention to sensory issues

Increasingly psychiatrists are acknowledging sensory issues in ASD (DSM-5) and other psychiatric disorders and are beginning to appreciate the impact of these on behaviour and mental well-being (Box 3). Sensory issues include difficulties in sensory integration along with hyper- and hypo-sensitivities to everyday sensory experiences (described in detail in several chapters of this book); sensory issues are identified in up to 90% of children with ASD[13] and found to be present in patients with diagnosed psychiatric disorders.[14,15,16] Sensory issues are major and potent triggers for upset, distress and out of control behaviours. Verbal individuals with ASD (ASD self-advocates) poignantly describe their exquisite sensitivities to our sensory world and their experience of being sensorily and emotionally overwhelmed which can result in what they and others describe as 'meltdowns' and 'shut downs' (Box 4). Recognising behaviours that point to sensory hyper-sensitivities (e.g. covering ears with hands, avoiding bright lights, snipping labels off clothes, refusing foods of certain textures) and those that point to hyposensitivities (e.g. banging objects, looking intensely at objects, seeking pressure by crawling under heavy objects)[17] are important skills for the psychiatrist to learn. In the absence of recognising behaviours associated these with sensory issues, consequent behavioural reactions may be misinterpreted leading to mistaken assumptions as to cause resulting in misguided interventions. For example, an individual refusing to go outside may be reported by caregivers as being 'noncompliant', not recognising that the individual is in sensory overload and afraid of going into meltdown (as meltdowns are distressing and even painful); in turn the psychiatrist may interpret this refusal as symptomatic of phobia, but not link the fear to sensory overload.

Meltdowns and shutdowns occur when we (or more correctly our physical bodies, because often it is out of conscious awareness) feel threatened and are triggered into automatic physiological responses.

Several symptoms and behaviours of meltdowns and shutdowns overlap with symptoms and behaviours that contribute to criteria for major psychiatric disorders (e.g. anxiety, mood and psychotic disorders). Diagnosing psychiatric disorder does not require identification of what has caused (triggered) the mental distress giving rise to symptoms and behaviours (adjustment

13 Leekam SR, Nieto C, Libby SJ, Wing L and Gould J (2007) Describing the sensory abnormalities of children and adults with autism. *Journal of Autism and Developmental Disorders* **37** (5) 894–910.

14 Mesquita Reis J, Queiroga L, Velasco Rodrigues R, Pinto Ferreira B, Padez Vieira F, Farinha M and Caldeira dS (2017) Sensory processing disorders and psychopathology. *European Psychiatry* **41** S2 16-7.

15 Serafini G, Engel-Yeger B, Vazquez GH, Pompili M and Amore M (2017) Sensory processing disorders are associated with duration of current episode and severity of side effects. *Psychiatry Investigation* **14** (1) 51–57.

16 Brown S, Shankar R and Smith K (2009) Borderline personality disorder and sensory processing impairment. *Progress in Neurology and Psychiatry* **13** (4) 10–6.

17 Bogdashina O (2003) *Sensory Perceptual Issues in Autism and Asperger Syndrome: Different sensory experiences – different perceptual worlds.* London: Jessica Kingsley.

disorder (Adj D) being an exception).[18,19] Meltdowns, particularly when seen in individuals unable to share their inner experiences (i.e. report their symptoms), may at first glance appear to meet criteria for psychiatric disorder, until it is recognised that the distress is subsequent to a specific trigger. Routinely screening for sensory issues and sensory triggers as possible precipitants to the mental distress reduces this risk of diagnostic error.

Differentiating between major psychiatric disorders, ASD-related reactions (meltdowns, shutdowns, sensory sensitivity-related fears and phobias) and developmental upsets seen in childhood ('temper tantrums') is crucial, as assessment, treatment and prevention are different.

## Supporting environments that minimise the negative impact of sensory concerns

The third interlocking fundamental to Responsive Communication is supporting an environment that minimises the negative impact of sensory issues and consequent sensory processing and emotional overload. The goal is to eliminate, where possible, sensory distress and overload by attention to sensory sensitivities and to assist with sensory integration. A Responsive Communication approach alerts the communicating partner (whether this is the psychiatrist or care provider informant) to possible sensory issues. These can be further investigated by a sensorially qualified occupational therapist. At present standard sensory assessments do not include the important issues of Irlen syndrome and emotional overload, so assessment for these two triggers may need to be specifically requested. Direct interventions consequent to a sensory assessment might include measures to correct sensitivities by use, for example, of tinted lenses to address scotopic sensitivity/Irlen syndrome; noise reduction headphones to help those who are hypersensitive to sound; pressure vests for those with poor boundaries or low reception for touch and trampolining for proprioceptive hyposensitivity, as well as eliminating 'sensory chaos' by attention to the characteristics of the physical environment (sights, sounds, textures).[20] The prudent psychiatrist screens for sensory issues and attends to these first before making a psychiatric diagnosis. Sadly, it is likely that people experiencing meltdowns and shutdowns from sensory and emotional overload have been labelled with a psychiatric diagnosis, or have been described as having behaviour problems and treatment initiated without recognising the underlying cause of the mental distress; an outcome which at best may not have been helpful and at worst may have been harmful.

18 American Psychiatric Association (2013) *Diagnostic and Statistical Manual of Mental Disorders: DSM-5 (5th edition)*. Arlington: American Psychiatric Association.

19 Bradley E, Hollins S, Korossy M and Levitas A (2018) Adjustment disorder in disorders of intellectual development. In: P Casey (Ed) *Adjustment Disorder: From controversy to clinical practice* (pp.141–172). Oxford: Oxford University Press.

20 Bogdashina O (2003) *Sensory Perceptual Issues in Autism and Asperger Syndrome*. London: Jessica Kingsley Publishers.

# More about shutdowns and meltdowns

## The experience of people with ASD

Autism self-advocates describe their experience of a continuum of agitated out of control behaviours (meltdown) through to withdrawal and zoning out (shutdown) (Box 4). Many with ASD or IDD however do not have the verbal or written skills to describe their experience of meltdowns and shutdowns, and here we benefit from reports of care givers and sensitive clinicians. Phoebe Caldwell reports the immense variety of autistic responses from the highly intelligent to the least able individual with ASD in these states of distress.[21] Drawing on over forty-five years' experience meeting and spending time with hundreds of children and adults and witnessing the extreme distress of meltdown or shutdown many times, Phoebe notes that less verbally able individuals with ASD do not respond well to someone speaking to them when in meltdown (however benignly delivered) – she has observed speech of any sort simply adds to the individual's confusion and worsens the meltdown. However when connection is attempted using sounds or rhythm patterns that empathetically support the individual's body language, meaningful connection can be made and the individual is able to respond, even though still in turmoil, and the episode is curtailed. Except on two occasions when individuals hit out, Caldwell reports successful engagement using body language to de-escalate meltdowns. On the two occasions when individuals hit out (Box 5A), she describes making an error of judgement about proximity.

'Freeze' behaviours, where the individual pauses in unusual postures for extended periods, are also seen in ASD.[22,23,24] Such behaviours have been described as a fear response.[25] Loos and Miller[26] describe in detail an eleven-year-old girl with ASD who, when pressured by an adult to perform tasks that were difficult, became unresponsive, sleepy, immobile and limp to the touch and then would fall asleep in a chair for several minutes up to two hours. They observed these shutdown states were always triggered by social stress of a certain kind and they became more severe and frequent over a period of about a year. Loos and Miller also propose shutdowns can easily be misinterpreted as 'avoidant' behaviour (i.e. considered by onlookers as intentional rather than triggered by perceived

21 Caldwell P (2018) Personal communication.

22 Hare DJ and Malone C (2004) Catatonia and autistic spectrum disorders. *Autism: The International Journal of Research and Practice* **8** (2) 183–195.

23 Wing L and Shah A (2000) Catatonia in autistic spectrum disorders. *The British Journal of Psychiatry* **176** 357–362.

24 Wing L and Shah A (2006) A systematic examination of catatonia-like clinical pictures in autism spectrum disorders. *International Review of Neurobiology* **72** 21–39.

25 Moskowitz AK (2004) 'Scared stiff': catatonia as an evolutionary-based fear response. *Psychological Review* **111** (4) 984–1002.

26 Loos Miller IM and Loos HG (2004) *Shutdowns and Stress in Autism* [online]. Available from: https://autismawarenesscentre.com/shutdowns-stress-autism/ (accessed March 2019).

threat). Stressful life events, loss of routine, experience of other losses and interpersonal conflicts, especially around expectations, are also described as precipitating circumstances to shutdowns.[27]

## The neurobiology of meltdowns and shutdowns

Polyvagal theory[28,29] provides a way for us to understand the neurological underpinnings of this spectrum of physiological triggered behaviours in response to threat (Box 2), whether this is physical (e.g. sensory issues), emotional (e.g. fear of going into sensory overload, disappointment, social expectations, bullying) or cognitive overload (too much information to process). Meltdowns and freeze behaviours, from a polyvagal perspective, result from activation of the sympathetic nervous system involving the myelinated ventral vagal network, while immobilisation and unresponsiveness describe activity of the unmyelinated dorsal vagal network (Box 2).

It is hard to appreciate something going on in others that has not been fully experienced by ourselves. And so, it is with the particulars of each of our sensory systems that we take our own sensory reception, perceptions and integration so much for granted. We tend to assume our experience is universal and do not think to question how someone else's sensory experience may be different. Related to the latter we find it hard to conceptualise, for example, that the restless behaviours we observe in the person sitting next to us, may be related to proprioceptive hypo-sensitivities and the person having to self-generate movements 'to know that I am alive' (as described by Tito Mukhopadhyay).[30,31] All of this is happening outside of our conscious awareness.

Neuroception (a concept introduced by Porges)[32] describes the automatic process by which the nervous system and brain evaluate risk, such as safety, danger and life threat, outside of awareness (Box 2). When our neuroceptors detect threat, physical or emotional, our bodies are activated to take action to ensure our survival. Our first line of defence is to activate our mammalian social strategies to stave off the threat through verbal and non-verbal communication. If this does not work we mobilise into fighting off the danger or running away, or just freezing on the spot, hoping we will not be noticed.

---

27 Dhossche DM (2014) Decalogue of catatonia in autism spectrum disorders. *Frontiers in Psychiatry* **5** 157.

28 Porges SW (2011) *The Poly Vagal Theory: Neurophysiological foundations of emotions, attachment, communication, self-regulation*. New York: W.W. Norton & Company.

29 Porges SW (2017) *The Pocket Guide to the Polyvagal Theory: The transformative power of feeling safe (first edition)*. New York: WW Norton & Company.

30 Mukhopadhyay TR (2008) *How Can I Talk if My Lips Don't Move: Inside my autistic mind*. New York: Arcade Publishing.

31 Mukhopadhyay T and Savarese R (2017) Classical Autism and the Instruction of Literature [video filmed at Duke Franklin Humanities Institute. Available at: https://www.youtube.com/watch?v=PamjosXYiKo (accessed March 2019).

32 Porges SW (2011) *The Poly Vagal Theory: Neurophysiological foundations of emotions, attachment, communication, self regulation*. New York: W.W. Norton & Company.

Response to threat depends on the physiological (physical and emotional) state of the individual and the intensity of the perceived threat.

If we perceive there is no escape, our phylogenetically older survival strategy takes over (para sympathetic nervous system) and we immobilise. In some mammals this behaviour is seen as 'feigning death' until the danger has passed (e.g. the predator has left); in humans feigning death has been likened to the trauma response (Box 2). These fight-flight-freeze-immobilisation are autonomic nervous system reactions automatically triggered by our neuroceptor threat detectors; they represent the biological substrates of meltdowns (fight-flight-freeze responses) and shutdowns (immobilisation) described by ASD self-advocates and care providers.

People with ASD are particularly at risk for being overwhelmed in their lives because of autism related sensory issues (as well as communication, cognitive and emotional overload) and being less able to activate the interpersonal social strategies in response to these. Studies of the autonomic nervous system of people with ASD confirms differences in ANS functioning.[33,34,35,36,37,38] It remains unclear whether these differences are part of the condition of ASD, or subsequent to a life time of greater frequency of perception of threat and activation of these survival responses, associated with living in a world that is in so many ways ASD unfriendly.

ASD self-advocates describe meltdowns and shutdowns as not so much triggered by one event but more in the context of a 'tipping point' that has arisen following an accumulation of stressful life circumstances. Sensory, cognitive and emotional overload combine to bring things to tipping point. Lipsky,[39] an adult with autism experiencing meltdowns and a consultant in meltdown management (as well as having professional experience in emergency and trauma management),

33 Groden J, Cautela J, Prince S and Berryman J (1994) The impact of stress and anxiety on individuals with autism and developmental disabilities. In: E Schopler & GB Mesibov (Eds) *Behavioral Issues in Autism* (pp.177–194). New York: Plenum: New York.

34 Kushki A, Drumm, Pla Mobarak M, Tanel N, Dupuis A, Chau T and Anagnostou E (2013) Investigating the autonomic nervous system response to anxiety in children with autism spectrum disorders. *PloS One* **8** (4). Available at: http://www.plosone.org/article/fetchObject.action?uri=info%3Adoi%2F10.1371%2Fjournal.pone.0059730&representation=PDF (accessed March 2019).

35 Kushki A, Brian J, Dupuis A and Anagnostou E (2014) Functional autonomic nervous system profile in children with autism spectrum disorder. *Molecular Autism*, **5** (39).

36 Lydon S, Healy O, Reed P, Mulhern T, Hughes BM and Goodwin MS (2016) A systematic review of physiological reactivity to stimuli in autism. *Developmental Neurorehabilitation* **19** (6) 335–355.

37 Woodruff B, Temkit M, Adams J and Goodman B (2016) Autonomic symptoms endorsed by adults with autism spectrum disorders. *Neurology*, **86** (16 supplement).

38 Goodman B (2016) Autonomic dysfunction in autism spectrum disorders (ASD). *Neurology* **86** (16 Supplement).

39 Lipsky D (2011) *From Anxiety to Meltdown: How individuals on the autism spectrum deal with anxiety, experience meltdowns, manifest tantrums, and how you can intervene effectively.* London: Jessica Kingsley Publishers.

differentiates between meltdowns and 'catastrophic reactions'. While both are unconscious physiological (adaptive) reactions to stressful situations, meltdowns occur in response to more prolonged exposure to sensory triggers, cognitive and emotional overload and being unable to get way from the overwhelming situation; a catastrophic reaction is an explosive, immediate involuntary reaction to something that has 'gone off script' or not gone according to plan.[40]

The two types of cessation of movement in mammals described in polyvagal theory (freezing and immobilisation) are uniquely adapted to our survival: 'freezing' describes momentarily remaining completely still (but with muscle tone) in response to danger (sympathetic nervous system activation), while immobilisation in response to life threat (vagal parasympathetic nervous system response) is without muscle tone (Box 2). These autonomic nervous system reactions and consequent behaviours overlap with an array of medical disorders involving movement, volition and behaviour generally referred to as catatonia: hyperkinetic catatonia includes such medical conditions as tardive dyskinesias, tics, compulsions, epilepsy and delirium and hypokinetic disorders include Parkinson's disease, neuroleptic malignant syndrome, delirium, coma.[41] The causes and pathophysiology of these medical conditions are not well understood. However catatonia-like behaviours and deterioration have been documented in between 12 and 18% of people with ASD).[42,43,44,45,46,47,48,49]
In autism at least, one factor underlying catatonic-like deterioration has been identified as ongoing stress involving: (a) external factors such as non-autism-friendly environments, loss of routine, structure; (b) psychological factors such as experience of conflict, pressure to conform and confusion and (c)

---

40 Lipsky D (2011) *From Anxiety to Meltdown: How individuals on the autism spectrum deal with anxiety, experience meltdowns, manifest tantrums, and how you can intervene effectively*. London: Jessica Kingsley Publishers.

41 Dhossche DM and Wachtel LE (2010) Catatonia is hidden in plain sight among different pediatric disorders: a review article. *Pediatric Neurology* **43** (5) 307–315.

42 Mazzone L, Postorino V, Valeri G and Vicari S (2014) Catatonia in patients with autism: prevalence and management. *CNS Drugs* **28** (3) 205–215.

43 Wing L and Shah A (2000) Catatonia in autistic spectrum disorders. *The British Journal of Psychiatry* **176** 357–362.

44 Wing L and Shah A (2006). A systematic examination of catatonia-like clinical pictures in autism spectrum disorders. *International Review of Neurobiology* **72** 21–39.

45 Shah A (2016) *Catatonia and Catatonia-Type Breakdown in Autism* [online]. Available from: https://network.autism.org.uk/good-practice/evidence-base/catatonia-and-catatonia-type-breakdown-autism (accessed March 2019).

46 Dhossche DM, Shah A and Wing L (2006) Blueprints for the assessment, treatment, and future study of catatonia in autism spectrum disorders. *International Review of Neurobiology* **72** 267–284.

47 Billstedt E, Gillberg IC and Gillberg C (2005) Autism after adolescence: population-based 13- to 22-year follow-up study of 120 individuals with autism diagnosed in childhood. *Journal of Autism and Developmental Disorders* **35** (3) 351–360.

48 Ghaziuddin N, Dhossche D and Marcotte K (2012) Retrospective chart review of catatonia in child and adolescent psychiatric patients. *Acta Psychiatrica Scandinavica* **125** (1) 33–38.

49 Mazzone L, Postorino V, Valeri G and Vicari S (2014) Catatonia in patients with autism: prevalence and management. *CNS Drugs* **28** (3) 205–215.

biological factors such as illness, pain and hormonal changes.[50] Psychological interventions targeting these three areas are effective. Other authors have described high doses of lorazepam and bilateral ECT used in a graded way according to severity, for the treatment of life-threatening autism-related catatonia and shutdowns.[51,52]

Lipsky[53] describes 'freezing' as switching from cognitive to instinctual functioning, a brief early symptom (or 'prodrome') prior to activation of the ANS fight or flight response. This latter conceptualisation is a reminder that successful intervention and support strategies along the stress-response continuum, will engage the individual differently depending on their functioning capacity at the time: once in instinctual mode, trying to engage the individual using cognitive behavioural strategies will no longer be effective and attending to individual safety (and that of others) takes priority.

## What to do about meltdowns and shutdowns

### Prevention is key

Identifying triggers, either single or several contributing to 'tipping point', is therefore necessary so as to plan how these might be prevented or minimised, and, where this is not possible, how the individual might be supported during an anticipated stressful time or trigger.[54] For example, Pat, a lady with autism and many sensory issues, showed an increase in meltdown and shutdown behaviours (getting 'stuck') associated with menses, urinary tract infection (UTI), constipation, the spring and autumn (allergies) and any changes in routine. Pat had a daily sensory diet (i.e. planned daily sensory activities designed by a sensorially qualified occupational therapist) and when out in the community carried with her a sensory backpack filled with items that helped her calm. Extra support and fewer expectations are planned around the times of her menses and at times of any anticipated changes in routine. 'Red flag' behaviour monitoring identifies possible UTIs, constipation and allergies so as to be able to step in early (e.g. with a GP visit or possible pre-prescribed PRN medication)

---

50 Shah A and Wing L (2006) Psychological approaches to chronic catatonia-like deterioration in autism spectrum disorders. *International Review of Neurobiology* **72** 245–264.

51 Dhossche DM, Shah A and Wing L (2006) Blueprints for the assessment, treatment, and future study of catatonia in autism spectrum disorders. *International Review of Neurobiology* **72** 267–284. Dhossche DM (2014) Decalogue of catatonia in autism spectrum disorders. *Frontiers in Psychiatry* **5** 157.

52 Fink M, Taylor MA and Ghaziuddin N (2006) Catatonia in autistic spectrum disorders: a medical treatment algorithm. *International Review of Neurobiology* **72** 233–244.

53 Lipsky D (2011) *From Anxiety to Meltdown: How individuals on the autism spectrum deal with anxiety, experience meltdowns, manifest tantrums, and how you can intervene effectively*. London: Jessica Kingsley Publishers.

54 National Autistic Society (NAS) (2016) *Meltdowns* [online]. Available at: https://www.autism.org.uk/about/behaviour/meltdowns.aspx# (accessed March 2019).

should concerns arise. Pat finds social stories especially helpful in helping her understand the structure of her day and in preparing for events.[55]

As meltdowns and shutdowns are triggered by 'threats' of any kind (biopsychosocial and environmental circumstances – from the individual's ASD IDD perspective), a sequential and systematic evaluation of the individual, as well as where they live and spend time, is needed to determine what these 'threats' are – for example, considering possible Health conditions, evaluation of their physical and support Environment and expectations on them, exploring whether they are Living with past traumas that have now been triggered or whether there is any Psychiatric concern (e.g. HELP approach).[56,57]

Reports by people with ASD of their feelings and behaviours when in meltdowns or shutdowns guide our approach as to how they wish to be supported at these times (Box 4).[58] Poignantly and frequently shared in these descriptions, is the desire for 'connection' during a meltdown – sometimes this is for a tight hug but more often it is the desire for someone just to be there (without any physical contact), for the course of the meltdown, to understand, not to judge, but instead to respect and appreciate how the person may be feeling. Meltdowns are described by ASD self-advocates as being exceptionally distressing, even painful in terms of the physiological changes that occur in the body, as well as the social embarrassment and humiliation experienced; meltdowns are traumatising. On a website sharing experiences of meltdowns,[59] autism self-advocates report that some reactions and behaviours of observers witnessing their meltdowns can add to their distress: they describe the following comments as not helpful (with autism self-advocate perspective in brackets): 'It's okay' ('It's not'); 'You need to pull yourself together' ('I will when I'm ready'); or 'Everything will be fine' ('I know'). The innate desire to have an understanding person present through such a terrifying event could be seen as involvement of the social engagement system (Box 2) to avoid going into complete shutdown (immobilisation). Likewise less verbally able individuals may be helped through a meltdown by

55 Bradley E and Caldwell P (2013) Mental health and autism: Promoting Autism FaVourable Environments (PAVE) [online]. *Journal on Developmental Disabilities* **19** (1) 8–23. Available at: https://oadd.org/wp-content/uploads/2013/01/41015_JoDD_19-1_8-23_Bradley_and_Caldwell.pdf (accessed March 2019).

56 Green L, McNeil K, Korossy M, Boyd K, Grier E, Ketchell M, Loh A, Lunsky Y, McMillan S, Sawyer A, Thakur A & Bradley E (2018) HELP for behaviours that challenge in adults with intellectual and developmental disabilities. *Canadian Family Physician Medecin De Famille Canadien* **64** (Suppl 2) S23–31.

57 Bradley E, Loh A, Grier E, Korossy M & Cameron D (2014) *Health Watch Table: Autism spectrum disorder (ASD)* [online]. Available at: http://ddprimarycare.surreyplace.ca/wp-content/uploads/2018/03/HWT_ASD.pdf (accessed March 2019).

58 Lipsky D (2011) *From Anxiety to Meltdown: How individuals on the autism spectrum deal with anxiety, experience meltdowns, manifest tantrums, and how you can intervene effectively.* London: Jessica Kingsley Publishers.

59 Musings of an Aspie (2012) *Anatomy of a Meltdown*. Available at: https://musingsofanaspie.com/2012/12/13/anatomy-of-a-meltdown (accessed March 2019).

engaging with their body language. For these less verbally able individuals, verbal engagement at these times is likely to contribute to sensory overload and escalate their distress.

Other preventive measures include low arousal and stress reducing approaches:

- Low arousal physical environments and social-interpersonal supports have been shown to reduce and prevent meltdowns.[60] McDonnell, who introduced the idea of low arousal approaches, suggests that this should include attention to staffing practices since, apart from service organisational structures and conflicting needs (e.g. the use of quick-fix practices such as restraint), it is we who support those on the spectrum who create high arousal situations and our body language can give rise to sensory overload.[61,62]
- Routinely screening for and eliminating individual, unique triggers in the physical and social environment also lowers arousal and prevents stress, especially for individuals with autism. Care givers may need guidance in recognising individual, unique sensory distress in response to painful features of their physical and social environment. For example, attention to wall colour, pattern and clutter, lighting, noise from TV and radio, overlapping speech, even specific characteristics of care givers such as pitch of voice and their choice of clothing may need to be considered. Architects and interior designers are already alert to the needs of those unable to see or to hear and increasingly are embracing the needs of people with autism.[63]
- Based on several decades of implementation and research in stress and coping in autism, Groden and colleagues have identified relaxation strategies that can be used with both verbal and non-verbal individuals.[64]
- Several research-clinicians offer comprehensive guidance on providing low stress environments and supports for individuals showing catatonia[65,66] and

60 Woodcock L and Page A (2010) *Managing Family Meltdown: The low arousal approach and autism*. London: Jessica Kingsley Publishers.

61 McDonnell AA (2010) *Managing Aggressive Behaviour in Care Settings: Understanding and applying low arousal approaches*. Chichester: Wiley-Blackwell. Further information at https://www.studio3.org/training-systems-for-managing-difficult-behaviour/low-arousal-approach-for-autism/ (accessed March 2019).

62 Caldwell P (2014) *The Anger Box: Sensory turmoil and pain in autism*. Brighton: Pavilion Publishing and Media Ltd.

63 McNally H, Morris D and McAllister K (2013) *Aldo Goes to Primary School: Experiencing primary school through the lens of the autistic spectrum* [online]. Belfast: McNally Morris Architects. Available at: http://mcnallymorris.com/Aldo_Goes_to_Primary_School_med_res_digital.pdf (accessed March 2019).

64 Groden J, Weidenman L and Diller A (2016) *Relaxation: A comprehensive manual for children and adults with autism and other developmental disabilities*. Champaign, IL: Research Press.

65 Shah A (2016) *Catatonia and Catatonia-Type Breakdown in Autism* [online]. Available at: https://network.autism.org.uk/good-practice/evidence-base/catatonia-and-catatonia-type-breakdown-autism (accessed March 2019).

66 Shah A and Wing L (2006) Psychological approaches to chronic catatonia-like deterioration in autism spectrum disorders. *International Review of Neurobiology* **72** 245–264.

complete meltdown[67] – the latter authors acknowledge the difficult balance between reducing stress and supporting participation in activities that are important for the individual's development.

- Meltdown prevention plans are available[68,69,70]. Lipsky[71] describes the need for 'scripts' and 'back up' plans (and back up of back up plans).

## Emerging technology

Individuals with autism are described as having difficulty recognising and reporting emotional feelings and sensations in their bodies (referred to as 'alexithymia'). Their body language communicating increasing distress (warning signals), may also not be picked up by others, including care givers.

Pickard and colleagues[72] have developed a sensor, worn like a watch on the wrist, that detects a person's heart rate, sweat levels, electrical activity, and skin temperature. The sensor can predict an impending meltdown (up to 3 mins before this occurs) with up to 70% accuracy. This is linked to a care provider device, e.g. mobile, alerting the care provider who can then step in to assist the individual. For more able individuals apps are being developed that can be downloaded onto their own mobile, providing access to personalised support when and where needed.[73]

## Vagal nerve stimulation

Vagal nerve stimulation involving subcutaneous (under the skin) placement of a stimulator has been effective for hard to control epilepsy for the past two

67 Loos Miller IM and Loos HG (2004) *Shutdowns and Stress in Autism* [online]. Available at: https://autismawarenesscentre.com/shutdowns-stress-autism/ (accessed March 2019).

68 National Autistic Society (NAS) (2017) *Anxiety in Autistic Adults* [online]. Available at: https://www.autism.org.uk/about/behaviour/anxiety.aspx (accessed March 2019).

69 National Autistic Society (NAS) (2016) *Meltdowns* [online]. Available at: https://www.autism.org.uk/about/behaviour/meltdowns.aspx# (accessed March 2019).

70 Murillo L (Unknown) *Ten Tips to Prevent Autism-related Shopping Meltdowns* [online]. Available at: https://www.autismspeaks.org/blog/2017/11/25/ten-tips-prevent-autism-related-shopping-meltdowns (accessed March 2019).

71 Lipsky D (2011) *From Anxiety to Meltdown: How individuals on the autism spectrum deal with anxiety, experience meltdowns, manifest tantrums, and how you can intervene effectively.* London: Jessica Kingsley Publishers.

72 Picard RW (2018) *How Emotion Technology can Improve Science and The Future of Autism.* INSAR May 2018. International Society for Autism Research Conference, Rotterdam, Netherlands. Available at: https://insar.confex.com/insar/2018/webprogram/Paper29310.html (accessed March 2019).
Picard R (2011) *Technology and Emotions.* TEDx Talk. Available from: https://www.youtube.com/watch?v=ujxriwApPP4 (accessed March 2019).

73 Brain in Hand Limited (2018) *Personalised Support from Your Mobile Phone – Reduce anxiety, feel safe, increase independence* [online]. Available at: http://braininhand.co.uk/ (accessed March 2019).

decades[74] and was approved for treatment resistant depression in 2005.[75,76] In a study to investigate over-eating behaviour in Prader-Willi syndrome, vagal nerve stimulation was found serendipitously to improve maladaptive behaviours, temperament and social functioning.[77]

- Clancy *et al*[78] piloted transcutaneous vagus nerve stimulation using a surface electrode place on the ear of healthy participants and measured heart rate variability (HRV), a measure of emotional arousal. Some participants received stimulation (active group) and others did not (control group). The normal beat to beat irregularity in heart rate (known as heart rate variability or HRV) significantly increased in the active stimulation group, indicating reduction of the fight or flight system and increase in body rest and digest functions.
- Lamb *et al*[79] studied hyperarousal and autonomic state in patients with post-traumatic stress disorder, also using transcutaneous vagal nerve stimulation to the ear. Measurements were made of postural HRV (as subjects lay on a motorised tilting bed) and skin conductance changes in response to acoustic startle while viewing emotional images. Vagal nerve stimulation resulted in down regulation (reduction) of the fight or flight response and upregulation (increased) activity of physiological state conducive to social engagement.

## Acoustic stimulation

Consistent with polyvagal theory[80] Porges *et al* found that auditory hypersensitivities in autism were reduced when neural tone was increased to middle ear muscles.[81] Improved auditory processing was found to be

74 Epilepsy Society UK (2016) *Vagus Nerve Stimulation* [online]. Available at: https://www.epilepsysociety.org.uk/vagus-nerve-stimulation#.W5lT_-L2Zom (accessed March 2019).

75 O'Reardon JP, Cristancho P and Peshek AD (2006) Vagus nerve stimulation (vns) and treatment of depression: to the brainstem and beyond. *Psychiatry* (Edgmont) **3** (5) 54–63. Available at: https://www.ncbi.nlm.nih.gov/pmc/articles/PMC2990624/ (accessed March 2019).

76 Taylor M (2016) *Using Vagus Nerve Stimulation (VNS) for Depression: is it recommended?* [online]. Available from: https://www.healthline.com/health/depression/vagus-nerve-stimulation (accessed March 2019).

77 Manning KE, McAllister CJ, Ring HA, Finer N, Kelly CL, Sylvester KP, Fletcher PC, Morrell NW, Garnett MR, Manford MR and Holland AJ (2016) Novel insights into maladaptive behaviours in Prader-Willi syndrome: serendipitous findings from an open trial of vagus nerve stimulation. *Journal of Intellectual Disability Research* **60** (2) 149–155.

78 Clancy JA, Mary DA, Witte KK, Greenwood JP, Deuchars SA and Deuchars J (2014) Non-invasive vagus nerve stimulation in healthy humans reduces sympathetic nerve activity. *Brain Stimulation* **7** (6) 871-877.

79 Lamb DG, Porges EC, Lewis GF and Williamson JB (2017) Non-invasive vagal nerve stimulation effects on hyperarousal and autonomic state in patients with posttraumatic stress disorder and history of mild traumatic brain injury: preliminary evidence. *Front Med (Lausanne)* **4** Article 124. Available at: https://www.ncbi.nlm.nih.gov/pmc/articles/PMC5534856/ (accessed March 2019).

80 Porges SW (2017) *The Pocket Guide to the Polyvagal Theory: The transformative power of feeling safe* (first edition). New York: W. W Norton & Company.

81 Porges SW, Bazhenova OV, Bal E, Carlson N, Sorokin Y, Heilman KJ, Cook EH and Lewis GF (2014) Reducing auditory hypersensitivities in autistic spectrum disorder: preliminary findings evaluating the listening project protocol. *Frontiers in Pediatrics* **2** 80. Also available at: https://www.ncbi.nlm.nih.gov/pmc/articles/PMC4117928/ (accessed March 2019).

associated with increased respiratory sinus arrhythmia (RSA), a measure of how the vagus nerve modulates heart rate activity and used to measure individual differences in stress reactivity. Reducing stress from auditory hypersensitivity removes threat that triggers fight or flight and promotes social engagement.[82]

## Medication

Psychotropic medications (e.g. antipsychotics) are frequently used to treat difficult to manage behaviours in non-verbal people with autism (behaviours that are sometimes referred to as 'challenging'). There are many concerns about this practice.[83,84] Problem behaviours causing risk to self and others are behaviours of distress. Therefore identifying the cause of this distress and treating the cause will stop the distress and therefore the difficult behaviours.[85] Unfortunately, some behaviours (such as aggression or self-injurious behaviours) that may occur when the individual goes into meltdown, or leading up to a meltdown, can be seen as behaviours to be managed rather than recognised as triggered behaviours in response to threat. This may lead to an equally unfortunate focus on trying to stop the behaviours with physical or chemical restraint, rather than focusing on the cause of the distress giving rise to the behaviours and removing the threat.[86]

Threat is both an objective reality that can be observed by others, as well as a subjective evaluation, a personal feeling; feelings of safety and trust alter the neuroception of threat. Therefore it is essential the evaluation considers the daily experience of the individual from their perspective; this will be communicated through their body language and behaviours where they are not able to share this verbally with care providers.

When we are stressed, the adrenal glands flood our body with adrenaline (epinephrine), a hormone that acts on most body tissues mobilising us

82 Porges SW, Macellaio M, Stanfill SD, McCue K, Lewis GF, Harden ER, Handelman M, Denver J, Bazhenova OV and Heilman KJ (2013) Respiratory sinus arrhythmia and auditory processing in autism: modifiable deficits of an integrated social engagement system? *International Journal of Psychophysiology: Official Journal of the International Organization of Psychophysiology*, **88** (3), 261–270. Also available at: https://www.ncbi.nlm.nih.gov/pmc/articles/PMC3610863/ (accessed March 2019).

83 NHS England (2016) *Stopping Over-Medication of People with Learning Disabilities [STOMPwLD]* [online]. NHS England. Available from: https://www.england.nhs.uk/wp-content/uploads/2016/06/stopping-over-medication.pdf (accessed March 2019).

84 Alexander RT, Branford D and Devapriam J (2016) Psychotropic drug prescribing for people with intellectual disability, mental health problems and/or behaviours that challenge: Practice guidelines (FR/ID/09). Available at: http://www.rcpsych.ac.uk/pdf/FR_ID_09_for_website.pdf (accessed March 2019).

85 Green L, McNeil K, Korossy M, Boyd K, Grier E, Ketchell M, Loh A, Lunsky Y, McMillan S, Sawyer A, Thakur A and Bradley E (2018) HELP for behaviours that challenge in adults with intellectual and developmental disabilities. *Canadian Family Physician Medecin De Famille Canadien* **64** (Suppl 2) S23-31.

86 Lipsky D (2011) *From Anxiety to Meltdown: How individuals on the autism spectrum deal with anxiety, experience meltdowns, manifest tantrums, and how you can intervene effectively*. London: Jessica Kingsley Publishers.

into action e.g. broncho dilation to let more air into the lungs, relaxation of the blood vessels to allow greater perfusion, blood redirected from gut, and increases in mass and contraction speed of muscles in preparation for fight or flight – essentially a cascade of physiological changes that may be felt as tachycardia, sweating, dry mouth, indigestion and general tension in many parts of the body and described as very unpleasant, even painful. Sympathetic nervous system activation (involving the neurotransmitter norepinephrine)[87] increases the rate of contractions of the heart, and this and epinephrine underlie the fight or flight response. Antiadrenergic medication, which reduces the influence of this epinephrine and norepinephrine activity on fight or flight responses, may be helpful, since beta blockers block the action of adrenaline receptors on body tissues, reducing these unpleasant body experiences and helping the individual remain calm even though trying to manage a difficult environmental trigger. For example, taking beta blocker medication prior to giving a public presentation or before examinations can have a calming effect.

Many with autism, prior to any triggering, have high levels of arousal (e.g. as measured by pulse rate). Treatment with beta blockers to reduce this hyperarousal involves monitoring heart rate daily, both when the individual is typically most anxious and when typically most relaxed and titrating response to medication against changes in pulse rate downwards.

Clonidine is another antiadrenergic medication that reduces noradrenaline activity in the brain. It is approved for the treatment of hypertension and ADHD but also reported to have some benefits in other psychiatric conditions, including anxiety related disorders, PTSD, sleep disturbances in children and adolescents as well as reducing hyperarousal behaviours in ASD.[88,89] It has been shown to block traumatic memories and fear responses in an animal model of PTSD.[90,91]

87 Drugs.com (2018) *Norepinephrine vs Epinephrine: What's the difference?* [online] Available at: https://www.drugs.com/answers/norepinephrine-epinephrine-difference-3132946.html (accessed March 2019).

88 Bezchlibnyk-Butler KZ and Jeffries JJ (2004) *Clinical Handbook of Psychotropic Drugs* (14th edition). Ashland, OH: Hogrefe and Huber.

89 Naguy A (2016) Clonidine use in psychiatry: panacea or panache. *Pharmacology* **98** (1-2) 87–92.

90 Holmes NM, Crane JW, Tang M, Fam J, Westbrook RF and Delaney AJ (2017) Alpha2-adrenoceptor-mediated inhibition in the central amygdala blocks fear-conditioning. *Scientific Reports* **7** (1).

91 Ogata N & Dodman NH (2011) The use of clonidine in the treatment of fear-based behavior problems in dogs: an open trial. *Journal of Veterinary Behavior: Clinical Applications and Research*, **6** (2) 130–137.

As noted previously on p.174, high doses of lorazepam have been used for the treatment of life-threatening autism-related catatonia.[92,93]

Any medication in autism should be used cautiously and conducted within the parameters of a trial, with careful documentation of target behaviours at baseline, monitoring for response and side effects with each increasing dose to determine overall effectiveness.[94] Temple Grandin, a person with autism and an astute observer of her own and other mammalian behaviour, provides an account of medications that have been helpful to her in managing autism related difficulties.[95]

## Responsive Communication and emerging understanding of mental distress in ASD and IDD

Psychopathology is a term used in clinical research to encompass some or all of emotional and behavioural distress, psychiatric symptoms and signs, as well as diagnosed psychiatric disorders. In recent years there has been greater recognition of (a) the impact of trauma in contributing to mental distress and psychopathology as well as (b) concerns about the accuracy of psychiatric diagnoses in ASD and IDD using conventional diagnostic and classificatory approaches.

These two themes are discussed separately in the coming pages, along with what a Responsive Communication approach might offer in addressing these two concerns.

### Trauma in the lives of people with ASD and IDD

Disability often confers societal disadvantage, which in turn impacts negatively on physical and emotional well-being, contributing to mental ill health. People with IDD and ASD suffer even greater disadvantage, adversity, negative life events and traumatic experiences compared to others not so affected. Many experience bullying at school, victimisation as adults and marginalisation from social inclusion and opportunities.

---

92 Dhossche DM (2014) Decalogue of catatonia in autism spectrum disorders. *Frontiers in Psychiatry* **5** 157.
Dhossche DM, Shah A and Wing L (2006) Blueprints for the assessment, treatment, and future study of catatonia in autism spectrum disorders. *International Review of Neurobiology* **72** 267–284.

93 Fink M, Taylor MA and Ghaziuddin N (2006) Catatonia in autistic spectrum disorders: a medical treatment algorithm. *International Review of Neurobiology* **72** 233–244.

94 Barrett M and Bradley E (2015) Autism spectrum disorders. In: S Bhaumik, D Branford & SK Gangadharan (Eds) *The Frith Prescribing Guidelines For People With Intellectual Disability* 3rd edition (pp.125–133). Chichester: Wiley Blackwell.

95 Grandin T (1998) Evaluating the effects of medication on people with autism. Available at: https://www.iidc.indiana.edu/pages/Evaluating-the-Effects-of-Medication (accessed March 2019).

Communication disabilities bestow particular disadvantage and increase the likelihood of social exclusion, difficulties accessing personal, community and health services and disconnection from emotional supports. Unique needs such as those related to sensory issues go unrecognised and unmet. Even at the start of their lives, a baby's sensory difficulties may make it difficult for them to recognise their mother's overtures, perhaps altering attachment processing. Demands of social acceptability add additional stress.

All contribute to daily challenges and struggles; we can anticipate many will have experienced traumatising situations (aside from meltdowns and shutdowns), including risk of experiencing trauma in general health and social care settings (e.g. sensory overload from noise and visual clutter in non-autism friendly environments communication and processing difficulties, emotional needs being overlooked). Behavioural escalation in response to this accumulation of distress may give rise to concerning care practices (e.g. physical restraint, behavioural programs or medication for 'behaviours'), along with re-traumatisation, as traditional services focus on their own organisational, health and safety needs before what feels safe from patients' perspectives (Box 2 and **Chapter 2** by Hope Lightowler in this book).

To date, key epidemiological studies of mental distress and psychopathology in this population have not considered the impact of trauma (or sensory issues in ASD), nor felt it necessary to identify possible triggers to the mental distress being studied[96]. However with the introduction in DSM-5 of a new category of 'trauma and stress-related disorders' (which includes both adjustment disorders and PTSD), there is now an opportunity to systematically identify trauma-related disorders in future population-based studies, as well as to review what diagnoses these individuals were given, in the absence of a trauma-related diagnosis being available in these otherwise robust studies. Meanwhile, given the ubiquity of trauma in the lives of people with IDD and ASD, a culture of trauma informed care in their service provision might offset risk of additional unintentional service-related trauma to an already vulnerable population.[97,98]

Responsive Communication embraces many elements of trauma informed care: focus on the individual; follows the individual's initiatives and interests, rather than imposing those of the therapist or care system; empowers and values the individual; learns about the individual directly through sensitive attunement

96 Bradley E, Hollins S, Korossy M and Levitas A (2018) Adjustment disorder in disorders of intellectual development. In: P Casey (Ed) *Adjustment Disorder: From Controversy to Clinical Practice* (pp.141–172). Oxford: Oxford University Press.

97 Alameda County Behavioral Health Care Services and Alameda County Trauma Informed Care (2013) *Trauma Informed Care vs. Trauma Specific Treatment* [online]. Available from: https://alamedacountytraumainformedcare.org/trauma-informed-care/trauma-informed-care-vs-trauma-specific-treatment-2/ (accessed March 2019).

98 Pitonyak D (2016) *Supporting a Person Who Is Experiencing Post Traumatic Stress Disorder* (PTSD) [online]. Available from: http://gatewayassociation.ca/wp-content/uploads/2018/07/supporting-a-person-who-is-experiencing-PTSD.pdf (accessed March 2019).

and observation; attends to social, emotional and attachment needs through relationship; through attunement assists with affect regulation; enhances skills through relationships; seeks to understand unique sensory issues and minimise the impact of these (Box 6).

Prompted by neuro anatomical and functional neurobiological research, a reconceptualisation of our ongoing sensory experiences, in and out of awareness, is informing our understanding of brain–body connection and what we mean by mental health. Along with this comes a realisation that some of our experiences, such as those related to trauma, are as much remembered in the physical body as embodied in our mental memories.[99] Responsive Communication offers the potential for individual trauma treatment for those who are functionally nonverbal by adapting strategies and constructs from existing body-based trauma therapies[100,101] so as to be available through body language (Box 6).

## Psychopathology and psychiatric diagnoses in ASD and IDD

Prevalence of mental ill-health is greater in people with ASD as well as in people with IDD compared to those without either condition. Additionally, measures of psychopathology are consistently greatest in those with IDD who have co existing ASD.[102,103] The extent to which this greater psychopathology may be directly related to trauma and autism-related sensory issues warrants urgent investigation. Meanwhile, however, an additional concern in understanding this greater prevalence of psychiatric disorder in routine clinical practice is how diagnoses are made.

Psychiatric assessment and specific subtyping of mental distress (psychiatric diagnosis) when the patient has ASD and IDD are very challenging. Psychiatric assessment involves determining whether the patient meets specific criteria for a specific diagnosis. Criteria are based on what can be observed (i.e. patient behaviours and patient affect) and what the patient shares about their inner experience (e.g. thoughts, emotional feelings – Box 1). In the absence of a direct account from the patient (when the patient has little or no verbal language), clinicians base their diagnosis entirely on behaviours observed or reported by others and the clinician's interpretation of these behaviours (i.e. what can be inferred from these behaviours about the patient's emotional feelings,

---

99 Van der Kolk BA (2014) *The Body Keeps the Score: Brain, mind, and body in the healing of trauma.* New York: Viking.

100 Ogden P (2015) *Sensorimotor Psychotherapy: Interventions for trauma and attachment.* New York: W.W. Norton & Company.

101 Emerson D (2015) *Trauma-sensitive Yoga in Therapy: Bringing the body into treatment.* New York: W.W. Norton & Company.

102 Niagara studies: Bradley EA, Ames CS and Bolton PF (2011) Psychiatric conditions and behavioural problems in adolescents with intellectual disabilities: correlates with autism. *Canadian Journal of Psychiatry* **56** (2) 102–109.

103 Bradley E and Bolton P (2006) Episodic psychiatric disorders in teenagers with learning disabilities with and without autism. *The British Journal of Psychiatry* **189** 361–366.

motivations, desires, intentions). Several aspects of this general psychiatric practice contribute to the potential for diagnostic errors unless measures are taken to prevent this. The first relates to where assessments are conducted and the second relates to the interpretations of motivations/intentions of the patient ascribed to these behaviours by the clinician.

### Where assessments are conducted

Ideally when conducting the psychiatric assessment, and particularly when the individual is unable to communicate verbally about their mental distress and the referring concerns are about behaviours that challenge, the patient with IDD or ASD should be seen and observed in the place where the concerns are manifest. Here the clinician can observe for any sensory issues or other circumstance that might be overwhelming and try to determine whether the individual feels safe in this environment (Boxes 2 and 6); this will usually require the psychiatrist to visit the patient rather than vice versa. This compares to the patient attending a typical outpatient clinic where clinical observations occur in an unfamiliar place (assuming the patient agrees to attend), with a smorgasbord board of sounds, lights, smells, intrusions into personal space (not a safe place – Boxes 2, 3 and 5B), increasing the risk of diagnostic error, e.g. making a psychiatric diagnosis of anxiety, depression, psychosis or personality disorder when the clinical presentation is due to unrecognised sensory issues or related to trauma (such as Hope Lightowler's experiences, described in this book).

While a Responsive Communication approach may be helpful in easing the individual's discomfort in a regular outpatient clinic, this is unlikely to be an environment conducive to promoting optimal therapeutic engagement to support ongoing psychological therapy, unless the therapist is able to negotiate circumstances that promote feelings of safety, such as attention to sensory needs and a process that imbues predictability, familiarity and consistency (Boxes 6 and 7).

### Interpretations of behaviours

If the clinician has little experience of ASD and IDD, or of the lives of his patients with ASD and IDD and associated unique circumstances such as sensory sensitivities and potential for sensory and emotional overload, consideration of these influences will be missing when determining what may be causing the patient's mental distress. For example, Jake was given a diagnosis of dog phobia as he was refusing to go out for fear of meeting dogs. Later it was learned that it was the noise of the dogs barking that was bothering him; wearing noise cancellation headphones, Jake is now able to go out and does not show any fear of dogs. Current psychiatric classification systems such as DSM and ICD, as these are applied to patients unable to articulate their inner experiences, characterise an 'outside-in approach'. For example, repetitive behaviours may be attributed to a symptom giving rise to the diagnosis of obsessive-compulsive disorder (DSM), yet verbal adults with ASD engaging in these behaviours tell us that they are trying to self-soothe in an environment that is overwhelming to them (an inside-out perspective).[104] The difference is important because treatment of OCD is different from intervention for an overwhelming environment.

Diagnostic errors in patients with ASD and IDD arise particularly related to psychosis and schizophrenia.[105,106,107] Again the issue here is in identifying what is causing the psychotic symptoms and behaviours. As sensory issues and the re-experiencing of trauma can also give rise to psychotic presentations, trauma and sensory screening should be done before making a psychotic disorder diagnosis.[108,109] In general, psychiatry concerns about psychosis also arise when people are seen as withdrawn into themselves or talking and behaving in unusual ways. When the individual has little or no verbal language and is unable to report what may be distressing them, working with their body language, tapping into their affect and how they engage and observing their responses to the sensory world, can help in determine whether indeed this is psychosis, a different disorder (e.g. mood or trauma related), or something entirely different, e.g. physical discomfort.

## Summary

Responsive Communication embraces careful and attentive observations of the individual's behaviour in response to their social and sensory environment. It also offers the examining psychiatrist opportunities for emotional attunement with the patient in the absence of the patient being able to share their inner world verbally. As such the approach illuminates key aspects of the mental state examination part of the psychiatric assessment which would otherwise be unavailable for examination.

Emerging neurobiological research is providing evidence for the intricate relationship between brain, body, mind and feelings: how we feel and how we respond to our environment has impact on our physical and mental health. This is another reminder that the nature of the environments in which people with ASD and IDD are supported also impacts on their physical and mental health. A complete psychiatric assessment of the patient with ASD or IDD should therefore include an assessment of the referred individual's living and work environments as well as their social/care provider supports.

104 Bradley E, Caldwell P and Underwood L (2014). Autism spectrum disorder. In: E Tsakanikos & J McCarthy (Eds) *Handbook of Psychopathology in Intellectual Disability: Research, practice and policy*. New York: Springer.

105 Palucka A M, Bradley E and Lunsky Y (2008) A case of unrecognized intellectual disability and autism misdiagnosed as schizophrenia: Are there lessons to be learned? *Mental Health Aspects of Developmental Disabilities,* **11**(2), 55-60.

106 Bertelli MO, Merli MP, Bradley E, Keller R, Varrucciu N, Furia CD and Panocchia N (2015) The diagnostic boundary between autism spectrum disorder, intellectual developmental disorder and schizophrenia spectrum disorders. *Advances in Mental Health and Intellectual Disabilities* **9** (5) 243–264.

107 Bradley E, Lunsky Y, Palucka A and Homitidis S (2011) Recognition of intellectual disabilities and autism in psychiatric inpatients diagnosed with schizophrenia and other psychotic disorders. *Advances in Mental Health* **5** (6) 4–18.

108 Bradley E (in press) Treating psychosis with respect. In: G. Parkes and V. Sinason (Eds) *Treating with Respect*. New York: Springer.

109 Chapter by Hope in this book.

In conclusion, Responsive Communication offers much to the psychiatrist supporting individuals with ASD or IDD or who are unable to articulate how they feel and what may be distressing them. Care givers embracing Responsive Communication could provide these adults with much needed emotional attunement and understanding; this combined with ASD-IDD friendly environments and trauma informed services would reduce exposure to unnecessary stressful situations and enhance mental well-being.

## Box 1: Feelings

Neurobiological research and insights from neuroanatomists and neuropsychologists (such as Damasio,[110] Craig,[111] Eagleman[112, 113] and Ehssen[114, 115]) are helping us understand our sensory bodies and are providing us with a language that connects our physical body to our feelings.

Feelings are mental experiences related to the body's sensory detection and physiology, and serve to regulate these processes through homeostasis. Feelings are the portrayal of our physiological state when we are having an emotion (Damasio).[116] Feelings are conscious and valenced, that is, they are experienced along a continuum of positive to negative attractiveness.

Emotions are action programs and can therefore be observed, whereas feelings can only be described by the person having the feelings.

Craig describes two types of feelings:

- Feelings that come from our bodies, e.g. 'my fingers feel cold'.
- Affective feelings that relate to our moods, e.g. 'I feel anxious, I do not feel safe'.

Both bodily feelings and affective feelings are a direct reflection of the physiological state of our bodies. Expression of our feelings is not just emotional (and verbal) but is also an expression of how our body feels and reacts. We use words to express our feelings but we also communicate our feelings through our actions including body language, facial expression and the tone of what we say.

When we do not have language to communicate our feelings, others make inferences (correctly or incorrectly) from these non-verbal expressions.

Feeling and understanding what is going on in our sensory and physiological body, such as the urge to go to the toilet, or feeling hungry or thirsty or in need of sleep, is called 'interoception'.

Interoception has been described as the eighth sensory system, the other sensory systems being tactile (touch), vestibular (balance), proprioception (body

110 Damasio AR (2018) *The Strange Order of Things: Life, feeling, and the making of the cultures*. Pantheon Books, New York and https://www.youtube.com/watch?v=CAmkDrVvJ68

111 Carreiro JE (2009) *An Osteopathic Approach for Children* (2nd edition). Amsterdam: Elsevier.

112 Eagleman D (2015) *The Brain*. New York: Pantheon Books.

113 Eagleman D (2015) *Can we Create New Senses for Humans?* Available at: https://www.ted.com/talks/david_eagleman_can_we_create_new_senses_for_humans (accessed March 2019).

114 Ehrsson HH (2007) The experimental induction of out-of-body experiences. *Science* **317** (5841) 1048. Available at: http://www.ehrssonlab.se/pdfs/Ehrsson-Science-2007-with-SOM.pdf.

115 Ehrsson HH (2016) *What If We Could Leave Our Body and Have a New One?* TED talk. Available at: https://www.youtube.com/watch?v=ZEhXX47PRvw (accessed March 2019).

116 Damasio A and Damasio H (2017) *The Strange Order of Things: Homeostasis, feeling, and the making of cultures.* The first lecture of Copernicus Festival 2017: Emotions. Available at: https://www.youtube.com/watch?v=CAmkDrVvJ68 (accessed March 2019).

awareness), visual (sight), auditory (hearing), gustatory (taste), olfactory (smell).[117] Interoception describes how our feelings are inextricably linked to the experienced physiology of our bodies both in awareness and outside of awareness, and consequently how we act moment to moment. Importantly, interoception draws our attention to how our body (physiological) state impacts our emotional state (and vice versa), influences our motivations, perceptions, thoughts and consequently impacts our physical and mental well-being.

Based on their research, both Craig and Damasio propose Descartes' proposition *'I think therefore I am'* might more appropriately be *'I feel therefore I am'* (Damasio) or *'I feel that I am'* (Craig, p.xvii).[118] This appreciation of how we feel is fundamentally important in driving our interests, passions, achievements and sense of fulfilment (rather than being driven by cognitions). It enhances ways in which we can empower people with severe ASD and IDD to feel fulfilled in their lives.

## Box 2: Feeling safe and the polyvagal theory

The autonomic nervous system (ANS) is part of the peripheral nervous system responsible for regulating involuntary body functions such as heart rate, breathing, blood flow, digestion and elimination. The largest nerve of the ANS is the vagus nerve.

Polyvagal theory (Porges) provides a cohesive theory involving the autonomic nervous system (ANS) and vagal nerve activation (the polyvagal theory) which is helpful in understanding neurobiological underpinnings of feeling safe and what happens when this felt sense is threatened.

He describes two vagal nerve distributions: the ventral vagal and the dorsal vagal:

- The dorsal vagal complex (unmyelinated – slower conduction) primarily supplies organs below the diaphragm (e.g. stomach, pancreas, gut), and is ordinarily involved in body maintenance, repair and regulation, e.g. digestion and elimination.
- the ventral vagal (myelinated – faster conduction) supplies organs above the diaphragm (e.g. heart, lungs). Importantly, the ventral vagal is part of the cranial nerve complex (involving cranial nerves V (trigeminal), VII (facial), IX (glossopharyngeal), X (vagus)) regulating the smooth muscles of the heart and bronchi through visceromotor pathways (myelinated). It also serves the striated muscles of mastication, middle ear, face, larynx, pharynx and neck through special visceral efferent pathways (myelinated) (Porges, 2011). Overall the ventral vagal system is involved specifically in maintenance, repair and regulation of the individual with the outside world – i.e. supports social interaction with others.

Porges has identified separate ventral and dorsal vagal activation in response to our sensory system detecting threat. He has introduced the concept of *neuroception* to describe the automatic process by which the nervous system and brain areas evaluate risk such as safety, danger and life threat, without awareness.[119] Once detected, body physiology adjusts to optimise survival (homeostasis).

Ventral vagal activation is associated with what he describes as the *social engagement system (SES)* present in mammals, including ourselves. This system is

117 Mahler K (2015) *Interoception: The eighth sensory system*. Kansas: AAPC publishing.

118 Craig AD (2015) *How Do You Feel? An interoceptive moment with your neurobiological self*. Princeton: Princeton University Press.

119 Porges SW (2017) *The Pocket Guide to the Polyvagal Theory: The transformative power of feeling safe*. New York: WW Norton & Company.

activated when threat is detected, mobilising social behaviours that attempt to avoid or avert the threat, e.g. smiling, vocalisation, listening, negotiating.

If this does not work then we fall back on phylogenetically earlier ways to respond to threat which involves activation of the sympathetic nervous system (SNS) to:

'Fight' (we fight off the threat)

'Flight' (we run away)

'Freeze' (we stop still in our tracks – an adaptive response, seen in reptiles for example, as predators are often attracted to prey by their movement).

In ASD 'fight' may be manifested as self-injurious behaviours, or hitting out at others or obstacles that happen to be in our way; 'flight' may be manifested as running, 'trying to get away', and 'freeze' is brief cessation of movement in a maintained posture.

When threat is so severe to be life threatening the body defaults to an even earlier phylogenetic survival strategy – that of 'feigning death' (immobilisation) – a dorsal vagal activity. In humans the equivalent of feigning death has been likened to a trauma response which includes behavioural collapse, fainting, urination, defecation and dissociation (being detached from physical and emotional experiences). These behaviours are not chosen or planned – rather they are biologically triggered. The threshold to their triggering is associated with the perceived degree of threat, prior trauma experiences, coping capacities and other physiological states of the body that may compromise resilience and coping, such as physical illness.[120]

Porges describes 'feeling safe' as an important moderator influencing the effectiveness of many medical procedures, psychological interventions and psychoeducation. Activating the SES supports health, growth and restoration of body function; in this state the autonomic nervous system (which includes the SNS and the vagal system) is not easily triggered into defensive responses (fight, flight, freeze, immobilisation). He promotes the principle of feeling safe as a precursor to treatment and advises vetting of the treatment environment for safety cues, e.g., related to sensory sensitivities, as eliminating these would prevent neuroceptor triggering of defensive states of the ANS, which in turn can be anticipated to interfere with engaging with others, learning and the effectiveness of any intervention.

Porges describes our 'tuned in' capacity to derive the state and intentions of others from the tone of their voices, their facial expressions, their gestures and postures (i.e. body language and activation of the SES system). We (our nervous systems) also rely on social support and predictable environments to self-regulate. Withdrawal or absence of social support, or loss of predictability are sufficient to trigger PTSD (p.58).

In summary our biological imperative is towards survival; in this context our nervous systems are constantly monitoring the environment for safety cues. Neuroception shifts the autonomic nervous system (ANS) into three broad states:

- safety (social engagement system),
- danger (meltdown – fight-flight-freeze) and
- life threat (immobilisation – complete shutdown) (p.21-22).[121]

120 Porges SW (2017) *The Pocket Guide to the Polyvagal Theory: The transformative power of feeling safe*. New York: WW Norton & Company.

121 *Ibid* Porges.

## Box 3: Our sensory bodies: outside, inside and knowing who we are

While psychiatry has traditionally focused on the brain and the mind in attempting to understand mental distress, structures below the brain, including sensory reception systems and modulation networks, are attracting greater attention as part of this understanding.

**Interoception** refers to sensations from the interior of the body.

**Exteroception** refers to sensations originating from events outside the body.

Recent research has identified distinct neural substrates supporting 'interoception' and 'exteroception' in our brains (Craig, 2002).

Exteroception includes:

- **teloreception** (sensory input activated from a distance, i.e. vision and audition)
- **chemoception** (taste and smell)
- **proprioception** (sensory input that relates to limb position)
- **thermoreception** (temperature)
- **nociception** (sensory input activated specifically by physically damaging or threatening stimuli – and causing pain).

Originally nociception (pain) and thermoreceptor (temperature) together with the sense of touch were considered only as aspects of exteroception, because all three sensations could be felt on the outside skin. Detailed neuroanatomical and neurophysiological research has confirmed a distinct interoceptive neural substrate that includes small diameter fibre sensory input from inside the whole body – not only from the viscera, muscles, joints and teeth but also from the skin, i.e. nociception and thermoception are also aspects of interoception.

Neuroception, the evaluation of risk (Porges; Box 2)[122] such as safety, danger and life threat without awareness, might be considered a higher order sensory system. As with other sensory systems a signal, once detected, adjusts body physiology to optimize survival (homeostasis).

These sensory systems continuously report what is going on outside and inside (exteroception and interoception) our bodies to our central nervous system and in particular to sub cortical structures in the brain known as the limbic system. The interoceptive (limbic) cortex involves a sensory component, the insula closely linked to a motor component (the anterior cingulate cortex); the insula functions as a sensory information integrating system and the motor centre initiates whatever response is needed to maintain the physiological condition of the body, essentially managing body energy expenditure to ensure optimal survival of the individual (homeostasis).

Such feelings from the body that signal its condition have been referred to as 'the material me'.[123] Functional imaging brain studies demonstrate subjective feelings (e.g. emotions, moods) correlated with interoceptive cortical activity (Craig, 2003), i.e. subjective awareness and 'the feeling me'.[124]

122 Porges SW (2017) *The Pocket Guide to the Polyvagal Theory: The transformative power of feeling safe*. New York: WW Norton & Company.

123 Craig AD (2002) How do you feel? Interoception: The sense of the physiological condition of the body. *Nature Reviews. Neuroscience,* **3** (8) 655–566.

124 Craig AD (2003) Interoception: the sense of the physiological condition of the body. *Current Opinion in Neurobiology* **13** (4) 500–555.

The way an individual processes and organises sensory input contributes to the formation of the sense of self, the perception of others and the experience of the physical environment throughout life; sensory integration and sensory modulation therapies are increasingly being used in medicine, e.g. to manage pain, discomfort, difficult thoughts (paranoia, confusion) and emotions (anger, sadness, fear), and in the treatment of trauma.[125]

Sensory hypersensitivities and difficulties in sensory processing result in overload of the 'material me'. Through neuroception our body experiences this as threatening, triggering the ANS defence system (fight-flight-freeze responses). The individual experiences emotional turmoil (the 'feeling me') and is observed to be in emotional overload.

## Box 4: Meltdown and shutdowns described by people with ASD (self-advocates)[126, 127, 128]

Meltdowns are physiological occurrences described by people with ASD as needing to run their course, typically lasting 5–10 mins (but may last much longer (hours) for non-verbal individuals) and typically the person feels better afterwards, provided the source of the build-up and trigger(s) have been removed.

Shutdowns they describe as not being accompanied by the same feeling of relief. Self-advocates refer to these events as 'explosions' (meltdowns) and 'implosions' (shutdowns). While these may appear to be triggered by some environmental circumstance, sufferers describe the experience more as a 'tipping point' consequent to an accumulation of stress.

Meltdowns may be more prevalent at younger ages, resurfacing around puberty and in adolescence, lessening in the twenties to be replaced by shutdowns at later ages.

Behaviours and feelings during a meltdown include:

- self-injury (head banging, scalp picking, skin picking, digging finger nails into palms), agitated repetitive behaviours, running, stomping, screaming, growling, uncontrollable crying
- aggression towards others perceived to be the trigger
- other triggered ANS behaviours in response to 'threat' of being overwhelmed, such as agitation, pacing and aggression, particularly in response to being contained or restrained
- feelings of head pressure and intense urge to head bang. They report sometimes being aware that their self-injurious behaviours are dangerous but are unable to resist the relief provided by these behaviours
- others describe the self-injury (SIB) as trying to head off the tipping point.

125 Champagne T (2018) *Sensory Modulation in Dementia Care: Assessment and activities for sensory-enriched care*. London: Jessica Kingsley Publishers, London, UK.

126 Musings of an Aspie (2012) *Anatomy of a Meltdown*. Seventy entries of people with ASD describing their experiences of meltdowns. Available at https://musingsofanaspie.com/2012/12/13/anatomy-of-a-meltdown/ (accessed March 2019).

127 Jance M (2018) *What It's Like to Have an Autism Meltdown*. Available at: https://www.autismsociety-nc.org/autism-meltdown/ (accessed March 2019).

128 Ryan M (2018) *How I Learned To Manage my Meltdowns.* Available at: https://www.sbs.com.au/topics/life/health/article/2018/05/02/how-i-learned-manage-my-meltdowns (accessed March 2019).

Creative ways to minimise the SIB but still get some relief are described:

- such as forceful writing with a pen through clothes, or hard skin pinching, especially the thighs.

Other behaviours to prevent going into meltdowns include:

- pacing, toe wiggling, rocking, finger biting, finger tapping, moving in certain patterns including hopping.

Behaviours during brief shutdowns include:

- withdrawal, zoning out, staring into space, curling up into a ball.

Lipsky[129] differentiates between catastrophic reactions and meltdowns.

Prolonged shutdowns and immobilisation, e.g. autism-related catatonic-like deterioration (p.172-173), are rare but may be life threatening as the individual is no longer independently able to meet basic needs e.g. related to nutrition and safety.

Stress leading to tipping point (p.172) arises from:

- life transitions
- thing not going according to plan, scripts or anticipation[130]
- breaks in routines or expectations
- unfamiliar places (or people)
- chaotic environments causing extreme anxiety
- any barrage to the senses – such as sounds, sights, smells.
- increasing demands surpassing coping skills
- conflict, social demands and confusion
- illness, pain, hormone related.

Sufferers describe often times already being in sensory overload (tipping point) and then even an event not usually upsetting, can trigger going into complete meltdown or shutdown.

## Box 5: Examples

**A) Ian deescalating a meltdown (p.170) using Responsive Communication approach:**

Let me introduce Ian. Ian comes into school, lies down in the foyer and bellows. He shouts, 'No, no, no', and kicks and screams. He is obviously in great distress. His teacher stands not too close but nearby, and says quietly, 'come along now, it's time to go to class'. This has no effect at all on Ian's despair. I suggest that his teacher stands back, and standing out of reach of Ian's lashing feet, I use a different approach. Every time he bellows, I answer him softly and empathetically with a contingent sound. After a few more bellows, he sits up suddenly, looks at me angrily, takes off his shoe and slams it on the floor. This is the first time that Ian has acknowledged my presence. It appears to me that he has projected his

---

129 Lipsky D (2011) *From Anxiety to Meltdown: How individuals on the autism spectrum deal with anxiety, experience meltdowns, manifest tantrums, and how you can intervene effectively.* London: Jessica Kingsley Publishers.

130 Lipsky D (2011) *From Anxiety to Meltdown: How individuals on the autism spectrum deal with anxiety, experience meltdowns, manifest tantrums, and how you can intervene effectively*. London: Jessica Kingsley Publishers.

desperation onto the shoe, showing me how he feels through his aggressive action. So I look pointedly at the shoe and empathise with it by making a sympathetic sound – 'aahhh'. Ian looks surprised and picks up the shoe and pulls it on but in so doing, he catches the back on his heel so it is uncomfy. Since we are now in contact I feel safe to use speech. I point to his heel and using a contingent circular gesture with my finger say, 'shall I make it comfy for you?' He sticks out his foot at once and I adjust the heel. After a few more muted bellows he gets up and takes his teacher's hand and off they go. The whole process took about five minutes instead of the normal hour.

(Personal communication, Phoebe Caldwell, 2019)

**B) The impact of the environment on behaviour and ability (p.184)**

For example, if a child is showing distress behaviour at school, it may be that the cause of their distress is that their desk is facing the window and they are hypersensitive to light, a condition that that can cause confusion and pain but may be corrected using tinted Irlen lenses. Or the teacher's voice may have a particular frequency which is painful and from which the child is trying to escape. In a respite centre, meltdowns occur because, in an effort to be cheerful, the hall walls have been painted with orange and purple diagonal stripes, which (not surprisingly) trigger visual processing difficulties. In this context, I am fortunate, in that I am able to visit the different environments in which the child or adult is placed. But this requires time and money, which are in short supply as services are arranged. However, in the longer term, anxiety can fall away and behaviour improve if the trigger is addressed. Sometimes improvements are dramatic, particularly when intellectual disability is the outcome of hyper- or hypo-sensitivities. For example, some children report that when they use noise reduction headphones, they feel calmer and they can hear what the teacher says – and the teacher reports that the level of their work has shot up immediately. As I said earlier in the book, we cannot assess the level of intellectual disability without first addressing sensory sensitivities.

(Personal communication, Phoebe Caldwell, 2019)

## Box 6: Psychotherapy: attachment, safety and Responsive Communication

Historically, psychological therapies for mental distress have relied on verbal exchange between therapist and patient. In more recent years greater understanding of trauma and attachment needs has highlighted ways in which these psychological therapies can be successfully adapted working with patients unable to engage verbally. Mental distress associated with trauma is remembered in the body as well as the brain.[131] Psychological therapies focusing specifically on the felt experience of the trauma in the physical body are now developing, e.g., sensorimotor psychotherapy, trauma sensitive yoga. However, these therapies still require the patient to adapt to the usual parameters of a therapy session. For the patient with ASD and IDD the therapist has to adapt to the circumstance in which the patient feels most comfortable, e.g., meeting in a place that is familiar but with any sensory triggers removed.

This need for familiarity is linked to attachment needs. Polyvagal theory provides us with a neurological basis for understanding early and later attachment behaviours, and the behavioural consequences when misattunements occur between individuals and care givers.

131 Van der Kolk BA (2014) *The Body Keeps the Score: Brain, mind, and body in the healing of trauma*. New York: Viking.

Working with children and adults with IDD and ASD, the communicating partner has a responsibility to make sure the environment is 'safe' from the individual's perspective – this would include attention to auditory (e.g. the communicating partner's pitch and tone of voice), visual (what they are wearing) and olfactory (e.g. perfume) cues of the communicating partner. Feeling safe and safe environments optimise healthy attachments, relationships and capacities to learn.

Responsive communication, through emotional engagement in a safe place and attention to any sensory sensitivities, offers the emotionally distressed individual the possibility of being felt deeply understood through their body language. This itself is therapeutic and healing; the impact on the therapist is equally deeply felt and the therapist in turn is now uniquely placed to work with care providers to ensure support provided is appropriately aligned to the individual's emotional needs.

## Box 7: Intersubjectivity and the psychiatric examination

Intersubjectivity refers to the 'mutual communication of ideas, feelings and intentions between two individuals that takes place even without the use of words. It is the tangible connection between two minds, the effortless bridging of the space between two people. Over and above the capacity to recognize and understand another's inner experiences, intersubjectivity also involves the desire to share and communicate those experiences. As such it is at the heart of every social interaction between two individuals'.[132] Responsive Communication provides a space for such intersubjective experiences to emerge; such 'moments of meeting' have a profound impact (psychologically and physiologically) on both communicating partners.

Psychiatric examination involves evaluation of the individual's **mood** and **affect**.

In the context of the constructs being offered by Craig and Damasio, mood might be considered emotional feelings shared verbally with the examiner. Affect is displayed in the individual's actions as well as through the intersubjective attunement felt by the examiner in response to the patient's emotions communicated through their body language.

132 Eagle RS (2007) *Help Him Make You Smile: The development of intersubjectivity in the atypical child*. Lanham: Jason Aronson.

# References

Alameda County Behavioral Health Care Services and Alameda County Trauma Informed Care (2013) *Trauma Informed Care vs. Trauma Specific Treatment* [online]. Available from: https://alamedacountytraumainformedcare.org/trauma-informed-care/trauma-informed-care-vs-trauma-specific-treatment-2/ (accessed March 2019).

Alexander RT, Branford D and Devapriam J (2016) *Psychotropic drug prescribing for people with intellectual disability, mental health problems and/or behaviours that challenge: Practice guidelines* (FR/ID/09). Available at: http://www.rcpsych.ac.uk/pdf/FR_ID_09_for_website.pdf (accessed March 2019).

American Psychiatric Association (2013) *Diagnostic and statistical manual of mental disorders: DSM-5 (5th edition)*. Arlington: American Psychiatric Association.

Barrett M and Bradley E (2015) Autism spectrum disorders. In: S Bhaumik, D Branford and SK Gangadharan (Eds) *The Frith Prescribing Guidelines for People with Intellectual Disability* 3rd edition (pp.125–133). Chichester: Wiley Blackwell.

Beebe B (2014) My journey in infant research and psychoanalysis: microanalysis, a social microscope. *Psychoanalytic Psychology* **31** (1) 4–25. Behavioral Issues in Autism (pp.177-194). New York: Plenum: New York.

Bertelli MO, Merli MP, Bradley E, Keller R, Varrucciu N, Furia CD and Panocchia N (2015) The diagnostic boundary between autism spectrum disorder, intellectual developmental disorder and schizophrenia spectrum disorders. *Advances in Mental Health and Intellectual Disabilities* **9** (5) 243–264.

Bezchlibnyk-Butler KZ & Jeffries JJ (2004) *Clinical Handbook of Psychotropic Drugs* (14th edition). Ashland, OH: Hogrefe and Huber.

Billstedt E, Gillberg IC and Gillberg C (2005) Autism after adolescence: population-based 13- to 22-year follow-up study of 120 individuals with autism diagnosed in childhood. *Journal of Autism and Developmental Disorders* **35** (3) 351–360.

Bogdashina O (2003) *Sensory Perceptual Issues in Autism and Asperger Syndrome: Different sensory experiences – different perceptual worlds*. London: Jessica Kingsley.

Bradley E and Bolton P (2006) Episodic psychiatric disorders in teenagers with learning disabilities with and without autism. *The British Journal of Psychiatry* **189** 361–366.

Bradley E and Caldwell P (2013) Mental health and autism: Promoting Autism FaVourable Environments (PAVE) [online]. *Journal on Developmental Disabilities* **19** (1) 8–23. Available at: https://oadd.org/wp-content/uploads/2013/01/41015_JoDD_19-1_8-23_Bradley_and_Caldwell.pdf (accessed March 2019).

Bradley E (in press) Treating psychosis with respect. In: G. Parkes and V. Sinason (Eds) *Treating with Respect*. New York: Springer.

Bradley E, Caldwell P and Underwood L (2014). Autism spectrum disorder. In: E Tsakanikos & J McCarthy (Eds) *Handbook of Psychopathology in Intellectual Disability: Research, practice and policy*. New York: Springer.

Bradley E, Hollins S, Korossy M and Levitas A (2018) Adjustment disorder in disorders of intellectual development. In: P Casey (Ed) *Adjustment Disorder: From controversy to clinical practice* (pp.141–172). Oxford: Oxford University Press.

Bradley E, Loh A, Grier E, Korossy M and Cameron D (2014) *Health Watch Table: Autism spectrum disorder (ASD)* [online]. Available at: http://ddprimarycare.surreyplace.ca/wp-content/uploads/2018/03/HWT_ASD.pdf (accessed March 2019).

Bradley E, Lunsky Y, Palucka A and Homitidis S (2011) Recognition of intellectual disabilities and autism in psychiatric inpatients diagnosed with schizophrenia and other psychotic disorders. *Advances in Mental Health* **5** (6) 4-18.

Brain in Hand Limited (2018) *Personalised Support from Your Mobile Phone – Reduce anxiety, feel safe, increase Independence* [online]. Available at: http://braininhand.co.uk/ (accessed March 2019).

Brown S, Shankar R and Smith K (2009) Borderline personality disorder and sensory processing impairment. *Progress in Neurology and Psychiatry* **13** (4) 10–16.

Caldwell P (2014) *The Anger Box: Sensory turmoil and pain in autism*. Brighton: Pavilion Publishing and Media Ltd.

Carreiro JE (2009) *An Osteopathic Approach for Children* (2nd edition). Amsterdam: Elsevier.

Champagne T (2018) *Sensory Modulation in Dementia Care: Assessment and activities for sensory-enriched care.* London: Jessica Kingsley Publishers.

Clancy JA, Mary DA, Witte KK, Greenwood JP, Deuchars SA and Deuchars J (2014) Non-invasive vagus nerve stimulation in healthy humans reduces sympathetic nerve activity. *Brain Stimulation* **7** (6) 871–877.

Craig AD (2003) Interoception: the sense of the physiological condition of the body. *Current Opinion in Neurobiology* **13** (4) 500–555.

Craig AD (2015) *How Do You Feel? An interoceptive moment with your neurobiological self.* Princeton: Princeton University Press.

Damasio A and Damasio H (2017) *The Strange Order of Things: Homeostasis, feeling, and the making of cultures.* The first lecture of Copernicus Festival 2017: Emotions. Available at: https://www.youtube.com/watch?v=CAmkDrVvJ68 (accessed March 2019).

Damasio AR (2018) *The Strange Order of Things: Life, feeling, and the making of the cultures.* Pantheon Books, New York.

Davies CE, Zeedyk MS, Walls S, Betts N and Parry S (2008) Using imitation to establish channels of communication with institutionalised children in Romania: Bridging the gap. In: MS Zeedyk (Ed) *Promoting Social Interaction for Individuals with Communicative Impairments: Making contact* (pp.84). London: Jessica Kingsley Publishers.

Dhossche DM (2014) Decalogue of catatonia in autism spectrum disorders. *Frontiers in Psychiatry* **5** 157.

Dhossche DM and Wachtel LE (2010) Catatonia is hidden in plain sight among different pediatric disorders: A review article. *Pediatric Neurology* **43** (5) 307–315.

Dhossche DM, Shah A and Wing L (2006) Blueprints for the assessment, treatment, and future study of catatonia in autism spectrum disorders. *International Review of Neurobiology* **72** 267–284.

Drugs.com (2018) *Norepinephrine vs Epinephrine: What's the difference?* [online] Available at: https://www.drugs.com/answers/norepinephrine-epinephrine-difference-3132946.html (accessed March 2019).

Eagle RS (2007) *Help Him Make You Smile: The development of intersubjectivity in the atypical child.* Lanham: Jason Aronson.

Eagleman D (2015) *Can we Create New Senses for Humans?* Available at: https://www.ted.com/talks/david_eagleman_can_we_create_new_senses_for_humans (accessed March 2019).

Eagleman D (2015) *The Brain*. New York: Pantheon Books.

Ehrsson HH (2007) The experimental induction of out-of-body experiences. *Science* **317** (5841) 1048. Available at: http://www.ehrssonlab.se/pdfs/Ehrsson-Science-2007-with-SOM.pdf (accessed March 2019).

Ehrsson HH (2016) *What If We Could Leave Our Body and Have a New One?* TED talk. Available at: https://www.youtube.com/watch?v=ZEhXX47PRvw (accessed March 2019).

Ellis M, Astell A and Scott S (2018) *Adaptive Interaction and Dementia: How to communicate without speech*. London: Jessica Kingsley Publishers.

Emerson D (2015) *Trauma-sensitive Yoga in Therapy: Bringing the body into treatment.* New York: W.W. Norton & Company.

Epilepsy Society UK (2016) *Vagus Nerve Stimulation* [online]. Available at: https://www.epilepsysociety.org.uk/vagus-nerve-stimulation#.W5lT_-L2Zom (accessed March 2019).

Farinha M and Caldeira dS (2017) Sensory processing disorders and psychopathology. *European Psychiatry* **41** S2 16-7.

Feil N (2015) *TEDx Talk: Validation, Communication through Empathy*. Available at https://www.youtube.com/watch?v=ESqfW_kyZq8 (accessed March 2019).

Fink M, Taylor MA and Ghaziuddin N (2006) Catatonia in autistic spectrum disorders: a medical treatment algorithm. *International Review of Neurobiology* **72** 233–244.

Ghaziuddin N, Dhossche D and Marcotte K (2012) Retrospective chart review of catatonia in child and adolescent psychiatric patients. *Acta Psychiatrica Scandinavica* **125** (1) 33–38.

Feil N (2009) *Gladys Wilson and Naomi Feil.* Available at: https://www.youtube.com/watch?v=CrZXz10FcVM (accessed March 2019).

Goodman B (2016) Autonomic dysfunction in autism spectrum disorders (ASD). *Neurology*, **86** (16 Supplement).

Grandin T (1998) *Evaluating the effects of medication on people with autism*. Available at: https://www.iidc.indiana.edu/pages/Evaluating-the-Effects-of-Medication (accessed March 2019).

Green L, McNeil K, Korossy M, Boyd K, Grier E, Ketchell M, Loh A, Lunsky Y, McMillan S, Sawyer A, Thakur A and Bradley E (2018) HELP for behaviours that challenge in adults with intellectual and developmental disabilities. *Canadian Family Physician Medecin De Famille Canadien* **64** (Suppl 2) S23–31.

Groden J, Cautela J, Prince S & Berryman J (1994) The impact of stress and anxiety on individuals with autism and developmental disabilities. In: E Schopler & GB Mesibov (Eds) Groden J, Weidenman L and Diller A (2016). *Relaxation: A comprehensive manual for children and adults with autism and other developmental disabilities*. Champaign, IL: Research Press.

Hare DJ & Malone C (2004) Catatonia and autistic spectrum disorders. *Autism: The International Journal of Research and Practice* **8** (2), 183-95.

Holmes NM, Crane JW, Tang M, Fam J, Westbrook RF and Delaney AJ (2017) Alpha2-adrenoceptor-mediated inhibition in the central amygdala blocks fear-conditioning. *Scientific Reports* **7** (1).

Jance M (2018) *What It's Like to Have an Autism Meltdown*. Available at: https://www.autismsociety-nc.org/autism-meltdown/ (accessed March 2019).

Kushki A, Brian J, Dupuis A and Anagnostou E (2014) Functional autonomic nervous system profile in children with autism spectrum disorder. *Molecular Autism* **5** (39).

Kushki A, Drumm, Pla Mobarak M, Tanel N, Dupuis A, Chau T and Anagnostou E (2013) Investigating the autonomic nervous system response to anxiety in children with autism spectrum disorders. *PloS One* **8** (4). Available at: http://www.plosone.org/article/fetchObject.action?uri=info%3Adoi%2F10.1371%2Fjournal.pone.0059730&representation=PDF (accessed March 2019).

Lamb DG, Porges EC, Lewis GF and Williamson JB (2017) Non-invasive vagal nerve stimulation effects on hyperarousal and autonomic state in patients with posttraumatic stress disorder and history of mild traumatic brain injury: preliminary evidence. *Front Med (Lausanne)* **4** Article 124. Available at: https://www.ncbi.nlm.nih.gov/pmc/articles/PMC5534856/ (accessed March 2019).

Leekam SR, Nieto C, Libby SJ, Wing L and Gould J (2007) Describing the sensory abnormalities of children and adults with autism. *Journal of Autism and Developmental Disorders* **37** (5) 894–910.

Lipsky D (2011) *From Anxiety to Meltdown: How individuals on the autism spectrum deal with anxiety, experience meltdowns, manifest tantrums, and how you can intervene effectively.* London: Jessica Kingsley Publishers.

Loos Miller IM and Loos HG (2004) *Shutdowns and Stress in Autism* [online]. Available from: https://autismawarenesscentre.com/shutdowns-stress-autism/ (accessed March 2019).

Lydon S, Healy O, Reed P, Mulhern T, Hughes BM and Goodwin MS (2016) A systematic review of physiological reactivity to stimuli in autism. *Developmental Neurorehabilitation* **19** (6) 335–355.

Mahler K (2015) *Interoception: The eighth sensory system*. Kansas: AAPC Publishing.

Manning KE, McAllister CJ, Ring HA, Finer N, Kelly CL, Sylvester KP, Fletcher PC, Morrell NW, Garnett MR, Manford MR and Holland AJ (2016) Novel insights into maladaptive behaviours in Prader-Willi syndrome: serendipitous findings from an open trial of vagus nerve stimulation. *Journal of Intellectual Disability Research* **60** (2) 149–155.

Mazzone L, Postorino V, Valeri G and Vicari S (2014) Catatonia in patients with autism: Prevalence and management. *CNS Drugs* **28** (3) 205–215.

McDonnell AA (2010) *Managing Aggressive Behaviour in Care Settings: Understanding and applying low arousal approaches*. Chichester: Wiley-Blackwell. Further information at https://www.studio3.org/training-systems-for-managing-difficult-behaviour/low-arousal-approach-for-autism/ (accessed March 2019).

McNally H, Morris D and McAllister K (2013) *Aldo Goes to Primary School: Experiencing primary school through the lens of the autistic spectrum* [online]. Belfast: McNally Morris Architects. Available at: http://mcnallymorris.com/Aldo_Goes_to_Primary_School_med_res_digital.pdf (accessed March 2019).

Mesquita Reis J, Queiroga L, Velasco Rodrigues R, Pinto Ferreira B, Padez Vieira F, Moskowitz AK (2004) 'Scared stiff': Catatonia as an evolutionary-based fear response. *Psychological Review* **111** (4) 984–1002.

Mukhopadhyay T and Savarese R (2017) *Classical Autism and the Instruction of Literature* [video filmed at Duke Franklin Humanities Institute]. Available at: https://www.youtube.com/watch?v=PamjosXYiKo (accessed March 2019).

Mukhopadhyay TR (2008. *How Can I Talk if My Lips Don't Move: Inside my autistic mind*. New York: Arcade Publishing.

Murillo L (undated) *Ten Tips to Prevent Autism-Related Shopping Meltdowns* [online]. Available at: https://www.autismspeaks.org/blog/2017/11/25/ten-tips-prevent-autism-related-shopping-meltdowns (accessed March 2019).

Musings of an Aspie (2012) *Anatomy of a Meltdown*. Seventy entries of people with ASD describing their experiences of meltdowns. Available at https://musingsofanaspie.com/2012/12/13/anatomy-of-a-meltdown/ (accessed March 2019).

Naguy A (2016) Clonidine use in psychiatry: Panacea or panache. *Pharmacology* **98** (1-2) 87–92.

National Autistic Society (NAS) (2016) *Meltdowns* [online]. Available at: https://www.autism.org.uk/about/behaviour/meltdowns.aspx# (accessed March 2019).

National Autistic Society (NAS) (2017) *Anxiety in Autistic Adults* [online]. Available at: https://www.autism.org.uk/about/behaviour/anxiety.aspx (accessed March 2019).

NHS England (2016) *Stopping Over-Medication of People with Learning Disabilities [STOMPwLD]* [online]. NHS England. Available from: https://www.england.nhs.uk/wp-content/uploads/2016/06/stopping-over-medication.pdf (accessed March 2019).

Niagara studies: Bradley EA, Ames CS & Bolton PF (2011) Psychiatric conditions and behavioural problems in adolescents with intellectual disabilities: Correlates with autism. *Canadian Journal of Psychiatry* **56** (2) 102–109.

O'Reardon JP, Cristancho P and Peshek AD (2006) Vagus nerve stimulation (vns) and treatment of depression: to the brainstem and beyond. *Psychiatry* (Edgmont) **3** (5) 54–63. Available at: https://www.ncbi.nlm.nih.gov/pmc/articles/PMC2990624/ (accessed March 2019).

Ogata N and Dodman NH (2011) The use of clonidine in the treatment of fear-based behavior problems in dogs: An open trial. *Journal of Veterinary Behavior: Clinical Applications and Research*, **6** (2) 130–137.

Ogden P (2015) *Sensorimotor Psychotherapy: Interventions for trauma and attachment.* New York: W.W. Norton & Company.

Palucka AM, Bradley E and Lunsky Y (2008) A case of unrecognized intellectual disability and autism misdiagnosed as schizophrenia: Are there lessons to be learned? *Mental Health Aspects of Developmental Disabilities* **11** (2) 55-60.

Picard R (2011) *Technology and Emotions.* TEDx Talk. Available at: https://www.youtube.com/watch?v=ujxriwApPP4 (accessed March 2019).

Picard RW (2018) *How Emotion Technology can Improve Science and The Future of Autism*. INSAR May 2018. International Society for Autism Research Conference, Rotterdam, Netherlands. Available at: https://insar.confex.com/insar/2018/videogateway.cgi/id/969?recordingid=969 (accessed March 2019).

Pitonyak D (2016) *Supporting a Person Who Is Experiencing Post Traumatic Stress Disorder* (PTSD) [online]. Available at: http://gatewayassociation.ca/wpcontent/uploads/2018/07/supporting-a-person-who-is-experiencing-PTSD.pdf (accessed March 2019).

Porges SW (2011) *The Poly Vagal Theory: Neurophysiological foundations of emotions, attachment, communication, self-regulation*. New York: W.W. Norton & Company.

Porges SW (2017) *The Pocket Guide to the Polyvagal Theory: The transformative power of feeling safe* (first edition). New York: W. W Norton & Company.

Porges SW, Bazhenova OV, Bal E, Carlson N, Sorokin Y, Heilman KJ, Cook EH and Lewis GF (2014) Reducing auditory hypersensitivities in autistic spectrum disorder: preliminary findings evaluating the listening project protocol. *Frontiers in Pediatrics* **2** 80.

Porges SW, Macellaio M, Stanfill SD, McCue K, Lewis GF, Harden ER, Handelman M, Denver J, Bazhenova OV and Heilman KJ (2013) Respiratory sinus arrhythmia and auditory processing in autism: modifiable deficits of an integrated social engagement system? *International Journal of Psychophysiology: Official Journal of the International Organization of Psychophysiology* **88** (3) 261–270. Also available at: https://www.ncbi.nlm.nih.gov/pmc/articles/PMC3610863/ (accessed March 2019).

Ryan M (2018) *How I Learned To Manage my Meltdowns*. Available at: https://www.sbs.com.au/topics/life/health/article/2018/05/02/how-i-learned-manage-my-meltdowns (accessed March 2019).

Serafini G, Engel-Yeger B, Vazquez GH, Pompili M & Amore M (2017) Sensory processing disorders are associated with duration of current episode and severity of side effects. *Psychiatry Investigation* **14** (1) 51–57.

Shah A & Wing L (2006) Psychological approaches to chronic catatonia-like deterioration in autism spectrum disorders. *International Review of Neurobiology* **72** 245–264.

Shah A (2016) *Catatonia and Catatonia-Type Breakdown in Autism* [online]. Available from: https://network.autism.org.uk/good-practice/evidence-base/catatonia-and-catatonia-type-breakdown-autism (accessed March 2019).

Stern DN (1985) *The interpersonal world of the infant: A view from psychoanalysis and developmental psychology*. Basic Books: New York.

Taylor M (2016) *Using Vagus Nerve Stimulation (VNS) for Depression: Is it recommended?* [online]. Available at: https://www.healthline.com/health/depression/vagus-nerve-stimulation (accessed March 2019).

The Caldwell Autism Foundation (2019) *Responsive Communication* [online]. Available at: http://thecaldwellautismfoundation.org.uk/index.php/responsive-communication/ (accessed March 2019).

Trevarthen C and Delafield-Butt JT (2017) Intersubjectivity in the imagination and feelings of the infant: Implications for education in the infant. In: EJ White & C Dalli (Eds) *Under-Three Year Olds in Policy And Practice* (pp.17-39). New York: Springer.

Trevarthen C (2016) *Pre-birth to Three: Professor Colwyn Trevarthen – Relationships*. Available at: https://www.youtube.com/watch?v=2kJI6G35TNk (accessed March 2019).

Van der Kolk BA (2014) *The Body Keeps the Score: Brain, mind, and body in the healing of trauma*. Viking: New York.

Wing L and Shah A (2000) Catatonia in autistic spectrum disorders. *The British Journal of Psychiatry* **176** 357–362.

Wing L and Shah A (2006) A systematic examination of catatonia-like clinical pictures in autism spectrum disorders. *International Review of Neurobiology* **72** 21–39.

Woodcock L and Page A (2010) *Managing Family Meltdown: The low arousal approach and autism*. London: Jessica Kingsley Publishers.

Woodruff B, Temkit M, Adams J and Goodman B (2016) Autonomic symptoms endorsed by adults with autism spectrum disorders. *Neurology* **86** (16 supplement).

Zeedyk MS (2008) *Promoting Social Interaction for Individuals with Communicative Impairments: Making contact.* London: Jessica Kingsley Publishers.

## Additional resource

*Responsive Communication: Tuning in to people with autism*. A free online video resource. Currently available at: http://thecaldwellautismfoundation.org.uk/index.php/responsive-communication-tuning-in-to-people-with-autism-a-free-online-video-resource/